GAY BAR

GAY BAR

Why We Went Out

Jeremy Atherton Lin

GRANTA

Granta Publications, 12 Addison Avenue, London W11 4QR

First published in Great Britain by Granta Books, 2021
Originally published in the United States in 2021 by Little, Brown and
Company, a division of Hachette Book Group, Inc., New York

A CIP catalogue record for this book is available from the
British Library.

1 3 5 7 9 10 8 6 4 2

ISBN 978 1 78378 581 0
eISBN 978 1 78378 582 7

Book design by Marie Mundaca
Offset by Avon DataSet Ltd, Arden Court, Alcester,
Warwickshire B49 6HN
Printed and bound by CPI Group (UK) Ltd, Croydon, CR0 4YY
www.granta.com

MIX
Paper from
responsible sources
FSC® C020471

This book is dedicated to its other daddy.

A long while amid the noises of coming and going, of drinking
        and oath and smutty jest,
There we two, content, happy in being together, speaking little,
        perhaps not a word.

                                        —Walt Whitman, 'A Glimpse'

CONTENTS

ix

THE DARK WALKS

LONDON

Historically, gay bars were the only spaces where queer people could be visible, as if that visibility could exist only within the imagined. Now it seems that reality outside the bar is so grim that people would rather preserve this fantasy, not just out of safety but as an emotional necessity.

—Hannah Quinlan and Rosie Hastings, 2017

It's starting to smell like penis in here.... His words hovered in the claggy dark. The other men laughed soundlessly. I couldn't be sure how I'd arrived in their circle. The room had become crowded like a bumper car rink, until I was no longer steering but carried along by collisions. I must have willed this, really. Still I hadn't discerned how these men formed one group. Their bodies circumscribed a turf, as on a playground or prison yard. If I'd encountered their type someplace else, I'd be averting eyes and stammering. I still was, but they not only sniggered, they touched me.

That is a ripe arse you have, man, the youngest and blondest had remarked in a maybe Irish accent. Whether or not I deserved the compliment, I would take it. I'd manifest the ass he desired. I would do so by tensing it slightly. *I'll have a piece of that, or you'll suck me,* the blond continued, pushing me to my knees as he and the others closed in. Someone else commanded, *G'on—suck it, you'll like it, it's the biggest one here,* like a benevolent bully. Then with a kind of brutal elegance, the group spread apart like the blades of a pocketknife.

That's when: *It's starting to smell like penis in here....* The voice was at once queeny and thuggish, the line nearly sung, a lewd *here we go again...* trailing off as he moved away, leaving me on my knees to the blond. The room did smell of penis, maybe. Like fog machine or nitrites, syrupy lager spilling over thick fists, smoker's breath, someone's citrusy cologne, the bleached vinyl seats. It reeked of toxic masculinity. It stank of the clammy skin of white Englishmen, which is like wet laundry hanging to dry without wind. Overhead, passing trains shook the black ceiling. The rumble disturbed the black partition that bisected the room at a diagonal, a false horizon promising someone better just out of reach.

The night's men-only rule was proclaimed on a print-out along with the name of the event, Brüt, in a tool-kit typeface connoting a narrow definition of gender. The men skulked in trackies, inhabiting or playacting working-class bodies. I thought then I had better not speak. My accent is too equivocal, scuppered somewhere on the Atlantic and apologizing. The point here was to be regular. The only distinguishing feature should be an erection the size of a Sky+ remote control. The haircuts were skinhead or fade. Leather daddies were present, but the group I'd fallen in with wore the uniform of rough council estates: polo shirt with collar popped, white trainers, white cap. It crossed my mind I was playing with men who emulated porn actors pretending to be rough trade.

I saw these men as being in their domain, depraved and sketchy, whereas I was just passing through. Then again, I understood I'm the company I keep: a man over forty with a Friday night hard-on, passing as desirable in the dark. I didn't end up here out of loneliness. I'd arrived with my companion, the Famous Blue Raincoat. We've been domestic for years. 'It may seem difficult to understand why two men who are happy with each other will take the risk of going to these places where the whole atmosphere of the group will tend to drive them apart,' wrote Gordon Westwood—a pseudonym—in his 1952 book *Society and the Homosexual*. It was the author's hunch there was no other spot for these coupled men to rendezvous. To the homosexuals, 'in a pathetic kind of way this place is their home.'

But that was another era. I hadn't been driven to The Bar by society's lack of understanding. Throughout the twentieth century, London pubs, cafés and clubs would be taken over—'selected' as Westwood put it—by a homosexual clientele. The unofficial meeting places could be so discreet most other customers wouldn't notice, and occasionally so brazen an orchestra would strike up a tribute when an attractive male entered the room. Proto-gays were segregated by class as much as anything else, sticking to the exclusive cellar bar at the Ritz on the one hand or an East End boozer on the other—or, in the case of privileged men in pursuit of a bit of rough, moving from the former to the latter. In this diffuse network of commercial spaces, the clientele might be tolerated to various degrees because it brought business. (Matt Houlbrook, an authority on London queer history, figures: 'The pink shilling was a potentially lucrative market, and men's demand for a "home" always ripe for exploitation.') Now we were being elaborately catered to: The Bar was designed for a demographic of masc-presenting homo satyrs.

The steel and brick and the exposed, girthy pipes declared this as manly terrain. The hint of disco in the

DJ's mix got me thinking about Andrew Holleran's 1978 novel *Dancer from the Dance*, in which hedonistic gays haunt Manhattan's derelict warehouses, abandoned factories and dilapidated piers. 'We were ghosts,' the narrator says. In 1918, the British war poet Wilfred Owen wrote of loitering along the wharves on the River Thames, where 'I am the shadow that walks there.' The final line—'I with another ghost am lain'—could reference troops in the trenches, but really must mean horny men who move that way to this day, as phantoms, with that slow walking, the opposite of rush-hour commuters who dart quickly but attempt to avoid collision. The cruiser ambles in pursuit of contact. It's a saunter that wills a larger terrain, populated by more attractive men. I'd determined myself into that pace. I had not gone upstairs to be anything but another ghost.

We go out to get some. On certain evenings Famous and I intuit we're going to end up in such a place without the need for discussion. We go out because we're thirsty. We go out to return to the thrill of the chase. We want to be in a room full of penises wherein each contains the strong possibility that it is, to use the old-fashioned queer initialism, tbh—to be had. That phrase looks forward to fondly looking back, all about the conquest and bragging about it later. But I could be at home, thumbing through a grid of tbh torsos on my phone. We go out for the aroma. Some nights just smell like trouble. The city at dusk carries the scent of all its citizens commingled. We head out on the dopamine. There are nights that have an audible pulse, so we dance.

I thought then of two lines from Paul Verlaine: 'I dance to save myself, and find / Swimming in sweat, it's in our common breath I fly.' We were not dancing, exactly, but the DJ was building up propulsive tracks, throbbing and hissing. I turned my cap backwards so the brim wouldn't impede my access to the blond's full shaft. I wanted my snout buried as much as anything else to prove my commitment to the scene. His pale foreskin was pulled back. The penis had been overhyped, but I decided still it was lovely. It was pleased with itself, like a toddler standing proudly at a scene of destruction. I plunged onto him, the decision to do so lagging behind the act. I reached to one side toward an onlooker, thinking: why not roll with this and grab a random dick. I touched something like a rubbery cauliflower. Its owner swatted my hand away. I left the voyeur to whatever that was: eccentric prosthesis or zealous case of HPV. He'd be happy enough just watching. Then the blond lad was yanking me toward the cubicles, and one of his mates fell in line.

In turn, I grabbed Famous, who pulled up his waistband and grinned as he joined us, abandoning unknown paramours. I got him those trackies—boys' size 13–14 he's so skinny. We formed a chain like kids on a field trip. Then, four in the box, we made a sight to peep from the glory holes, pressing together and kissing like an onanistic king rat. Other limbs tried to force the door ajar, as the blond shoved it closed with his forearm. When men barricade in a dark room, it turns certain other contenders into zombies. You're never sure which ones they are, because they lay in wait until your consummation begins. Then, out of sight lines, they try to wedge their way in, to prize open doors, pound on them.

Suddenly, the blond lad pulled back and stumbled out,

muttering either *need a cigarette* or *not feeling it*. It was brighter in the cubicle, and the light must have disabused him of the impression of me as one archetypal thing. His mate was unamused: *What th' FUCK, the fuck ya goin'?* The blond moved across the corridor crabwise past men who leaned against walls with flat palms as if load-bearing. He was shaking his head in the inebriate way that indicates an aversion to listening.

Downstairs, near the bar, a couple of younger guys actually danced. A wryness tugged at their lips. One had brown skin. A tall figure in high heels swayed near the DJ, as if they'd walked from the nonbinary present day into a clone scene from the seventies—checked their pronoun at the cloakroom, hoping the bouncers wouldn't look down at their feet. For over a century, policing queer sites entailed the persecution of the effeminate, the *screamers*—in powder and perfume, perched on a knee, calling one another girl or queen. After the late thirties, the monitoring of London venues shifted from surveying the people inside to targeting the premises, so that a landlord could be accused of keeping a disorderly house if he was host to gender deviance. Masculine—*normal*—men with stealthy predilections could be invisible and thereby beyond the law. Properly behaved places were left alone. This encouraged what Matt Houlbrook describes as a collusion between proprietors and patrons 'to construct a queer consumer who was not obviously queer.' At The Bar, masculinity had been twisted into something perverted, yet still functioned to banish effeminacy. We were now self-policing—and frankly that contributed to the arousal. But I for one was pleased to see those high heels slip through.

The Bar had been trading less than a year. When it opened in 2017, everyone said gay bars were doomed. (*Financial Times*: 'The party is coming to an end.') More than half in London had folded within ten years. This was blamed on property developers, apps, assimilation. In Britain, the steep decline came not long after civil partnerships were introduced in 2005. When same-sex marriage was legalized in New York in 2011, the journalist June Thomas wrote, 'I can't help wondering whether, as gay rights move forward, the gay bar—the place where it all began—may get left behind.'

The name of a gay bar, Stonewall, provides the metonym for gay liberation. It figures the place was a dump. The Stonewall Inn, like other gay bars, was mafia-owned, selling watered-down drinks to a clientele of both the furtive and the flagrant. The 1969 uprising against police raids there—the fabled brick crashing through the window—makes a fabulous origin myth. But gays had been acting up in their chosen watering holes and all-night cafeterias for years. Just around the block from the Stonewall Inn is Julius'—where, three years before the Stonewall rebellion, a trio of activists drew attention to exclusion by pronouncing their homosexuality to the guy working the bar. He took his cue to turn them away. An image of the bartender placing his hand over a glass was snapped by photographer Fred W. McDarrah. This raffish provocation—a *sip-in*—marked a step toward establishing the right of gays to assemble in the state. Younger-generation gays stand on the shoulders of such insurgent bar patrons, but we form a precarious pyramid. We're shaky on details, partly down to the booze.

Certain pivotal events come across as staged: when the *New York Times* covered the sip-in, the headline was '3 Deviates Invite Exclusion by Bars' with the subhead 'But They Visit Four Before Being Refused Service. . . .'

Now our turf was under threat not so much by police, but a juncture of economic factors like unchecked property speculation and an upsurge in stay-at-home gays. I responded to the closures with an automatic, nearly filial sense of loss, followed by profound ambivalence. The gay bars of my life have consistently disappointed. Activists claim they should be kept open to facilitate knowledge passing between generations. Had I ever received wisdom on a barstool? Not really. Instead, I recalled a dive in Los Angeles that I'd timidly entered in my youth, only to be told *You're too good for this place.* The gentleman rested his hand on my thigh with an infuriating lack of intent. Not long ago I looked that bar up online, and read a pundit's one-star review complaining that the crowd there groped him when all he wanted was to celebrate New Year's Eve with his wife and friends ('all Heteros,' as he wrote). 'I certainly don't expect to have my physical space violated just because I may choose to party in a gay area,' he asserted. I thought: to be violated *was* my expectation back when I ventured in.

Perhaps the bars were only ever meant to be a transitional phase. When a BBC article queried 'Do gay people still need gay bars?,' I wondered which people and what places. It's been proposed that in less liberal countries the advent of gay bars will be eclipsed by hookup apps. Was the BBC talking about those citizens? About lesbians, who barely had any places left anywhere, or young queers who anyway tend to prefer roving parties that reflect their fluidity? Was the BBC talking about *me?* I had to consider whether gay bars promised a sense of belonging then lured us into a trap. In a gay bar, am I penned into minority status, swallowing drinks that nourish my oppression—have gay bars kept me in my place?

The BBC could just as well have asked 'Do gay *bars* still need gay *people?'* Straight drinkers now blithely invade our territory like the gaggle of sloppy strangers who show up at the end of a house party. The *New York Times* put it this way: 'How "Gay" Should a Gay Bar Be?' The article discussed another spot I used to know in West Hollywood, where it eventually got to the point that every table was booked by bachelorette parties; the owner placed a moratorium on their presence until gay marriage legislation passed. When that happened federally in 2015, and the gals piled back in to take group photos with the go-go hunks, the management opened an adjacent space devoted to a clientele of actual gay men.

'What are they doing at the hall of the outcasts on this night?' wrote Donald Webster Cory—another pseudonym—back in his 1951 book *The Homosexual in America: A Subjective Approach.* 'Did they arrive by accident, or have they friends or brothers here, or are they among those rare souls who especially enjoy the company of gay folk, although they are not themselves gay? Or perhaps, are they thrill-seekers and slummers who have merely looked in upon another world?' We'd since been outnumbered: more fag hags than fags. The misogynistic old trope of a lonely heart attached to sexual criminals out of compatible ostracization had been replaced by one of basic bitches latching on because the gays turned out to be winners. They'd shove

11

me out of their way and cry *yasss*. When Famous and I returned after many years to a rustic gay saloon in the woods of northern California, a bartender approached midway through our first Lagunitas. *I want to thank you for coming,* he said. *And for being, I presume, gay.* Not sure how to respond, I tried: *You, too.* He continued, *It's changing here, now that 'gay is accepted.'* A bar rag hung from his air quote. *Weekends all you'll see is bachelorette parties.* I nodded. *Frankly, it was better when we were unacceptable,* he said ominously.

And yet: in 2017, a poll revealed homophobic attacks in the UK had surged eighty percent in the previous four years. In the States, the year 2016 marked the most violence against gays ever recorded, even without the forty-nine casualties at the Pulse nightclub in Orlando. A *Vanity Fair* article on the tragedy was headlined 'Mass Murder at the Gay Bar: When a Refuge Becomes the Target.' The journalist Dave Cullen began by disclosing his position. After publishing a book on the school massacre at Columbine, he'd become a go-to consultant every time a mass shooting occurred. 'And then, when my part is over, I need a drink. I'm gay, so that means a gay bar,' he wrote. I recognize myself in that line—and how what seems obvious to him (and to me) may need pointing out to readers who've never frequented such a place. He declares an affiliation—leading me to wonder why it is that certain of us don't hesitate to regard the gay bar as our natural terrain.

If the habitat—the gay bar—faces extinction, the possibility arises that gay identity is an endangered species. I'm talking about gay rimmed in lightbulbs, GAY shouted in all caps, G-A-Y spelled out like the namesake of the British nightclub chain. To many, that's nothing worth preserving.

But, confronted with the husks of gay bars on city streets, I found myself increasingly in support of that brand of gay—as in blatant, an embarrassment, a blight. I've found myself drawn back to the ghetto, where groups of gay men converge to lick one another's wounds, or pour salt on them, and in other ways behave inappropriately. If my experiences in gay bars have been disappointing, what I wouldn't want to lose is the expectation of a better night. Gay is an identity of longing, and there is a wistfulness to beholding it in the form of a building, like how the sight of a theater stirs the imagination.

The closing gay bars had me thinking about the finitude of gay. The American activist Harry Britt once said, 'When gays are spatially scattered, they are not gay, because they are invisible.' The question becomes whether that dissolution of identity is the ultimate civil rights achievement. By 2018, an opinion piece in the Israeli newspaper *Haaretz* declared, 'Being Gay Is Passé.' A few years prior, one poll showed half of young people in Britain were identifying as not completely hetero, with most of those placing themselves in a nonbinary area on a scale of sexuality. So, not completely gay. I came across a statement online by a woke young person expressing his consternation that cis gay males remained the most culturally validated type of queer. He himself identified as a gay man—but as much as anything, he clarified, as *a reminder of his privilege*. I questioned how I would speak with him about his daddies if given the chance—they were far from perfect, some outright villainous, but they'd been through it. And they aren't a monolith. I struggled with how we could reframe the narrative when we were each trepidatious about the word *gay*, yet both still inclined to use it. The identity, foisted upon me since the days when other boys in my scout troop noticed my bubbly handwriting, had come to have a faded quality. I considered I might have Stockholm syndrome for the epithet. But more and more I heard myself defaulting to *queer,* somehow both theoretically radical and appropriate in polite company. The word *gay* was intoned like a joke or an elegy.

Then in London a handful of new venues popped up, often not gay bars but queer spaces. Many folded in no time. Itinerant parties were a more feasible or cooler option (a return to the peripatetic socializing of London before gay bars, when homos assembled at whichever spot was in favor). Sober nights were tried out as a thing. Events were developed for trans, femmes and womxn of color. There, *inclusivity* might not mean *everybody.* It could indicate *the rest of us.* Inclusivity could be enforced by a strict door policy, raising the question of how identity is legible—how to differentiate, for example, a questioning person from a voyeur. Some parties issued charters that proscribed judging and patriarchy, as well as groping and leching—all of the stuff encrusted like grime in the gay bars I'd known.

———

The Bar was a throwback—randy and problematic. At a glance, the *homo-* prefix meant not just same sex but same gender, race, class. It seemed to me it was not only the dominant demographic of white men that hearkened to an earlier time, but the propensity for barebacking. The club opened on the brink of the distribution of PrEP. (Patrick Califia predicted in 1998: 'When there is a vaccine or an effective treatment or, please Goddess, both, some will return to pre-AIDS sexual behavior. And that's as it should be. Because there was nothing wrong with that behavior in the first place.') England's National Health Service enrolled ten thousand people on a PrEP trial starting in the autumn. Promiscuous gays seemed to think they got their magic bullet, and apparently then all went to The Bar.

It was in Vauxhall, just south of the River Thames, having taken the space over from a hip-hop club shut with ignominy after a series of violent incidents, culminating in the death of an aspiring pilot after being held down by the bouncers. By contrast, The Bar's application for a late license played the gay card, brandishing words like *community, cabaret, eclectic, diverse*. A member of the House of Lords wrote a letter of support in which he elucidated the need for *safe spaces*—a term entered into the Merriam-Webster dictionary that year. The letter alluded to the dangers associated with meeting strangers online, suggesting that gay bars facilitate a vetting and self-monitoring among members of a community. The year before, the Old Bailey had handed down life imprisonment to a serial killer who drugged, raped and murdered four young men whom he'd met on apps.

In actuality, the place turned out to be, if by no means unfriendly, not exactly what the term *safe space* brings to mind. *Whatt'ya need a Viagra for,* an ursine bartender grumbled to a bouncing young man fiendishly trying to secure a pill. *You kids today,* he added kindly, as the boy began to totter and sway. The place offered *that* kind of camaraderie—a gruff maternalism simultaneously defaulting to certain Vauxhall stereotypes: masculinist, debauched, dodgy. Vauxhall was saddled with a reputation in the aughts as a destination for those with a death wish—heavy drug users and bug-chasers, the bad seeds of the gay populace. The risk taking seemed to have been sublimated into a risky aesthetic. Crossing the empty dance floor at The Bar, Famous and I were once stopped by a manager and asked to present more *fetishistically*. Famous shrugged and took off his t-shirt. I winced and pulled mine over my shoulders like a harness. *That'll do*, the man said.

Our first time there, it was just before Christmas. We'd been down the street at the Eagle London watching yule-tide *Golden Girls* episodes. The Eagle too once had a dark room and sold poppers, but after someone collapsed naked on the dance floor, it cleaned up its act—planted ivy on the roof and began hosting vegan barbecues. The Eagle is part of an informal network of leather bars going by the same name in several different cities—at its peak, there were some fifty in the convocation. Since its makeover, the London iteration had become a spot for healthy-looking men with neat beards and t-shirts with social media slogans (#mascfag)—the type Famous and I call happy gays. But on this night, there was hardly anyone there, just a couple of nicotine-stained men and their bosomy friend hacking over Sophia's insults and Blanche's side-eye. The beer went down cold in the empty room. Gay bars can be festive—a bunch of bears singing along to 'All I Want for Christmas Is You.' (On Christmas day of the previous year, Famous and I found ourselves at another Eagle, in Los Angeles, dancing to George Michael songs just hours after it was announced the singer was dead.)

Having had our fill of Rose's idioms, we thought we'd

walk to The Bar, a new cruise club in the arches I'd seen listed in *XY*. It was barren there, too. A brawny little Polish guy made out with us briefly, then declared he preferred one-on-one, also noting that the scene paled in comparison with that of Berlin. We wound up giving head to a man who told us it was his birthday and that he didn't want to blow his load—he'd been edging for days—but we finished him off, bringing his party to a fizzle. Because he was pock-marked with big feet, I'd perceived him as brutish. But, awkwardly waiting next to him at coat check, I clocked his outerwear, a practical navy number from Michael Kors, and any such delusion faded.

On subsequent visits, there was far more action. For a time, Famous and I found The Bar made a suitable last resort. I'd bite a blue pill, and we'd each wash half down with the lager that came with the door fee. On a good night, each gesture and grab, even chortle or rejection, enhanced a cumulative fever. Men sat side by side along the edge of the room in a lustful stupor. Certain duos or threesomes drew a crowd who circled to watch intently as if it were blood sports. Guys in jockstraps positioned themselves on all fours on the benches. One had FUCK THIS with an arrow written on his ass cheeks. I held on to the thick chain around the long neck of a greedy lad who tongued my face like a lizard; the next time I was there, he did the same thing again. More than once, a man followed Famous and glowered when I came into proximity. Men inhaled poppers, some while genuflecting at my erection, and I was flattered by their thrall. A twink begged me to finish in his gaping mouth as I kissed another man. I glanced down; the boy looked polite, the type to be well liked and reliable in the office. He crouched like a gargoyle on haunches, then slipped down to his knees. After splattering onto him, I was compelled to disregard him immediately, sensing that must be what he wanted. As Michel Foucault put it, 'You meet men there who are to you as you are to them: nothing but a body with which combinations and productions of pleasure are possible. You cease to be imprisoned in your own face, in your own past, in your own identity.'

I'd rouse myself from the reverie of getting blown by a dubious-looking lover with talented lips, in order to keep an eye out that Famous wasn't doing anything I wouldn't do, or moreover wasn't involved in something better than what I ended up with. I'd push off the two middle-management types burrowed into my armpits, alternating drags of my stink with nitrite hits, and make my way, parting voyeurs, toward Famous and the lithe brown-haired lad whom he tentatively caressed. My final time there before the bar shut for good, I topped a lout in a cubicle who wanted me to finish inside him. I could tell he was unconcerned about whether I was wearing a rubber, and may have preferred if I wasn't. I was, but had rolled it on so hastily it was more like a beanie atop my glans than a sheath. *Come in me*, he panted, probably amped on PrEP. Bored, I pretended to finish. As we left the cubicle, he laughed heartily with his mate, who, I now realized, had been peeping from next door.

One night as we approached, Famous and I encountered a young man befuddled at the back door. I was aware the venue alternated that entrance in the alley with a street-facing one; I muttered as much and we all walked around, at a distance, to the other side. He was tall and towheaded, looked Swiss or at least like a scion who's inherited his father's Swiss watch: upright, careful, well bred. An hour or so later, in the scrum upstairs, I caught sight of the young man watching some fucking. He hadn't come to the wrong place, after all. I moved closer to him. He took off an ordinary sweater to reveal a leather harness across his fluffy blond chest. I began to kiss him, grabbing onto the straps. I slipped my hand down his unbuttoned fly, but had no access; his crotch was a smooth leather mound. The harness, I realized, extended into a chastity contraption, so that there was no way he could get fully erect beneath. His pleasure was distinctly not about his penis; or rather it totally was but in a theoretical way. Its containment drew attention to the everything else of his body; it made him into a whole, not just a setting for the phallus. Soon I found my face in his pit, ripe and wet. It was grassy, wild and vast—a savannah. He grinned. We'd exchanged an intimacy I never would have anticipated on the street. I passed him to Famous who inhaled the blueblood deeply. Another time, in the toilets downstairs, Famous and I found ourselves burrowed into either armpit of a short brunette. His aroma was bituminous and sweet. He grinned and told us he was celebrating his thirtieth birthday. *Thank you, boys,* he sang as he drifted away, with the familiar timbre of a dirty-minded twink.

In each case, the encounter was something more or other than maschalagnia—it was tender. Roland Barthes proposed that a touch of sentimentality might be the ultimate transgression: 'the transgression of transgression.' I experienced for those boys a genuine fondness. I nestled into that place that causes embarrassment daily, that is rebuffed with antiperspirant, where we confess our passion and fret as it deliquesces, where we check for malignant lumps, where we years ago discovered puberty and marveled at what sort of men we might be.

———

Maybe it's borrowed nostalgia, but to me the destination of Vauxhall still promises seediness. Vauxhall lies in the shadow of the hulking MI6 headquarters, the building blocks the view of the river. Its architecture is intimidating yet goofy, influenced not just by local industrial edifices from the thirties, but Aztec and Mayan temples. Like the men around here, it's a little too much and gives itself away. The neighborhood is being encroached by development to the west, including the new American embassy. The cranes and glassy high rises hover like chaperones. Vauxhall is for passing through. Cars rush by after crossing the river. The bus station is sheltered by a cantilevered split roof sticking into the air like a pair of skis. Trains pass above every few minutes on the brick viaduct.

The Bar occupied one of the railway arches, flanked by a sauna and another nightclub. The first time we exited, through the back door in the wee hours, a member of staff called out, *Come again*. I found myself announcing I might apply for a job. *Come see us in the new year*, he hollered cheerily. But the place required the presence of beings more definitive—bartenders with nipples that protrude like duckbills, poking from tight black t-shirts, men built like chesterfields. I could never be a part of that furniture. Outside, the air smelled faintly of garbage, and I detected the whiff of stale jacuzzi from the sauna next door. A pipe spilled chlorinated water. The brickwork had grown mossy down the length of its trajectory, like a viridescent trail to adventure on the building's belly. It seemed at once sad and to muster a kind of comical hope. I thought of the essay by the artist Robert Smithson in which he portrays a great pipe on a riverbank as 'secretly sodomizing.' This one was jerking off. It probably actually was leaking semen into the alley.

The sauna was the last remaining in what was once a group of four. When this location opened in 2006, a Starbucks followed nearby soon after. The way the urban scholar Johan Andersson saw it, the businesses did not represent competing visions but neoliberal neighbors: 'Rather than being "pushed" out by gentrification, public sex has been commercialised and incorporated into the high street as yet another chain branch.' The former Starbucks CEO Howard Schultz is credited for popularizing the sociologist Ray Oldenburg's term *third place*, a social spot between home and work. In free market terms, there may be no reason to distinguish coffeehouse from gay bathhouse, to monitor what people want from their steam.

In total, the viaduct is two miles long, comprising eighty million bricks and nearly three hundred arches. There have been other raunchy clubs and cheesy bars in these arches, though more and more have gone out of business. The Portuguese family restaurants seem to persevere. A small theater puts on gay plays. A neon sign in a handwritten script mounted over one pedestrian tunnel reads *Pleasure*, a frivolous play on the Vauxhall Pleasure Gardens, which once sprawled across this terrain.

When the viaduct was constructed in 1848, it was designed to circumvent those renowned grounds, at one time the top visitor attraction in England, but by that point becoming lusterless and verging on closure. From the late seventeenth century, the shaded land was said to harbor strumpets and other deviants. Over time, the gardens were made reputable and illuminated at nightfall by oil lamps ignited ceremoniously. Still, rustlings from the penumbra continued to arouse suspicion. The avenue Druid's Walk—or Lover's Walk—remained unlit. Disused boats swayed from tree branches, occupied by men who nestled there to smoke. Among the boughs, a series of roofed arbors, some adapted from old coaches, provided nooks for assignations. They had names like pubs—the Royal George, Checker, King's Head. The gardens were reputed to be rife with dandies and queers. Princess Seraphina, named John Cooper at birth, was known to have attended the Ridotto al Fresco ball in June 1732, the same night one waiter became so drunk he excited himself into a gown. Though Lover's Walk was finally under lamplight by the late eighteenth century, it intersected another avenue at the gardens' far edge. This was known as Dark Walk, an unlit stretch giving shelter to the concupiscent. In the novel *Vanity Fair*, Thackeray alludes to the terrain in plural: 'the dark walks, so favourable to the interviews of young lovers.'

The gardens have since been reduced to a manicured, undulating public green. It's pleasant enough. There's a basketball court. Joggers circulate. At lunchtime, office workers stroll the paths. A man might hold my eye contact briefly—very different from the carnivorous stares inside the clubs.

My personal favorite Vauxhall monument must be—on a traffic island in the busy intersection where the bus and train stations meet—a concrete and metal pissoir, brutalist in style, with a sign that reads Urinal in the trustworthy Transport for London typeface. It's a very British architecture. It just stands there, dour, gray, with that blunt word in the sky, calling to mind a nineteenth-century neologism: first *Urning* in German, coined by Karl Heinrich Ulrichs in his bold and iffy hypothesis of a third sex—basically, a male body with a female sex drive—then adopted by Victorian emancipators as *Uranian*, mythical code word for comradely love.

Public toilets have been repurposed for homosexual encounters to the extent of requiring new descriptors: *tea room* in America or *cottage* in Britain. In London, various architectural defenses—brighter lights, partitions—have been implemented to deter frisky goings-on. In the case of this Vauxhall pissoir, it is the notably open design—no doors and a trough only semiconcealed by low walls—that foils untoward activity. Even a wayward glance would be conspicuous. (Foucault: 'visibility is a trap.')

In 1937, the publishing firm Routledge brought out *For Your Convenience*, a little green book later posited as the original gay city guide; it is ostensibly an overheard conversation in a private gentleman's club regarding how to follow drainage routes in order to cruise for sex. The design is replete with an illustrated map of central London public toilets as endpaper. In his book *Queer London*, Matt Houlbrook postulates how an association with degraded places helped construct homosexual identity as filthy: 'notions of the queer's character were derived from the nature of that site at which he was most often arrested.' In 1954, one police constable testified: 'I think they get a great deal of satisfaction from the chase, shall I call it, the chase. These urinals have got a certain odor inside them, staleness, and it does excite them, there is no doubt about it.' Scrubbed clean, he declared, they stayed away, until the antiseptic aroma wore off and once again 'you can see these people definitely working themselves up into a frenzy inside, and once they are on heat, that is the way to describe it, it is like the bitch, once they have the scent there is no holding them, they are oblivious to everything else.'

In 1985, Vauxhall's liberal local council decreed a ten-minute maximum for police officers in public lavatories. The *Sun* headline: 'Lefties to "Clock" Cops in the Loo!' The new law attempted to put an end to the decades-long tradition of assigning so-called pretty police to London toilets with the intention of ensnaring insatiable homos. With the change in law, attendants became responsible for reporting any cop who prolonged their visit.

———

There's another pissoir, on the pavement beside the Royal Vauxhall Tavern. This one waits dormant underground until rising to street level vampirically at dusk. It stands embarrassingly close to the picnic tables at which chummy pubgoers sit smoking. The regular crowd at the RVT comprises cuddly bears in checked flannels, weedy bespectacled types, dykes with facial piercings. The RVT is in many ways the opposite of the sketchy scene at The Bar across the alley. Everyone here looks like they were in drama as a teenager, maybe as members of stage crew.

If I were to picture the last gay bar standing, it might look like the Royal Vauxhall Tavern. The building is uniquely isolated, as if on a corner without streets: It was built as the vertex of two Victorian terraces, and when the vicinal houses were knocked down in the seventies, only the pub remained, which explains its distinctive wedge shape; it looks like a slice of a cake. The RVT was built in the years after the pleasure gardens ceased operations in 1859, along what had been its western edge. Throughout the barroom are six cast-iron pillars with Corinthian capitals, and another half dozen line the pub's bowed facade. The columns are thought to have been purchased at auction from the gardens, which would make them the only known material relics of that famed site to subsist locally. A curving bar once snaked alongside these posts, doubling as a catwalk for twiggy drag artists lip-syncing to bubblegum pop. (One act by a swinging sixties type climaxed with the popping of her balloon-pregnant belly against a column.) The serpentine bar was later removed but the columns remain, still swung from by performers during barnstormers like 'Survivor' or 'It's Not Right but It's Okay.'

These columns, and the queens wrapped around them, won the pub a Grade II listing from Historic England in 2015, the first instance of a public site achieving this status based largely on its queer history. The RVT came out as a gay bar gradually: after the Second World War, the clientele combined returning servicemen and local homosexuals. Truck drivers and market traders sat in their own section behind engraved glass. It's held to be among the oldest gay pubs in the country, that way inclined since at least 1950. I would have thought its historical listing to be a fait accompli; there are Grade II listed phone booths in this country. Enough time has passed that gay bars, once a scourge, have become monumental in their own way. But their vastly undocumented history requires transcribing. As the critic Ben Walters wrote in the building's listing application, the queer archive is 'fragile from fear and forgetting, too often written in whispers and saved in scraps.'

Gay history tends to make an antagonist of authority. In January 1987, thirty-five police officers raided the RVT. One burst into the dressing room of the preening drag queen Lily Savage, who took him for a stripper. Eleven people were arrested, essentially for being drunk at a pub. The cops wore surgical rubber gloves, contending it was a precaution over the threat of contracting AIDS or hepatitis B by way of a needle (the cops being squeamish about the blood they were prepared to shed), as well as protection against the spillage of amyl nitrite. But it's said that on that night nobody was actually searched for drugs. 'Instead,' as Ben Walters has written, 'the gloves seemed like a perfect symbol of oppressive marginalization, speaking to a deep-seated abhorrence of queer bodies.' He adds: 'But they also had tremendous camp value, looking rather prissy in themselves and being just a dash of poetic license away from the rubber gloves used for washing-up—a classic accessory of feminized domesticity.'

Onstage a few nights later, the drag queen Adrella brought forth a container of fake blood. She suggested that if it came to it, the gay men in the audience could squirt it onto their skin to put a scare into fearful cops. This was met with hearty laughter—tiny release amid a crisis. Every day, another friend was diagnosed or succumbed. The pub was hosting funerals. Gay men, recently identified as the most affluent minority in the nation, were more visible but no more popular. They were endangered not only by the virus but vigilantes, not just by the police but Members of Parliament.

The listing of the pub was orchestrated by a scrappy cohort of customers, event promoters and performers who called themselves RVT Future. They were strategic in making their case by imbuing the bar with an almost traditionalist sense of value. Tales that play off the *royal* in the pub's name were accentuated, namely the legend that Princess Diana was once there. The perhaps tenuous connections to the historical pleasure gardens were convincingly underscored. They found a champion in not just the swish actor Sir Ian McKellen but in Boris Johnson, then the mayor of London. Their mission expressly did not have the support of the pub's managing director or the building's owner, an Austrian company that specializes in converting historical properties into luxury accommodation. The company launched its own petition in opposition to the listing, which campaigners decried as an example of astroturfing, as in fake grass roots. Subsequent to the successful Grade II listing, the pub's clearly annoyed managing director updated his bio on the RVT website to include a line about how the place now operates under 'onerous restrictions.'

For the campaigners, preservation was a political statement, a way of archiving gay history in the form of a building. It was activism by way of paperwork, putting in mind the critic Gayle Rubin's proposal of queering bureaucracy. Rubin admits that bureaucracy lacks glamour and charisma, and that queers are prone to live for the moment. But: 'momentary excitements are intrinsically fragile, evanescent, and unstable. Part of the reason for our impaired memory of the older strata of queer knowledges is that the institutions and organizations that produced them are gone. Queer life is full of examples of fabulous explosions that left little or no detectable trace.' The question is whether the spark is extinguished when an official story is made of the blast.

—————

In 2017, the British establishment was ready to institutionalize the subculture as heritage: queerness was a national treasure. The year marked the fiftieth anniversary of the Sexual Offences Act of 1967, which partially decriminalized sex between men in England and Wales. Commemoration was widespread. It seemed that employees and volunteers of nearly every major institution were being issued rainbow lanyards. Around the necks of old codgers and pimply teenagers, this lent a respectively woebegone or awkward effect.

The normally fusty National Trust re-created a place called the Caravan club. The original, on Endell Street in London's West End, was only open for around six weeks, in July and August 1934, in the basement of a building notorious for prostitution and gambling. A card circulated, full of genteelisms: 'London's Greatest Bohemian Rendezvous...said to be the most unconventional spot in town...ALL NIGHT GAIETY.' During its brief existence, hundreds of people from disparate social strata became members. After the commissioner of police received an anonymous note calling the Caravan 'absolutely a sink of iniquity' that was 'only frequented by sexual perverts, lesbians and sodomites,' a sting operation was put into motion. The statements by undercover cops paint a colorful picture.

The constables were in agreement that the place was run by a figure called Iron Foot Jack, and that couples in a variety of gender combinations lay about on cushions. Effeminate men, pipe-smoking lesbians and 'coloured people' were present. The single bathroom was an oversubscribed destination, with same-sex couples going in for three to twelve minutes at a time, to be asked 'Was it thrilling' by their peers upon exit. One man was observed sitting on the toilet blackening another's eyelashes.

Police Constable Miller detailed how men kissed and fondled, touching one another on the buttocks while passing endearing remarks. PC Bryant testified that one reveler put his right hand on the fly of another man's trousers. ('I heard one of them say: "Oh darling."') PC Slatterly noted that PC Mortimer dutifully socialized and danced with male prostitutes. The latter reported, 'Men were dancing together and whilst doing so, paused, and went through the motions of sexual intercourse. Such expressions as "You need not do it anymore, I've come" and "Oh you bitch" were freely used.' The fastidious constable watched two men gyrating together for one hour and eighteen minutes. Mortimer also found himself importuned by a male regular named Josephine, who promised to don turquoise blue the following evening in anticipation of his return.

From under the divans, evidence was collected: An assortment of lipsticks, eyebrow brushes and powder puffs, just beneath where two sailors had been sitting. A knuckleduster. A used rubber. A slip of paper that read, in part: 'This certifies that I, the undersigned, a female about to enjoy sexual intercourse with _____ am above the age of consent, am in my right mind, and not under the influence of any drug or narcotic. I am in no fear of him whatever, do not expect or want to marry him, don't know whether he is married or not, and don't care.' One officer brought the process of collecting evidence into the realm of ritual humiliation when he rubbed blotting paper on the cheeks of men in order to prove they wore rouge.

On the August night the club was raided, dozens were apprehended and twenty-seven eventually brought to criminal court. It was documented that one of them, Cyril de Leon, told the officer in charge: 'I don't mind this beastly raid, but I would like to know if you could let me have one of your nice boys to come home with me. I am really rather good.' When the accused—largely flamboyant men—were brought into trial at Bow Street Magistrates' Court, the media had trouble discerning whether the crowd who'd gathered outside, including porters from the nearby Covent Garden Market, were jeering or cheering them on.

The project of simulating the short-lived nightclub to commemorate the Sexual Offences Act seemed to operate on this thought experiment: if only the Caravan had opened *after* the law changes of 1967, or if the act had gone through decades *earlier*—what good, libertine fun everyone would have had at a place like that, without interference from misguided police. In reality, while the Sexual Offences Act represented certain progress, its language was cautionary. At the law's passage, one of its proponents, the Earl of Arran, spoke: 'I ask one thing and I ask it earnestly. I ask those who have, as it were, been in bondage and for whom the prison doors are now open to show their thanks by comporting themselves quietly and with dignity. This is no occasion for jubilation, certainly not for celebration. Any form of ostentatious behaviour, now or in the future, any form of public flaunting, would be utterly distasteful and would, I believe, make the sponsors of the Bill regret that they have done what they have done. Homosexuals must continue to remember that while there may be nothing bad in being a homosexual, there is certainly nothing good.'

The act specified the right of two men—never three or more—to be intimate within totally private spaces. This actually reinforced the culpability of men caught publicly, whether in flagrante delicto or in the process of seduction. The exemption of private space privileged wealthier men whose residences were more secluded. Any site was deemed public as soon as a third person was present, and a commercial venue that allowed lewd acts was considered to be a brothel. In other words, the same accusations that shut down the Caravan would have held up after the passing of the act, perhaps more so. It's been reported that the number of men convicted of gross indecency jumped from four hundred and twenty in 1966, the year before the new laws went into effect, to one thousand seven hundred and eleven in 1974. To my mind, the anniversary celebrations were marked by revisionism, as that equivocal piece of legislation was roundly characterized as emancipatory. In the process, once covert citizens involved with the scene were rendered public personalities. I saw it as a conundrum of whether such subcultures are *heritagable* at all.

When I say *gay bar*, you might picture a salon of effete dandies engaged in witty banter, a lair of brutes in black leather, a pathetic spot on the edge of town flying a lack-luster rainbow flag for its sole denizen—one lonely hard drinker. Of course, a gay bar can be all these things and more. Many of us have believed finding a home in such a place meant finding oneself. Late at night, all the men in the room are referred to as boys (*Hello, boys*, shouts the drag queen) and this approximation of neverland evinces a mind-set of perennial searching.

A gay bar, it will be said, affords refuge. The Latin root *refugium* positions a *refuge* as a place to which one *flees back*—indicating regression, withdrawal and retreat. A gay bar could be seen as the last refuge of those addicted to sex or alcohol, to their own abasement or oblivion. The question arises as to what distinguishes an enclave from a

32

quarantine, and whether either is any longer necessary. The young homos in my South London neighborhood create a parallel universe in mixed company. The blippy alert of an incoming Grindr message in a straight pub punches between worlds. A territory is not conquered, but complicated— revealed to be permeable. (Not to mention, in some cases, the pub in question once went through a gay phase.) The boys are comfortable enough in the desegregated space, but may keep one thumb on an app, migrating not their bodies but their attention to a ghetto of common lingo and desire. Is it enough to have a gay bar in the palm of your hand?

I've come across two separate interviews in which Alex Green, a campaigner for the reopening of London's historic gay venue the Black Cap, has likened going into his beloved gay bar at the end of the day to unburdening himself of a backpack...or rather hoisting one on, a big gay backpack—he couldn't be sure which way the analogy worked. This proverbial backpack makes sense to me: gay identity is a paradox of freedom and containment. The critic and activist Simon Watney once wrote of the sense of relief upon finding a gay bar in a new city, promising the chance to meet other people like us: 'And yet the question remains, in what sense "like" us?'

Each time I step into a gay bar, I sense my identity being calibrated—a fleeting introspection at the threshold, sending ripples through my time there. The glance-over you get at the door, at sleazier spots entailing a request to strip down. The more banal costume change at a standard coat check, when I decide which layers to discharge and what significations attach to the clothes I keep on. But in a gay bar, do I become more or less gay? Is the mark of my queerness attenuated when contrasted with others more flaming than me? Is it absorbed by the dimness—or more fully exposed, as if under ultraviolet? Depends, in part, on the place. But no matter which type, in gay bars, if such a thing is possible, my self-awareness and sense of ease amplify concurrently. Twink, top, masc, queen, member of a throuple, tweaker, tourist, voyeur, exhibitionist, pee-shy, among friends, lonely, terrified of disease. In gay bars, I have been each of these things. I've found my identity affirmed and challenged. I have been tugged between isolation and camaraderie. As with other men, I suspect, my goal is to be basic, to blend in—but, with a snobbishness, to not appear like a native to the territory.

An acquaintance of mine, after an elegant company event, led a group of colleagues to G-A-Y, the bar in Soho. Standards had by that point resolutely lowered. While Mark generously ordered rounds, a thief observed him type in his PIN, then lifted his card. At the bank the next morning, the teller told a rueful Mark that he would read out a list of purchases. Mark was to determine where his spending ceased and the perpetrator's spree began. The teller looked at a screen, which revealed the previous night's transactions from G-A-Y. *Okay*, boomed the teller. *These are the purchases that were processed in that period.* Mark nodded his head.

10:45. £19.50. GAY.
11:10. £13.00. GAY.
11:50. £37.50. GAY.
12:15. £26.00. GAY.

In telling the story, Mark reenacted glancing around the bank, wishing the teller had a quieter voice or the bar a different name. We laughed with him because a mundane interaction had become an incidental humiliation. Wayne Koestenbaum writes, 'Humiliation is always personal, even when it lands on an individual because of group characteristics.' Mark wasn't the guilty one, though somehow exposed, as if he were a sitcom character, either closeted and at risk of being inadvertently called out or straight and misidentified by association. Plus, there does remain something embarrassing about a gay bar. It's so conclusive, especially one that spells out its own name.

I often think of that bank teller, as if he were the embodiment of social policing. I hear it in my mind: *gay* four times pronounced with a guttural *g* followed by a diphthong vowel, accentuating how that word manages to convey an abstract onomatopoeia. Nobody thinks of themselves as just another homosexual, but it's what the teller sees on the screen. Sometimes labels are funny, as are patterns of behavior, stigmas, even stereotypes, being interpellated in a bank. I consider myself lucky to be in on the stolen bank card joke, swinging off that gay diphthong flamboyantly.

The word *gay* may have suggested dissoluteness from as early as the fourteenth century, and its meanings over time have implied a carefree quality but also a looseness of morals. According to *The Oxford English Dictionary*, historical senses have included: bright, lively-looking, brilliant, showy; finely or showily dressed; lighthearted, disposed to joy and mirth; exuberantly cheerful, merry, sportive; offhand or airy (probably dismissively); a dog's tail carried high or erect; wanton, lewd, lascivious—obsolete since the mid-fifteenth century, but also promiscuous, frivolous, wild, crazy, flamboyant; a female living by prostitution; a male living by prostitution (if a *gay boy* or *gay cat*, as opposed to a *gay man*, who was a womanizer); attractive, charming; specious; in rude health; forward, impertinent, too free in conduct, overfamiliar or reckless (when phrased as: *to get gay*); foolish, stupid, socially inappropriate; a noble lady or gallant man; a childish amusement, trifle or whim; a picture in a children's book; various lighthearted matters, as contrasted with the grave.

Gertrude Stein may have been the first to publish the word meaning homosexuality, in 1922. It being Stein, who knows what she meant. She deployed it with characteristic recursiveness: 'They were together then and traveled to another place and stayed there and were gay there, not very gay there, just gay there. They were both gay there.' Elsewhere in the text: 'They were...gay, they learned little things that are things in being gay...they were quite regularly gay.' The first occurrence of the term *gay bar* in print is thought to be in the 1947 diary of the comedian Kenneth Williams, who wrote from Singapore: 'Went round to the gay bar which wasn't in the least gay....' His usage is timeless in the way it expresses ironic disappointment. Three years later, what's considered to be the first recorded use of *gay* as a self-description for a homosexual man, in *Sir!* magazine, was even fuller of despair: 'I have yet to meet a happy homosexual. They have a way of describing themselves as gay but the term is a misnomer. Those who are habitues of the bars frequented by others of the kind, are about the saddest people I've ever seen.' With queer etymologies, usage is often ironic or counterintuitive from the start. One of the earliest published occurrences of *coming out* in the sense of revealing sexual orientation appeared in an article on gay London life published in *The Observer* in 1971: "'I enjoy my double life," said a delicate youth wearing a gold chain belt in a Chelsea pub. "I don't want to come out.'"

A friend of mine, Robbie, used to wear his brown hair to his shoulders, and threadbare t-shirts of bands like the Breeders. One night he stood in line for G-A-Y Late, the sister club to G-A-Y Bar. The bouncer denied him entry at the door. *Why not!* Robbie barked back. *Because,* she said, *you don't look gay.* Robbie was bemused, possibly a little flattered. *But I am,* Robbie contested. *Like, one hundred percent.* The bouncer appraised him again. *Well, you don't look like it,* she said, removing him from the queue. These stories circulate because, whether being unintentionally proclaimed gay or told you're not gay enough, there will always be a slight misfit. A friend's complexities have been flattened, and the punch line is how someone can get it right yet so wrong.

———

We go out to be gay. We crave this when once again growing bored with the straight world. I will announce to Famous: *I want to be gay this weekend.* This carries an ineffable but precise connotation along the lines of *white girl wasted.* It means we don't want to, for example, attend a recital of minimalist composition. That's something we might otherwise do. But when we decide *to be gay,* we want to dance to 'Starships' by Nicki Minaj, and go downhill from there. On nights when we crave not dick but ridiculousness—the bad taste and nostalgia—we head to a venue less sleazy, more cheesy, where every queen appears to believe their own hype. They invent tiny melodramas. Group conversation involves a lot of squawking in pursuit of a collective cackle. A gay bar can be a repository for all the extra that doesn't fit into other spaces. When a gay person remarks they're being *a bad gay*, it doesn't mean unethical, but that they haven't been conforming to type. It means they've been a bad gay culturally. Hence: *I really should go out; I've been such a bad gay.* We pretend we go out as an obligation.

'Queer scenes are the true *salons des refusés*,' wrote the critic Michael Warner, 'where the most heterogeneous people are brought into great intimacy by their common experience of being despised and rejected in a world of norms that they now recognize as false morality.' I imagine that Warner, a theorist prone to questioning presumptions of gay identity, would also recognize how in these spaces we don't just find *great intimacy* in the face of *false morality*, but fall into *false intimacy*. This doesn't have to be a problem. To me, it's a draw. Gay bars are sites of genuine artifice. We go out to be real, which in gay argot can mean fake it.

We go out to be on the inside. Once, Famous and I disembarked at Waterloo station with the intention of walking along the bank of the Thames to the Royal Vauxhall Tavern. Approaching the river, we came upon an elaborate queer party en plein air. I assumed this to be a product of Sadiq Khan's affirmation of the city's nightlife in the face of its many setbacks. Khan published his vision for a twenty-four-hour London shortly after becoming mayor in 2016. He created the esoteric-sounding role of night czar and appointed Amy Lamé, a gregarious fixture of the RVT scene. (She's been at it for decades; the last time I saw her hosting, she wore Birkenstocks but still bellowed to the crowd *Snog a stranger!* from the stage.) Together, the pair hailed the 'night-time economy' as a means of revenue and place-making. Khan's vision must've looked something like what we now stood before: a large crowd singing along to 'Smalltown Boy' and 'I'm Coming Out' under a synthetic snowdrift. Everyone likes a gay anthem of transformation and freedom. I gave in, but with a sense of dislocation, almost as if I was appropriating my own culture. The drag queens on the bandstand began to berate the staff of the adjacent bar. *The performers are entitled to free cocktails*, they squalled into the microphones. *And somebody better bring shots. That's how it works.* The staff of the tourist trap apparently did not know gay bar etiquette. After a dance, Famous and I continued on our way to the RVT. We didn't mind paying the cover charge. We wanted to cross its threshold, be inside the walls, where the codes are self-evident.

We go out to be nobodies. We head for a gay bar when we want to be anonymous homosexuals, what the sociologist Erving Goffman called 'eventful to no one.' At my preferred type of gay bar, there's no obligation to network; I'm there to be with people not because of what I do but who I fuck. Another night at the RVT, a Saturday—it was nearing Christmas again—having escaped from a *salon* in a lavish town house piled with cocaine and decorated in humongous black-and-white photographs of the unfortunate and impecunious, we were received by the glamorous vampire who works the door. They're a tall, glassy-eyed creature with lank hair and a way of coolly receiving us as if we were expected—and not for being *us*, thankfully, but just two more soused midnight shadows. We gave them our cash and moved into the humid jostle. 'He's on the Phone' by Saint Etienne was playing, the lyrics quintessentially London—lipstick and Leicester Square—painting the city as an ocean of ships passing in the night. I took a hit of Amsterdam Gold during Robyn's 'Dancing on My Own.' After the small talk of that middlebrow art gathering, we both prayed not to see anyone else we knew. Maybe, I thought, we could go to The Bar in the arches afterward, and abandon any remaining semblance of respectability. Famous whispered into my ear, *I like being in places where I don't know anyone.* I concurred. *Fuck that salon,* I said, as we swiveled to the Magician remix of Lykke Li's 'I Follow Rivers.'

The only time she was inside the RVT, Princess Diana went there explicitly to be an anonymous homosexual. It was 1988. The actress Cleo Rocos has written that she and her television costar Kenny Everett had begun drinking peach bellinis with Diana at a brasserie in Kensington earlier in the day. They ended up at Kenny's penthouse up the road to watch *Golden Girls*. Eventually, Freddie Mercury showed up. According to Rocos, the four of them sat on the sofa in front of the show, and Kenny turned the volume down so they could replace the dialogue with their own ribald improvisations. Diana played Dorothy. They became giddy, with Diana burying her giggles in a cushion. Freddie reported they'd be going to the Vauxhall Tavern; Diana said she'd like to come along. There was much protesting as everyone feared she'd be found out there. Kenny warned it would be full of manly, hairy gay men. But Diana was resolute, and was soon in a cab adorned in Kenny's fatigue jacket, leather cap and aviators. When they arrived at the RVT it was full. The group pushed toward the bar, greeting acquaintances along the way. 'Our hearts pounded with every new leather-clad hairy body that approached,' Rocos reports, 'but no one, absolutely no one, recognized Diana.' The goal of the princess was to order a drink undetected; that accomplished, she was back in a taxi to Kensington Palace, waving goodbye to the boys gathered outside.

The line I've read that best distinguishes a gay bar may be from the journalist June Thomas. She wrote, 'There's more literature in gay bars'—meaning the magazines, health pamphlets, guides, maps and flyers that pile up on the peripheries. At the RVT, I spied a booklet, beer-soaked and footprinted, on the sticky floor at the base of one of the columns. It was not a small square concertina like HIV-prevention pamphlets, nor a glossy listings magazine. Picking up the matte-yellow stapled journal, I saw it was the publication of the Urban Laboratory at University College London, which had become the authoritative force in the study of London's precarious sites. I took it home and dried it on the radiator.

The pamphlet compiled essays from those who work in queer spaces or study them academically, or both. One contributor, Joe Parslow, wrote an essay that refers to the critic José Esteban Muñoz's paralleling of the word *stage* in the sense of a platform for performance with *stage* as a phase that queers are told to get over—as when parents contend it's just a blip. In 2009, Muñoz wrote, 'Today I write back from that stage that my mother and father hoped I would quickly vacate. Instead, I dwell on and in this stage.' Parslow explains how he was inspired to think from the stage outward when he designed his own venue, Her Upstairs, one of those few places that opened against the wave of bar closures; it shut down after only a short spell.

In his listing application for the RVT, Ben Walters offered another symbolic interpretation of the stage. When Pat and Breda McConnon took over the tavern in 1979, they made the decision to put an end to the messy tradition of bartenders serving drinks between the legs of the drag queens atop the curving bar. But rather than cancel the entertainment, they renovated the interior, removing that bar and installing a bespoke stage. Walters points out the meaningfulness of this move. Performing on the bar had meant that a drag queen could be swiftly cleared away and the performance denied at the sign of a police raid. The McConnons permanently ensconced queer performance in the materiality of the building. Their stage was not a phase.

Another thing that marks out gay bars: the mirrors over the urinals in the men's bathrooms. This used to disturb me. I remember the first time I experienced it, years ago. Famous had taken me to Heaven. I was aghast at the mirrors directly above the trough, including one angled strategically in the corner like those used to monitor shoplifters. In general, urinals in England come with their own set of challenges. British men are prone to making conversation there, a comment about the night, the state of the toilets, sports. This puts me in an awkward position. When I open my mouth, as a friend says of himself, my handbag falls out. It's less, these days, a fear of being bashed, more a matter of not wanting to embarrass my neighbor. I don't want to watch him adjust to my gayness, to act like it's cool—as if gay is not a lot to do with enjoyment of penis. Then I am ashamed that I am ashamed that he is ashamed that I am ashamed. I shake myself, and leave with dripping hands as I don't want to stand under the dryer any longer than necessary. I scurry away. Scurrying is also a telltale trait—the way so many gays always appear like they're about to miss a train—but at least I'm on my way out.

In a gay bar bathroom, the dynamic is less predictable. After years of recoiling, my dick a shy slug, I've discovered my exhibitionist streak. This must have changed after the time I'd taken too much of my mom's cannabis tincture before going to the Eagle LA when we were back on the West Coast. She *had* warned me, reporting that once on two droppers of the stuff, she lost all sense of linear time while chopping onions. But I ignored her advice, took a second dose and by the night's end was at the corner toilet giving a peep show in the dim light. Since then, overconfident from the generally positive response, I have stood with the open hips of a yogi. I make *other* men pee-shy. The next time I went to the Eagle LA, I found myself, inebriated, starting up the same act. Just when I thought I was about to bask in other men's admiration, one shouted, *We're all here just waiting—are you going to piss or what?*

At the Royal Vauxhall Tavern, there are mirrors but, because of the tone of the place, they seem more flirty than licentious. An attractive man glanced at me with a smile and said cutely, *Now I can't go.* Soon after, I saw him on the dance floor, whispering to his friend and nodding at me. We all knew he still had to pee. Fleeting, gently pervy interactions like that may be the closest I get to experiencing a sense of gay community.

It was last call at the RVT. Famous stole away to the toilets. 'Family Affair' by Mary J. Blige began to play—a song meant for the start of the night. I danced on my own by the door, near the shelf of condoms and literature. I recalled another time I'd been there recently. I'd given my coat check ticket to the most boyish and poised of the bartenders, the one who moves with a distinct admixture of flirtatiousness and efficiency. He brought my jacket from the cloakroom, the blue nylon I wear when I predict I'll end up going out, because it promises to wipe clean easily. About to hand it to me over the bar, he said, *You know what…* and brought himself around the hatch, with shoulders alert like a pantomime butler. He held up my jacket with alacrity to indicate I should turn around so he could slip me into it. I momentarily forgot that I don't smile in gay bars. He both served and took the upper hand: to get into the jacket, I had to turn my back to him, and yet into the sleeves it was I who inserted. I submitted, but he received.

On this night, I glanced over and saw that the bartender was busy, holding someone else's attention in a brief exchange. He fetched them their extraneous last drink. Famous bounced forth. I caught his eye and pointed my index finger to the speakers. *This song*, I mouthed. Famous tilted his head. We pushed through the doors into the wind. I'd put my jacket on myself this time, without ceremony. But leaving on a good song also makes a fine exit. Mary J. Blige sang at our backs about starting the party as we took long strides down the street.

THE FACTORY

LOS ANGELES

When I was young the absence of the past was a terror. That's why I wrote autobiography.

—Derek Jarman, 1992

I can't remember my first. It was someplace in Los Angeles. If it counts, my first gay bar was an ex–gay bar. Probe, on North Highland Avenue, was once a raunchy private club for gay men. I wasn't aware of this. The name should have provided a clue to its past, but to my mind *probe* just telegraphed a generic nightlife vibe. Anyway, we didn't refer to the name of the venue. By the time I arrived in town to attend college in 1992, it was used by different promoters each night of the week for rotating 18+ events—goth Helter Skelter, industrial Kontrol Faktory, the disco costume party Club 1970.

I skipped to the front of the line to that last one, having arrived with two doll-like girls from the dorms. But I think I was first driven to Probe by my roommate, not long after the school year began. Tim was a skater in trousers so wide you couldn't see his feet. We were there for Citrusonic, a weekly party of happy hardcore—cartoon noises over tribal drums with occasional lyrics about the ecstasy kicking in. I nodded my head stiffly, pretending I was on something.

47

Tim danced only briefly—an impassive bob as if he were about to breakdance but never did—before catching the attention of a girl who played the daughter on a sitcom I grew up watching. They sat together atop a speaker for the rest of our time there.

I danced alone. I kept my head down as if that's what heterosexuals did, while actually the straight ravers around me grinned at one another in druggy fellowship. Little did I know the place used to be resolutely homosexual. In the early seventies, the club was the Paradise Ballroom, one of the Hollywood spots where black and brown gay men developed a style of dance called posing. They'd freeze in various positions at each *boom* of 'Papa Was a Rolling Stone,' looking like photos of Greta Garbo and Marlene Dietrich and Gloria Swanson. Some on the scene also appeared as dancers on *Soul Train,* and brought aspects of posing from disco to TV screen. Dance historians disagree over the extent to which posing cross-pollinated with the *Soul Train* house style of locking—quick moves interspersed with halts, said to have been invented as a means of coolly handling a flub. However it happened, an evolution of posing was dubbed punking, an allusion to the slur for homosexual men. (Over the years, *punk* has been used to indicate a catamite, sissy, faggot, bottom, prison bitch and boy who accompanies a hobo to be used for sex.) Punking—or waacking, as it became widely known to avoid the pejorative—would eventually go on to hook up with voguing on the East Coast.

In 1978, the site became Probe, with an exclusive membership of leathermen and clones, macho men so alike they could have replicated in a lab. They gathered together to look the same in the same places. By 1979, an American sociologist reported 'the fastest proliferating type of establishment in the gay bar business is a place where gay men can declare with gusto that they are not like women.' At one Halloween party at Probe, guests in drag were turned away at the door, told cross-dressing wasn't appropriate to the event's theme, Sodom and Gomorrah.

Probe appears in the 1980 movie *American Gigolo*, playing the role that nightclubs often do on film: a location of depravity where a protagonist is faced with specters of their fallen self. The concrete facade looks austere like a bunker or tomb. Inside, Richard Gere scooches past somnambulant clones wearing hard hats and passing poppers between them. The parties at Probe were elaborately themed: Adam and Yves. Undersea. Working the Nile. The prom. Halloween in a New Orleans mansion. War games (to which, went the poster, 'Probe invites all able-bodied men...').

The marathon DJ sets at the annual Black Party stretched for fifteen hours. In preparation, the resident DJ would sleep long nights for a month and never skip the gym. Records were carefully selected from dozens of promos arriving each week. The playlist formed an arc that would build, swell, peak and release. In the early hours of the morning, a diva might sing live. Into the day, slower, sometimes melancholic comedown tracks played—like 'Close to Perfection' by Miquel Brown or 'Come to Me' by France Joli—in the genre variously called morning music or, in something of a misnomer, sleaze.

In 1984, the membership criteria tightened, even as the lights were further dimmed. At flashlight underwear parties, guests were encouraged to 'probe the darkness' with their handheld lamp while a White Hot Intellibeam occasionally swept across the floor to expose sporadic wild scenes. A flyer for an event the next year called Marquis de Sade's Playroom described a long hallway of complete darkness, with the sound of dripping water echoing through the catacombs and men waiting behind walls of cold stone. Into the nineties, such events still took place there on occasion. Just months before I came to town, the Black Party was themed Nightstalkers, presumably after the nickname of the California serial killer who inspired terror in me as a kid. The Nightstalkers flyer promised 'A Chilling Walk in the Realms of the Unknown.' It detailed a scenario: 'He had arrived in the rain and his boots stunk of wet leather. I found that I liked it. If my mother knew, I'd be so ashamed. He took me to a corner of the club. He made me do all sorts of things. . . . He acted as if he was stalking me actually. Like an animal. I shivered.'

Such debauchery always took place on other nights, belonging to other men. Of all human categories, adult gay males were among the least familiar to me. Many of them were dead. In 1992, the year I moved to L.A., over four thousand new cases of AIDS were diagnosed in the county; the death toll there was nearing fourteen thousand in the ten years since reporting began. Men who slept with men constituted the vast majority of those cases. According to one study, gay men in Los Angeles knew an average of eighteen infected persons each. It was in 1992 that the disease was declared the nation's leading cause of death for young men.

An essay published that year, 'The Pursuit of the Wish,' quoted one gay man as saying that while it was no longer so, sex used to be like brushing his teeth. Its author, E. Michael Gorman, pointed out that men who'd laid claim to exaggerated masculinity in the wake of gay liberation were now finding themselves filling a role of caretaker—sissified by the disease. Some of the men that Gorman interviewed were sanguine. One responded: 'In between the play and the grief we find ourselves.' Gorman observed: 'One interesting change seems to be the decline of the bar as the prototypical gay institution.' The Probe management responded to shifts in how men vetted one another (and got off) through the introduction of a voicemail service, 976-PROBE. The venue gave way to hosting various nights, popular with students, maladjusted teenagers, ravers, straights. Its elite mailing list dwindled; it was no longer exclusively gay. Probe became a vessel for other people's parties.

The Los Angeles I moved into was a city of vacancies. There was a surfeit of empty apartments. I arrived in September, just as I turned eighteen. The air was dry and unmoving, following a period of exceptionally strong winds. The sky had been blackened from the cars and buildings and palm trees set alight during the Rodney King riots the preceding March. AIDS was all around, but the visible symptoms—and the mourning—were shuttered away. There is no particular way to describe what I was intuiting around me. Maybe there isn't a term for a sense of loss when you don't know what you're missing.

———

It was 1992 and I was against gay visibility. The visible gays did not make life any easier for me. They gave corporeal form to the suspicions that followed me around high school. I didn't want the public to be forced to think about gays. I certainly didn't want my roommate to have to think about them. At the start of the school year, I arrived first. Our room was so small I could sit on my bed and put my feet on his. I had a vision of him requesting to switch to another room, but Tim was more worldly than that. He had taken a year off from school. His eyeballs oscillated slightly, people suspected from the pills he'd swallowed at raves. Other skaters came to our dorm room to suck balloons inflated from his nitrous tank or sit on the floor clipping their toenails while a skate VHS with a Dinosaur Jr. soundtrack juddered away. Tim was kind to everyone and unimpressed by the university. He never washed his bedsheets. I took to Scotch-taping a sheet of Bounce to an electric fan to deodorize the room. We listened to the Pharcyde and mix tapes from Beat Non Stop, the DJ shop on Melrose Avenue.

When Tim went home for the weekend or stayed out late with a girl, I lay in the dark and played Barbra Streisand's cover of 'Somewhere,' in which astral synthesizers evoke outer space. Alone in the dark, I felt comforted, embarrassed and duplicitous.

I was on the lookout for other students who were voting Bill Clinton. The first person I met was Xuan. At orientation, she approached and asked what music I liked. With the trace of a Vietnamese accent, she launched this inquisition almost defensively—as if seeking a password. I answered The Smiths. *Fine*, she snapped. *Let's go to coffee.* Xuan spoke everything in monotone and constantly scowled. (She told me her childhood nickname was Sour Yogurt, which rhymes in Vietnamese.) She listened to British guitar bands with four-letter names. She ordered both lipsticks and photographs in matte finish. Once the autumn term had settled in, we found each other again, and sat in her dorm room under the September cover of *Harper's Bazaar*, which she'd pinned to the wall. Linda Evangelista formed an accent aigu with her wrist. Xuan wore a spritz of Tresor on hers. By filling our conversation with topics from far-flung locations, we cemented our discrete but mutual otherness. We were allied. We quickly formed a habit of bickering, but it never reached the deep trauma of in-fighting because our stigmas were not a match. Instead, our stigmas jostled against each other. Hers was manifest in a half-moon indented on her upper arm, indicating she'd been born in a place they still jabbed for smallpox and arrived in the US by boat. *We are freaks*, Xuan would say to me at all manner of normal white people events, digging her fingers into my arm.

Back home, I covered by going out with girls, but told

friends I would fuck either Morrissey or Snoop Dogg, a comment tossed out as if no big deal, figuring it positioned me as one of those secure enough to admit same-sex desire without actually fitting into a category. But in L.A., people didn't humor such equivocations or self-deceit. The taxonomic mentality of Hollywood prevailed, and my new peers had the mind-set of blunt casting directors to whom I was incontrovertibly gay. As far as Xuan was concerned, I needed to have gay sex with haste. Someone else acted on this by introducing me to Matias. He lived off campus already. He'd managed to skip the dorms and swiftly settle into a Westwood apartment with a dining room table and salt in the kitchen and housemates who held car keys in hand as they chatted in passing about utility bills. Matias was chubby with baby skin and eyes that sparkled like diabolical gems. He wore a male symbol earring in his right ear. He was gay in a way not fathomable in my Silicon Valley high school. It was as if, I thought, he got to be gay the way black kids got to be black: with an attitude that made others want in. He'd shift his head from side to side like a sassy dashboard ornament. He agreed to drive me to the boulevard, if only to placate my newfound champions.

The nightlife stretch of Santa Monica Boulevard in West Hollywood hummed like a neon tube. Bright pink shops sold homoerotic mugs and magnets. The party atmosphere was entrenched but subdued. Groups of gays gossiped al fresco over amaretto sours. West Hollywood, incorporated as its own city in 1984, had been dubbed the Gay Camelot and then officially marketed as the Creative City in an effort to draw not just gay bar tourists but design aficionados.

Creative was a way to connote gays zhoosing up the place. Gays were thought to be especially well adapted to the postindustrial economy, experts in leisure and aesthetics. A 1985 issue of *Urban Geography* put it this way: gay people 'emphasize exchange-value.' In other words, their hype and flourish raise costs for everyone else. In actuality, the organizing principle in establishing West Hollywood's cityhood had been a push for strict rent control. Ultimately, anyway, nobody referred to it as the Creative City. It was Boystown.

I didn't have a fake ID yet, so mostly the bars were just background noise. Come to think of it, the first gay threshold I crossed must have been that coffeehouse on the boulevard. It buzzed like a normal café with intermittent shrieking. Matias and I joined some other students he knew. They wore sweatshirts rolled above the wrist. I could tell right off the most amiable by far was Oliver, a tall ballet dancer with soft black skin who had the habit of smoothing his eyebrow with his middle finger, palm fanning out. He smiled at me slyly, his eyes kind even as he angled his face at a lordly oblique. Taller still was the chiseled sophomore who carried himself with the indignance of a politician's son. There were older men at our table and adjoining, with raw sausage fingers groping cigarettes and stubble as dense as sand. They cackled, *UCL-GAY!*, meaning homosexuals abounded. I'd so far only heard the other crack: *University of Caucasians Lost among Asians*. I was the butt of both of these jokes but had little attachment to either distinction. Still, a part of me flinched at being corralled into a punch line.

The guys at the table seemed so confident—jaded already.

They sat with impudent elbows and ankles. I'd heard it said that gays were perpetually adolescent, but I was convinced this particular sampling had never been boys in the first place. They assessed instead of greeted. They laughed like they'd already butt-fucked. They looked down long noses with the pride of a man with an ass made only for fucking, as if there never was shit. They used phrases like *fresh meat* as they recrossed their legs. They spoke as if words were handed to them to disgrace. They were swishy—not mincing, but like a sword slicing air. They were satisfied with cliché. They dismissed whole populations with one sting. Bottoms and tops were fixed positions. To have a clear racial preference was a highly amusing character trait. It became a part of their repertoire of innuendos. If someone liked black men, for instance, *He goes to Catch One* was all that needed to be said.

Eventually Matias ran into an acquaintance who was more like what I'd been expecting, in that he showed some interest in me. I thought I must have misheard when he introduced himself as Rock. He threw his muscular body around frantically, while his face was deadly serious. His hair was shaved to the scalp, and a large ring hung from his septum like a bull. Then that name, so commanding yet ridiculous. *He's a dancer,* a girl whispered. *A go-go dancer,* Matias qualified. *And modern,* said Rock. *And ballet.* He seemed too compact, almost stocky, for that. Rock smelled sickeningly sweet. I would learn the cologne was bright pink in color, and that its name ended in an exclamation mark. Rock held up his chin to scrutinize me, as though he wore a cap with a brim that shaded his vision. He held his lips tightly to one side.

Jer-ah-me, he repeated my name, in three distinct syllables, the last one possessive. He spoke through a stuffy nose, the audacity of his own name slightly mitigated by the way he pronounced it as a honk. He pulled up the wide jeans he'd let fall to divulge a Calvin Klein waistband. Before leaving, he made a show of finding a pen, then pressed into my hand a folded slip of paper. *ROCK*, I read in the dim of Matias's backseat, with a 714 area code number and a heart pierced by an arrow. *Bye. Jer-ah-me*, he had said, as if the words were two complete sentences, as if he were making fun of me. Rock: I thought of a boxer, and then of being knocked out. I waited the customary two days which I'd never waited to phone another boy. *I knew you would*, he said when I did.

We made plans to meet at the gay coffeehouse, and I got a lift from Matias again in his battered Cabriolet. Around the corner from the boulevard, Rock and I stole away from the never-been-boys and sat on a curbside. The Boystown appellation was relevant only to us. We were tykes. The others had bloated muscles but shaved chests, a paradox of alpha and infantile. The men moved past on their way between bars, amazing with the tightness of their t-shirts. Looking askance was the neutral expression. They walked in redoubtable threes. I finally confronted this identity, one I'd both been handed and told to forsake. In West Hollywood, I began to think it was something you had to work at. Everyone else looked like they were auditioning for a toothpaste commercial. They obviously went to the gym. I figured after all I might not be gay.

A jeep drove by with no roof; the frat boys inside shouted *faggot!* It was hurled toward me as much as anyone else. Rock

57

leaned in. *That's just bound to happen,* he said. *Here?* I marveled. *Especially.* He actually had a girlfriend. But *faggot* did not quite bounce off him, and neither did it quite bounce off me. We sat marked. He told me he wanted to kiss me. I wanted him to want that a little bit longer. I extolled the virtues of a book called *Geek Love,* in which a couple works in the circus, and the wife imbibes all manner of toxins every time she becomes pregnant in order to guarantee job security for their freak offspring. *It's a parable some of us can relate to,* I said unnecessarily. Rock's praise for my exegesis was excessive. *I like you just how you are,* he added. He spoke as if his lines had been scripted. I wished on a streetlamp that the one person who liked me would not prove to be a fake.

1992 was the year Calvin Klein underwear was modeled by Marky Mark. Rumor had it his third nipple was airbrushed out of the image. Other than that, he was anatomically perfect: an epilated Adonis with a shit-eating grin. His name alone was a collision of narcissism and neoteny—duplicated with a diminutive. He was phallus and eunuch, all about the dick he was compulsively grabbing and therefore covering up. Because he was straight, his unattainability equaled safe sex. On the boulevard, the parading men emulated his aggressive wholesomeness. A Marky Mark poster snickered from nearly every bus stop shelter. On Matias's apartment wall, the scale shifted and it looked enormous. *How'd you get it?* He'd thrown a rock—*I was drunk*—and shattered the glass. *I had to have it.* How did Matias already know what he had to have? I precisely did not. I held no judgment about his looting. But the exploitative aspect of the treasure bothered me: Calvin Klein seemed like some nefarious mastermind who'd branded this white boy foundling and turned him into a honey trap. Gay men were falling over themselves to get into those pants, meaning to buy a pair, and to get ahold of the poster through acts of vandalism.

I tried not to be ungrateful. Matias was letting Rock and me use his couch for a tryst. We lay parallel and Rock fingered me painfully. I couldn't help but think he wanted it to hurt. I wanted him to enjoy doing so if that's what he desired, and worried it might stink. Afterward, I couldn't sleep. Rock kept building me up, but in a way that reiterated he was the only one who could possibly like me. He'd remind me about the allegory of the ugly duckling. He told me I had a great look, could try brightening it with loose face powder by Clinique. I should definitely consider a nose ring. He wrote me letters in which I did not recognize myself in his flattery. I saw instead what he wanted me to be, but had to admit that I wanted to be that person, too. I took in the courtyard through the miniblinds across the window. I was paranoid about neighbors peeping. The view through the slats was fragmented like a titillating eighties film poster, *American Gigolo* or *Body Double*. Now I was living in the sort of R-rated film I'd not long ago been banned from seeing.

Of course I can't remember my first gay bar—I was drunk. Subsequent forays into nightlife went something like: dragged from a party in the hills where students hung like cuff links off older men, shoved into the back of Matias's sedan, released onto a throbbing dance floor. At Circus, we entered through a malicious clown's grin.

The club was designed as what architecture critics call a decorated shed—a simple box overwhelmed by its signage, in this case not just the maniacal clown portal, but a tiger jumping off the roof and flanking elephants. Inside, hunks danced topless to show off their glabrous pecs. My impressions were gleaned through strobes and fog machines. Fists pumped in silhouette to a deific DJ. I learned that another massive club, Arena, was a former ice factory, and after that pictured it as a giant block of ice. It was a largely Latino crowd there and its energy was amplified by extravagantly costumed club kids.

Then there was the nondescript one which we never seemed to refer to by name, on a side street off the boulevard and up a stairwell. It was pulsing and busy, but generic. Its advantage over the legendary Mickey's on the boulevard was that it allowed under-21s on Thursdays and Sundays. So I never set foot in Mickey's and wound up in this place instead. The purplish lights behind the bar were like mosquito zappers, making each drink iridescent. I recoiled from the cloying cologne in the air, as sickly as vomited rum and Coke. The crowd was prissy and impenetrably groomed.

I had no concept of the place's exterior. We could have been anywhere; we just rushed up the stairwell high on the weed smoked from a glass pipe in Matias's Cabriolet. I was unaware that we were in the Factory Building. It was originally constructed in 1929 and home to the Mitchell Camera Corporation, makers of the heavy, expensive, Mickey Mouse–ear cameras emblematic of the film industry. The Factory Building was unassuming—an *undecorated* shed—but sprawled between streets, so that it could be accessed by either North La Peer Drive or North Robertson

Boulevard to the east. Embossed metal sidewalls and steel sash windows were fitted over a prefabricated Truscon steel frame. It is rumored that during the Second World War, the site manufactured Norden bombsights, used to drop the atomic bomb on Hiroshima from the Enola Gay. After the camera business moved to the Valley in 1946, the property underwent various incarnations, often concurrently in different sections. In 1967, the old plant was converted into a private club—The Factory—by a consortium of investors including Paul Newman. Groovy waiters were hired for their model-like looks, and the tips came in hundred-dollar bills. Celebrities joined waitstaff smoking weed on the roof. (The opening line of the club's profile in *New York* magazine: 'Bejeweled, Balenciaga'd, trailing ostrich plumes, the matron from Dallas who is determined to be fashionable sets down her yummy pineapple daiquiri and as her husband and friends slap their knees and bray, the matron sails off with a blond, curly-haired bartender to get the most fashionable kick since cocaine: invading the men's room at The Factory for a look at the graffiti on the walls.')

In 1974, the main upper space was transformed into Studio One by Scott Forbes, a former optometrist. The windows were painted black, and ground-floor exterior walls erected. Inside, men peeled off their shirts, basking under seven disco balls and a neon Pegasus. The dance floor was lined in mirrors, an interior design trope common in the city. (Edmund White: 'L.A. has the most beautiful men in the world, and it is only appropriate that it should celebrate them with their multiplied images.') The *Los Angeles Times* depicted the club as the inside of a jukebox—'a futuristic inferno.' Men danced atop speakers with tambourines and fans. The club was revamped three years in. A review of the reopening read, 'Faces were smiling; shirts were removed to reveal glistening, muscled bodies; tight, revealing jeans and melon-buns abounded!' At its peak, a thousand, maybe sixteen hundred bodies filled the space on a single night. Divas cooed from the speakers. 'Total drama, that's what I shoot for,' said the lighting designer. His signature was to keep the lights on the floor low, ensuring the experience was for the dancers, not onlookers.

Outside the club, Scott Forbes raised gay visibility. He organized a takeover of Disneyland in 1978, forcing the park to unwittingly host the first of its unofficial gay days. Reports estimate some eighteen thousand people attended. The code of conduct included: no drag, no pot, no poppers, no t-shirts with lewd slogans. Meanwhile, Studio One became a draw for celebrities. By 1979, a sociological paper announced: 'Gay bars are not what they used to be—clandestine hideaways where a few of the more brazen gay people sought one another out in secret.' A-list stars spotted at Studio One were indicative of a trend: 'For them to parade in, unconcerned by—even because of—the fact that the place is gay, is a testament to the new status of gay establishments.' Forbes qualified to the *Los Angeles Times*: 'Disco to a gay person is very much a social necessity. To a straight person it's more like a trendy thing.'

But that prescribed social necessity began to give some gay men pause. A thirty-seven-year-old Studio One regular spoke with ambivalence to the *Times* in 1976. 'Even the dances have a depersonalized quality to them. The Hustle and The Bus Stop, for instance. In both, you have 50 or 100 people lined up, dancing the same way, completely unattached to each other, simply doing the same move-ments, like robots. Like lemmings, they begin to form those lines.' He went on to prognosticate a dystopian future, what he called the ultimate discotheque: 'I can envision the day when we all just walk up to the entrance to a disco, put a bunch of quarters in a slot, enter and become immediately surrounded by music. Then each of us will go into a space the size of a telephone booth and dance by ourselves.'

Forbes operated Studio One from the year I was born until just before I moved to Los Angeles in 1992. I was quin-tessentially late to the party. Studio One was no longer that legend whose name was chanted in a Village People song. It was just *there*. At some point, the venue was rechristened Axis. The 18+ nights underwent a series of creepy names to entice ephebes and their admirers: Young & Restless, Campus, Playground, Intros. I had no wristband for the bar. Someone would try to give me theirs, stretching it out to wrestle over their wrist. I'd arrive with or mostly without Rock. 'Show Me Love' would inevitably play. House-music tracks had become so pushy—they demanded rather than seduced. The songs were 'A Deeper Love' and 'Deeper and Deeper' and 'Deep Inside.' If I was with Xuan I'd be alert to how tacky it all was as she scrutinized the scene. But we danced like adorable cyborgs. The thing to do was add a judder, as if nearly not scaling the beat. I developed a mode of moving in which my left hand stayed at the small of my back like a matador, my right swinging a phantom string of pearls. My face was acceptably matte under the lights, one tone paler than my natural skin tone from the powder Rock recommended.

I'd slip away from the crew I arrived with in order to experience the place on my own. What was house music if not
a place to inhabit. I wanted to be enclosed. I wouldn't mind
rubbing against some other boy, but couldn't face the rejection if he awaited something better, something oiled like
the men dancing on platforms, like Rock did other nights of
the week. I wouldn't mind being forced by some anonymous
older man, shoved into a corner. I'd suffer his grip with mixed
feelings. The music boomed. I couldn't discern all the lyrics,
so the messages became mine to interpret. What I heard
was a longing to be perturbed, for a hairy arm to wriggle
its way in. I walked very slowly through a dark passageway,
to encounter nothing but a noncommittal glance from one
stumbling man. I came upon the back room, where a cabaret
was in progress, and found a place at the edge, trying to
shrink and blend in. Suddenly I was under the spotlight—a
Madonna impersonator writhed against me as she lip-synced

to 'Deeper and Deeper,' working the disco look from the video: the flares, the snow-cone afro. Were all the words to all the songs about deepness? Deep was a huge penis so far up a body it pokes organs, disturbs the whole household. Deep was the trouble I would one day be in. Deep was my virginity. I was too terrified to dance with the queen, though it would have been the sporting thing to do. Another type of boy, with overplucked eyebrows, would have taken his cue to shimmy like a Slinky. Instead, I stood stiffly with half a grin, and it dawned on me I had in that moment adopted another role, one that conveyed a desirable archetype of its own: the sheepish boy next door.

———

It was becoming apparent that being homo did not amount to being the same: I clearly was not like other gays. But neither did this revelation make me unique. Disassociation is a gay ritual as much as any other. Axis, née Studio One, was not a sanctuary in which to find my true self. I found it both tacky and forbidding. But if my overriding impression was *whatever,* neither was the building particularly glad to see me. The place had been afflicted for years with more acute conflicts of sameness and difference. Some claim that Studio One had not provided a refuge to all, its legacy blemished by a door policy that favored white boys above the rest. Brown and black men would have been less numerous on the dance floor a few years prior. Someone who looked like me might also have been denied entrance. I was under the impression I was always late to the party, but in fact I may not have been invited.

In 1975, the *Los Angeles Free Press* ran the headline 'Studio One Hit with Charges of Racism, Sexist Discrimination.' The reporter trained his eye on the door, recording thirty-five instances of women or people of color being turned away within forty-five minutes, and not a single such situation involving white men. The next year, a *Los Angeles Times* reporter broached the subject of sexism at the club's door. Scott Forbes retorted: 'This was established for gay people. We only advertise to gay people. We only entice gay people. Gay people like to go where there are other gay people, where they can feel relaxed.' The article further outlined the claims made by black and Chicano men that they were frequently denied entrance. 'The secret to a discotheque's longevity is the door,' Forbes maintained. He pointed out how, for instance, 'if you smell bad, you don't get in.' Pressed, Forbes explained it was the straight black men who amounted to the bad element—along with heterosexuals in general. ('Because they only go out now and then, they always overreact.') Two—eventually three—pieces of ID were required of nonwhites and women. A golden boy with a fake California license fared better than an immigrant from Asia with a valid green card. Under the scrutiny of subjective criteria, passing the multiple-ID check was a virtual impossibility. The policy was commonplace at other clubs and also imposed upon transgender people, drag queens and other 'freaks'—with whom, in the words of one club owner speaking anonymously, 'gay people are loath to be reminded that they are associated.' Gay men of color came to the door of Studio One increasingly prepared. For some, getting in was a triumph of principle. Once inside, they might glance around then leave. Brown and black gays knew other enclaves—Other Side, Gino's II, Circus, the legendary Jewel's Catch One.

There are those who maintain these are simply aspersions cast on Studio One; the ban against open-toed shoes was not a strategy for deterring women, just insurance—a party that good is sure to end in broken glass; Forbes's own associates were hardly all white males; Manny Slali, the club's lauded DJ, was of Mexican and Arab heritage. But activists were unconvinced. Out front, flyers calling for a boycott were distributed by the Gay Community Mobilization Committee and Ad Hoc Group of Women and Men of the Community Seeking an End to Racism and Sexism. The literature insisted that discriminatory bar owners 'are not sisters and brothers but exploiters and profiteers.' By the nineties, any such discrimination may have been of a subtler kind. I was not denied entrance. It was up to me to step inside, look around and stir up an existential crisis on my own.

———

I went out to tag along. But I made it seem like I'd been dragged out. Therein I found some unaccountable version of agency. I could convince myself I was passive, even a victim, and easily seduced, even swayed. Gay, in other words, was not something that I was pursuing. Gay was happening to me.

Rock was scheduled to dance at Studio One on a Saturday night, meaning 21+ only. I arranged to meet him beforehand at a party near my college campus hosted by Oliver, the ballet dancer. I was pleased that this plan got me an invitation to Oliver's place. His crowd was glamorous in a way that reminded me of Madonna's dance troupe, who amounted to my first impression of gays. Those dancers loved being poncy. They did not act like they were imitating women, but one another. At sixteen, I'd sat in a nearly sold-out cinema watching the tour documentary *Madonna: Truth or Dare*, and when two of them french-kissed, the audience groaned in repulsion. I took it personally, whereas they were impervious on the other side of the screen. Now I lived under the Hollywood sign, and attended parties with regal flamers nearly that chic.

I got to Oliver's just in time to catch Rock on the way out. He was patronizing. *I have to go*, he said, *to work.* I realized I hardly knew anyone else at the party. A bombastic dandy reminded me of André Leon Talley, and I decided he must have just returned from the Champs-Élysées. He elongated his vowels. I knew I'd have nothing interesting to say to anyone who feigned interest. I could only think to continue to associate myself with Rock. The rest of them glanced at one another at the mention of his name in a way that made me unsure of what status that gave me.

I slurped down sweet drinks until I began to spin. In the bathroom, I sat on the toilet and then leaned into the tub and vomited. I turned on the tap to keep the sound from carrying. The retching was of less concern than the farting. I tried to clean up the floor but was dizzy. Someone was knocking on the door and saying, *Y'ok?* I felt sorry for myself and moreover the people who lived there. I kept my head down, stumbling past the person waiting, through the foyer and into the street. *Y'ok?*, a voice called after me. I gave them the back of my hand, trying to do so politely. The night air seemed clean-cut and sparkling, lit by the citadel-like campus. A boy and girl danced by, hippies, and I was sure their pursuits were wholesome compared to this mess I was in.

I pushed forward to Matias's house, the only refuge I could think of, the site of the epic house party where I'd joined the electric slide to 'Mistadobalina' then dissolved on the doorstep after the tab of LSD kicked in. At my second ring, the frumpier of the roommates (not the cool girl who'd landed a role in *Sister Act* 2) answered the door wearing a cable-knit cardigan. I recognized then how different she was from Matias, how sensible. *He's not home,* she sighed. *I'm really not well,* I pleaded. *You can take the couch, I guess,* she said. I went to the bathroom first, then somehow ended up in Matias's bed. It was large enough I was able to go fetal in a corner at the foot, my rank face far away from his pillow.

Then I was stammering apologies to Matias, who stood tsking above me. *I saw your boy dance tonight,* he slurred. *Everyone in West Hollywood saw him. Everyone in West Hollywood has had him. That's why everyone knows the size of his dick.* He rolled his shoulders in an old Hollywood way, when the femme fatale embraces her true evilness. *Rock is trash,* he said. *And you had better watch out for that.* The light poured in from the hall so that he was in silhouette. *Try this,* Matias instructed. *What is it?* I asked. *It'll make you feel better. Sniff it deep.* He held a small bottle to my nostril. Then I was no longer just spinning but looking down at myself from the ceiling. He snatched the poppers away and dragged me into the front room. I stood staring at that poster of Marky Mark. I feared Matias was right. Even if delivered as a warning, it was cruel of him to say. I had never heard somebody talk about *everyone* meaning the denizens of West Hollywood: I was momentarily

impressed with my life, that my boyfriend was a celebrity. I
had also never heard anybody talk shit about another man's
penis. He must have been insinuating it wasn't big. I didn't
care what other people thought. They were underestimat-
ing it based on envy. I just liked that it became hard for me.
It was an obelisk; it was the Washington Monument. I felt
included by the erectness of it, patriotic. Then I thought:
Were other people really aware of his body? It was unlikely
Rock had not been disloyal. After all, he had a girlfriend
when we started all this.

I patted my nostril, wondering if it would swell up again like
it did when I had it pierced. That was done by Rock's friend,
who worked in a hair salon equipped with a piercing gun
and no studs, so he'd used one from his own earlobe, dipped
in peroxide. I'd been thinking about AIDS ever since. It was
as though I'd been adopted by the wrong family—these
nightclub people, thriving on secrets and risk. Even Rock's
dorm room was a nightclub. I'd taken a bus out of the city to
the canyons, where Rock attended a small university. The
night was darker there, the campus hushed. Each student
had their own en suite. I'd been eager to see Rock away from
nightlife, and deflated when I saw how it followed him. As I
swallowed his treacly jizz, as he later commented about how
cumming would be bad for his skin, techno played from a
boom box and beams of light in alternating colors rotated
on the wall. The bulb in the bathroom had been changed to
blue. I considered a nightclub a place to come home from,
an excursion to wash away. I saw then that to Rock, a nightclub was a habitat he carried with him like a carapace.

Now, as Matias glazed over from his own hit of poppers, I
was disturbed by what my life had come to look like: pages

from a tawdry gay magazine, brashly hued and glossy and filled with flash photos of shirtless men with gel in their hair, sheen upon arrogant sheen. Everything about being gay was so *crowded*: the ads for bars and escorts and waxing services rammed together, shallow and histrionic and imperious. I'd been indoctrinated by the kinds of gays that give *gay* a bad name and, because of the fact that I'd allowed that to happen, figured I must be no better than them. I faced the possibility I was a degraded cliché.

———

I could no longer make another excuse not to visit my father's friends—a large Chinese family from Taipei who'd resettled in an Orange County suburb dominated by their extensive network of evangelicals. I agreed to attend Sunday dinner at the home of someone in their congregation. A part of me looked forward to it. These Chinese family gatherings were chaotic and wholesome: no alcohol, just a lot of interruption and gadgets, then a prayer before eating. I'd be grilled but for once wouldn't be drunk. I hoped some of the progeny were still young enough to play children's games to occupy me. The doorbell was a familiar suburban two-tone, not a hard buzz like in the city. At the euphonious sound I decided to enjoy myself. I was about to have a secret again, to remember what it feels like to move through a space like a nice young man, normal, nothing other than what is expected of a good university student.

I took off my shoes and placed them alongside all the others: toddler sandals, teenager sneakers, the tiny loafers of senior citizens. From the kitchen came vinegar smells

71

and the sound of sizzling. I was introduced to this auntie and that uncle, terms broadly used for elders. The oldest of them displayed no interest in me whatsoever because I was not kin. They tut-tutted at one another's maneuver in the kitchen or poorly chosen item of clothing. There was much simultaneous lecturing. Eventually, one of the older boys brought me upstairs to a bedroom. It was lit only by a desk lamp and glowing fish tank. A teenager sat there who hadn't come downstairs all evening. Something about his bearing told me it would be rude to look at him directly. I glimpsed the lower half of his face, covered in scar tissue, which amassed on one side so there was little distinction between jaw and neck. I then felt ashamed for not looking at him directly. His hair was orange from Sun In. He smiled, but it appeared involuntary or mocking, or both. He gave the impression of being self-contained, a little jaded. He interacted lightly with the boy who brought me in, muttering bits of Mandarin. His sideways glances were aimed at the floor.

There were drawings and various art supplies on the desk. I scanned photographs on the wall until my eyes came to rest on an uncanny image. A series of prints had been tacked together to form a panoramic stretch of city blocks. It was *the boulevard*: the wide sidewalks and skinny trees, boxy stucco shop fronts, beer patios, the neon signs waiting to be switched on. The images had been taken under bright afternoon sun. A few figures were about, young men strutting beneath rainbow flags. There's where Matias parked, in front of the café. Around the corner, I fell for the charismatic Rock. Out of frame to the south was where we went dancing at Studio One.

I thought surely a family member who came across this

photomontage would decipher the location and be scandalized. But then again, I had learned the codes, knew what type of videos were available at Drake's and what sort of man hung out at Trunks. The boy had taken the photos himself, that much was clear from their consistency with the other images around the room. The gaze was homoerotic, but not at bodies. Details from West Hollywood—signage, streetlamps—were rendered monumental. I'd wasted so much energy disparaging the boulevard, castigating it out of a bitterness that I could never truly belong—not attractive enough, not white enough. The scene confronted me with a gym-body ideal, forcing me to look farther afield to figure out what else gay could be and to understand what I was up against. I hadn't considered how it might be something other than a territory to be inside or excluded from, but a geography *apart*—held in thrall from afar. *Santa Monica Boulevard,* I blurted. The boy mumbled, *I love it there...* but to the tune of: *Obviously.* The boy had hung on his wall a real place made mythic, like Proust's Balbec. I considered how a cultural scene could function not as a box with a clear outside and in, but as a signal, like a searchlight across the sky. He had depicted a landscape. I'd been experiencing the place as a movie set where I was vying for a part. He looked around himself and interpreted, and through that became attached. I was only ever concerned with how I appeared in it, with the stressful situation of men looking at other men. To me, West Hollywood was a state of mind (and a tacky one: *WeHo, ugh*), not a unique city that, for all of its problems, gay people had built themselves.

———

The refrain 'out of the bars and into the streets' became a classic of gay rights activism because traversing the two terrains summed up what it is to be publicly gay. I'd contend Los Angeles contributed to this as much as San Francisco or New York City. Pedestrian actions in Los Angeles appear especially strange to onlookers, so have in their own way great impact. In 1970, protesters marched down Santa Monica Boulevard from Gardner to Doheny; among them, the Commie-Jew-Fag-Bastard Kazoo Band was buzzing show tunes. The march was provoked by the 'no touch' rule at the West Hollywood hot spot the Farm, which like many gay bars was run by mobsters. In theory, the homosexuals were granted a place to congregate, while the management's proscription of contact between them kept the cops away. This routine was getting old. The protest began at the bar days earlier, as the Gay Liberation Front stalwart Don Kilhefner called out instructions for his brothers to link arms and stay put when the police arrived, which they did until the cops backed down. After the ensuing march, Kilhefner and his comrades laid claim to victory. A poster was tacked up: 'Gay People's Victory No Demonstration Tonight "The Farm" Is Liberated!'

It's been said the nation's first gay pride parade was a motorcade in Los Angeles; held in 1966, it comprised thirteen or so cars heading down Cahuenga Boulevard to Sunset Boulevard to protest the exclusion of gays from the armed forces. (Nobody got hurt, so it didn't make the news.) That New Year's Eve, a bunch of queens pressed into the Black Cat in Silver Lake. Three Christmas trees were still up. A trio of black women known as the Rhythm Queens sang a rock version of 'Auld Lang Syne.' As balloons fell and midnight smooches began, a dozen plainclothes vice officers sprang into action, tearing down the decorations and wielding truncheons. Sixteen were arrested. Cops chased two men across the street to another bar, New Faces, where the owner was knocked down and two bartenders beaten unconscious. One was hospitalized with a ruptured spleen, and upon recovery charged with felony assault. A jury voted to convict all six men accused of lewd contact (kissing other men for ten seconds). A protest was organized in early February. Men and women marched with simple placards. The word *gay* did not appear. 'Blue Fascism Must Go!,' read one sign. 'Abolish arbitrary arrests.' 'No more abuse of our rights and dignity.' Among the hundreds there were young people of color and Sunset Strip youth, not necessarily queer but joining in solidarity against persecution at the hands of the LAPD. The protest continued over several days. Three thousand flyers were printed. As the street was scarce of passersby, they were handed mostly to motorists.

Clearly, the Black Cat protests did not make the impact
Stonewall did two and a half years later. The scholars Elizabeth A. Armstrong and Suzanna M. Crage have proposed
that this is partly due to geography. New York's Greenwich
Village was dense and gossipy. On the night of the rebellion, *Village Voice* reporter Howard Smith only had to glance
out his window to note the fracas below on Christopher
Street. The author Edmund White chanced upon the scene,
as did the activist Marsha P. Johnson.

In the aftermath, media-savvy liberationists were on it
with the outreach. The groundwork for a commemorative
event was already in place: a well-behaved homophile
demonstration called the Annual Reminder first occurred
in Philadelphia on the Fourth of July 1965 to speak up
for those denied their right to liberty and the pursuit of
happiness. New York activists determined the event should
be moved to the last Saturday in June. The Fourth of
July was spoken for anyway. The Annual Reminder would
now have something specific, the Stonewall uprising, to
remind people about. It would be renamed Christopher
Street Liberation Day and rolled out nationally. True to
their contrarian fashion, San Francisco activists held off
on participating. In Los Angeles, however, the gay rights
leader Morris Kight convened his network to begin plans
for a march down Hollywood Boulevard. The L.A. police
chief stated he might as well be granting a parade permit to
thieves. But the California Superior Court ultimately issued
an approval, plus required the LAPD to provide protection.
It was in part these efforts in Los Angeles that helped elevate

Stonewall into the prevailing gay bar liberation narrative. Furthermore, news about Stonewall was circulated by *The Advocate*, a publication founded in Los Angeles after editors Dick Michaels and Bill Rand were stirred by the raid of the Black Cat.

Dick and Bill happened to be present one momentous Saturday night in August 1968 at the Patch, a bar in the L.A. suburb of Wilmington frequented by gay men and some lesbians from the nearby roller derby. Its proprietor, Lee Glaze—known as the Blond Darling—was under orders by the local police commission to prohibit drag, groping, male-male dancing and the presence of more than one customer in the restroom at a time. These rules proved bad for business, so Glaze reinstated the dancing. He'd put 'God Save the Queen' on the jukebox to indicate that members of the vice squad were present, signaling the crowd to cease shows of affection. On the night in question, Glaze took to the stage and thanked the LAPD for sending an unprepossessing batch of officers, as they provided weak temptation and had been easy to discern in the mix. Everyone, including the vice cops, appeared to get a kick out of this. Around midnight, though, as the crowd was coming up on a few hundred, the officers led in uniformed police. Two arrests were made, tipping the Blond Darling over the edge. He jumped onto the stage again, this time blasting: 'It's not against the law to be a homosexual, and it's not a crime to be in a gay bar!' A boy in the crowd shouted, 'We're Americans, too!'

Glaze pledged to help pay bail and legal fees, then asked if anyone in the crowd happened to own a flower shop, which someone in fact did. Glaze proceeded to buy out all his flowers—according to Dick Michaels, 'gladioli, mums, daisies, carnations and roses (but no pansies).' With about twenty-five others, he composed agitprop bouquets and took them to the station. The stone-faced desk sergeant at the Harbor Division cautioned the crowd to shush if they intended to stay. Cops wandered out to get a look at the motley crew and their assemblage of flora. Around five in the morning, the first of the prisoners was freed, and immediately garlanded to much fanfare. A half hour later, the second man was also covered with bouquets upon being released.

———

I walked among gay bar landmarks, but saw only their latest incarnations. Buildings which could have been edifying had been repainted and renamed, or neglected. I didn't know where to begin seeking out gay history. Maybe I didn't want to. Gay yesteryear gave me the creeps. For instance: a branch of the thrift store Out of the Closet opened on Fairfax Avenue. The profits went to medical assistance for people living with AIDS and HIV. The stucco storefront was painted a lurid pink accented in Palm Springs teal, and the sign's neon tubing formed the shapes of a chair, cowboy boot, hanger and Hawaiian shirt. I cringed when I passed it, imagining the store to be filled with stuff scavenged from the homes of dead queens—musty baroque junk from all the inferior Liberaces. That thrift store became my mental picture of gay history: tacky old shit, moth-eaten and be-grimed, in a belligerently gaudy building. Each artifact was soiled and stigmatized. I hadn't found a way to consider the multifarious story of my people—and to read it with, but not *through*, the disease.

For our third year of college, Xuan and I rented an apartment together in West Hollywood. The location was just far enough from the campus to feel dangerous. We unintentionally moved into a very homosexual building. Each dismal apartment faced onto a lush courtyard garden, which echoed with the sounds of warm weather: someone's parrot, the murmur of canned laughter on television and vocal scales in a light opera style when the manager gave lessons in the afternoon. Upstairs, two guys shouted their intercourse with great might. They grunted and barked, calling out commands and affirmation. It sounded painful on purpose. Their racket clearly evoked anus and dick.

The thick Harley in front of our building I figured belonged to the top. Sometimes, it was joined by another motorcycle, a pale blue old Honda. This belonged to Juan. I'd met him first, but he fell for Xuan. I was deeply envious. He would kiss me only at a party with an audience. Nobody who kissed me in private had his romantic brown curls and his effortless style. The gays wore painstakingly chosen, box-fresh clothes; Juan's perfectly plain things looked like they'd always been there on the bedroom floor. On occasion, I'd ride on the back of his Honda, clutching his bony frame as we took the curves of Sunset Boulevard. All the good ones, I worried, weren't gay.

Our apartment building was off Genesee, parallel to Santa Monica Boulevard, a mile or so east from the night-life epicenter, where Boystown grew haggard and lowered its standards. At the supermarket, gay men released heavy sighs as their pace collided with that of the elder Hasidim in black hats and tightly curled payess. Our building backed onto the parking lot of a sex shop. Each time I took the garbage out, I was looking to be scandalized. Farther east still, the cars slowed as drivers craned their necks at the prostitutes on the corners—boys dressed as boys, or as girls. I rode my skateboard to Astro Burger, where I sat, preferably in the back booth, over a veggie with pickles browsing for under-21 nights in the *LA Weekly*.

The Tomkat all-male cinema had a stately deco facade, but my primary impression was of the dirty puns in block letters on the marquee. I was stunned to behold scenarios of fellow troopers or cellmates written in foot-tall letters. When I finally gathered the courage to go in, I followed behind an attractive man, somewhere around thirty. Inside, there was nobody else like him. He slinked into the seat beside me and pulled it out, no big deal, like a pack of cigarettes. He let me grasp the shaft only briefly before firmly moving my hand away. He made for mine, but it was limp. He looked at me without intensity and shot a thick load onto the back of the seat in front of him, then zipped up and left. His exit was silhouetted by the light pouring in from the lobby. I romantically watched what he'd left behind drip. That seemed such a territorial, manly thing to do. The other men were getting up and moving seats periodically, so I followed suit and tried the other side of the auditorium. A guy swooped into the row behind and blew on my earlobe. I rose again to avoid hearing him repeat whatever he'd said. On my next seat, I landed in a puddle of cum with a squelch. The following morning at the laundromat, I felt conspicuous and debased. I sat on the curb under the hard sun while the machine soaked my jeans, washing away someone else's sins.

Down the block was Circus of Books. I bought a magazine from the eighties there, in which two tan stepbrothers with wispy hair falling over their ears pulled on top of each other eagerly. Their pubic bushes were prelapsarian. Their taut bodies helped me have less rudimentary orgasms. Then I fell back onto my futon and thought about whether they'd since fallen down dead, lesions defiling their velveteen skin. Across La Jolla Avenue was the Gold Coast bar. I found something about its stale beer scent inviting. I surmised the men who went there did so without fear of disappointment, settled as they were into their low expectations and leathery skin. Soon after I turned twenty-one, I took myself on a lonely tour of dives populated by spoken-for sugar daddies: final stop, a wooden bench bisecting the room at the Gold Coast. Men played pool behind me. Those at the bar glanced over their shoulders, barely stirring. The one who sat down next to me was rough-skinned and reeked of cigarettes, but still I flushed. He patted my thigh paternally, and told me I was too good for the place. I couldn't see how that was possible—I'd made the choice to go in.

At a new wave night called Velvet, a boy whose calls I'd stopped returning smashed a glass on the dance floor in anger, and I was impressed that I could hold sway over his emotions. I went to after-hours parties thrown in disused offices, spun out on crystal meth—sometimes beige-yellow and looking incorrect, other times like diamonds that made me coo, laid out in six-inch lines by a slippery character who used the drugs to get me to fuck him, which backfired when I got too high to perform. At one of these dens, I suffered palpitations but was too embarrassed to mention to the strangers around me that I was sure I was dying. In the next room, Rock, who'd reappeared as if out of nowhere, danced with the enabler I wasn't screwing.

I went out to get attention—or rather, to refract it by way of a costume. I wore short shorts and face powder to a mainstream club on the westside; in the women's bathroom, they shouted at me to leave, but I was terrified to go into the men's. I went back to Probe on a mixed night, and danced atop a platform backed in mirrors, wearing stacked Adidas and, tucked into my hair, smelly daisies snipped from Xuan's kitchen-table bouquet. I flashed back to being five years old or so, when my grandfather yanked me off the side table on which I danced dressed as Pinocchio. Now I felt—not like a star, more like an extra in other people's movies. I wasn't arriving into my true self, but escaping. Eventually, I ventured farther east, to Silver Lake leather bars and mucky dives where Vaginal Creme Davis took to the stage. I'd slurp a Coke then leave in order to avoid anything happening, or worse still be caught out waiting in vain.

Mostly, though, I went out vicariously through magazines. Now the Calvin Klein ads were for CK One, the unisex eau de toilette, with a black-and-white photo of scruffy types in a line, revising a composition of the crowd from Andy Warhol's Factory taken by Avedon. Their hair was either very long and lank or severely shorn. The diesel dyke Jenny Shimizu crouched. On her biceps was a tattoo of a pinup girl riding a wrench. She had actually worked as a mechanic. The message was authenticity. A boy in a beanie standing in a contrapposto pose held his arm above his head to reveal a thick bush, as if CK One smelled of his armpit, though in actuality the sample was disappointingly astringent. One morning, a scented advertisement was inserted into every college newspaper. The whole campus reeked of the stuff. It should smell, I thought, tangy like the ditch between scrotum and thigh, or of mud or gasoline. Instead, it just reminded me of Tower Records on Sunset Boulevard—where they sold bottles from freestanding displays. The fragrance blended seamlessly with the plastic of shrink-wrapped CDs. At Tower Records, instead of the cologne, I bought the box set of the Velvet Underground, the house band of Warhol's Factory. The song 'All Tomorrow's Parties' was existential—all about the *never enough* of nightlife, a dirge for the satiable, for moderation. It was as though I did not hear the song so much as live inside it.

I watched and rewatched *Absolutely Fabulous* episodes: the one where it's New Year's Eve and they've got glamorous plans but wind up not leaving the house—that said everything. I'd phone the Hello Happy Line, a number printed in the liner notes of a Deee-Lite album—basically a voicemail giving info about a rave, but to me Lady Miss Kier wishing everyone a groovy time was a mental health service. I leafed through books on the Factory and identified the cute men. I pored over the photos in a Wolfgang Tillmans monograph, sweaty and blunt, showing ecstatic nights out and cigarette-scented domestic scenes in which people who looked like beautiful weeds were half dressed in army surplus and sequins. Nightlife was theater, their disarrayed apartments the backstage. I memorized pictures of other people clubbing in the pages of *Edge, Spunk, Planet Homo, Paper* and *Project X*. I wore out the spines of British magazines, especially *i-D*. The *i-D* logo was rotated clockwise to resemble a winking smiley face. Whoever modeled on the cover winked. In October 1995, *i-D* ran a fifteenth-anniversary issue. The cover was mirrored, the gimmick being that this time the reader was the cover star. The club reviews were in the back. This issue featured a new London night called Popstarz: 'Skinny glam-indie throwdown that's aimed at gay men and dykes.' Two boys were pictured, both in vintage tartan trousers with gangly pale arms, one decorated with tattoos. They each scowled self-consciously. I returned to the page again and again. Popstarz seemed like the place for me, and the silly spelling of its name made it less intimidating.

One evening, I found myself back at the Factory Building—entering by the opposite side from where I used to run up the steps nearly four years before to Studio One. It was the opening night of a club called Cherry, which I could tell was going to be a big deal. The tone of the promotions was bratty—gay in a way that co-opted seventies glam rockers who'd co-opted gay. I borrowed a pair of enormous yellow sunglasses from Xuan, and one of her shaggiest coats, which I wore over a pair of gym shorts, looking like Little Edie Beale forced to step out of the house. At the club, I was shooed to the front of the line, just after an actress I recognized from *Melrose Place*.

Inside, a figure sloshed toward me like a shot of whisky carelessly poured. It was the Warhol superstar Holly Wood-lawn. She was an actress with a name like a destination. She'd finally made the move to Hollywood, and brought along something mordant with her from back east (the

Woodlawn is named for a Bronx cemetery). According to what I'd read in the club zines, she'd been gagging to leave New York City. She was an alumna of the *real* Factory: Andy Warhol's. She was transgender, I guess, depending on who you ask or how you define it. She had an air about her of both arrival and being still on her way. She was born in Puerto Rico, grew up in Miami, and her journey to New York City inspired the first verse in Lou Reed's classic 'Walk on the Wild Side.' Now she was stumbling around another Factory. She was in residence at the Backlot Theatre, somewhere in the building. I imagined her show involved a lot of anecdotal digression as her index finger swirled a martini.

Her eyes were alight. *Honey,* she blasted, and gave me a theatrical once-over. *Even I wouldn't try getting away with THAT.* We stood locked for a second. The mud-cracks of her face seemed to wish me no harm. I knew she was being sardonic, but also that she was admiring. I looked ridiculous but good. I lacked polish, but then look at her films. They were set in the gap between aspiration and realness. I recognized that liminal location. It was the only place I dwelled that wasn't just rented.

Holly Woodlawn stood before me, now *in residence* in this building which shared her knack for survival—inebriate, feisty—and for transformation. But gay bars have not always welcomed her kind of difference. On the scene back east, the mean gay boys gave Holly the slur 'hormone queen.' They perceived themselves as natives in their bodies and their location. Gay boys can be so territorial, and too wrapped up in the moment to see how their gay bars are actually transitioning—in that they've likely been something else, and will change again in the future.

It wasn't full yet, and those present seemed already drunk. I recognized Alexis Arquette, sometimes boy, tonight woman, dancing alone with intensity on the stage. The music was not house, but rock. Holly Woodlawn inspected me like she couldn't tell which way I was headed: actress or mean boy — or some other species, considering my outfit was that much of a mess. I didn't know, either, but was beginning to feel like a part of a lineage. I didn't know how else to learn history but to try it on. Someone whisked her away, and soon after I left.

THE ADELPHI

LONDON

If coming out isn't a coming home, then it would mean that homos were still lost souls who have to face the universe alone. And that would be a bit of a downer, really.

—Mark Simpson, 1996

The nineties were all about leaving. For me, coming out but not *into* a particular scene, identity was a perpetual state of departure, like the slogan straight boys gave their assholes—*exit only*. My defining gay film was Gus Van Sant's *My Own Private Idaho*, which I first watched just after turning seventeen, and which wasn't actually gay, because the vagabond hustlers at the heart of its story never stop long enough to settle into the identity. 'I'm a connoisseur of roads,' says River, shifty but earnest. 'I've been tasting roads my whole life.' Keanu, as a slumming fils de famille, goes, 'When I left home, the maid asked me where I was off to. I said, "Wherever. Whatever. Have a nice day."' That line is so Generation X, as in exodus.

But the gay rights movement was about standing ground ('we're here, we're queer, get used to it'). In the spring of 1993, just as I came out, one million of my people marched on Washington, D.C. The area's gay paper, the *Washington Blade*, ran its largest edition to date—over two hundred pages including a double-page ad from the distinctly middle-class department store Nordstrom. *The Nation* ran the headline 'The Gay Moment.' *Vanity Fair* went with 'The Gay Nineties.' This sense of arrival and assimilation ran counter to the more alluring mood of shoving off and hitting the road. The gays were making a big ta-da when it would have been au courant to roll their eyes and shrug. At the nexus of pride and whatever, of course some homosexuals were compelled to detach from gay, inducing much chatter about what form a counterculture to the subculture could take.

In Britain, a coterie of journalists tried out *post-gay*. The term swished through the pages of newspapers and magazines in op-eds that were cleverly, if flippantly, critical of gays acting smug and excessively shopping. To be post-gay was to be out, but over it. The vague concept took a material form in *Attitude*, a semigloss lifestyle magazine founded in 1994. It gave post-gay an aesthetic: this was not overtly masculine, which was considered *super-gay* after the clones had taken to disco dancing in hard hats. 'Out with the gay look, in with the straight look,' the editors of *Attitude* decreed in their guide to post-gay culture. But they equated the former with muscles and jeans, the latter with an androgynous, louche style—*straight* as in Jagger and Bowie. Post-gay, according to the guide, was long hair, no gym, pouting and Britpop guitar music ('real music') as played by fey straight men. (Brett Anderson, the sylphlike vocalist in the band Suede, identified as a bisexual who'd never had a homosexual experience; this was met by the post-gay pundits with much approbation.)

The *Attitude* columnist Mark Simpson took it further, editing the essay anthology *Anti-Gay*. He proposed *de-gaying* as 'the inevitable result of postmodernism finally catching up with gay and fragmenting its pretentious "grand narrative." People are leaving gay because they no longer believe its claims to interpret the world or make it a better place.' The post- and anti-gay writers recited tenets of academic queer theory, wherein sexual identity is taken to be socially constructed—a fallacy that perpetuates hegemonic norms. If desire is an unpredictable wind, then identity is a broken weather vane pointing in one arbitrary direction—gay, lesbian, bi, straight—rather than turning on the breeze.

In his book *On Flirtation*, published in the autumn of 1994, the British psychoanalyst Adam Phillips suggested this could amount to another type of dogma: 'the new pieties of the contemporary academic sexual enlightenment—that it is both more truthful and better not to know who you are, that it is preferable to slip, shift or float than to know, stop or stay.' In that September's issue of *Attitude*, one article was based on the question 'What exactly is the queer appeal of Keanu Reeves?' Its author took his answer in the form of an observation by one of Keanu's directors: he seems aloof and noncommittal, as if always heading off on a bus.

———

Also that September, an eighteen-year-old boy in Gloucestershire left his family home. He had slouched through adolescence under scraggly long hair, a lock of which was, for a brief period, wrapped in varicolored thread. He wore a floppy purple sweater that reeked of weed and a Dinosaur Jr. t-shirt, also purple and baggy—but then most things drowned his skinny frame. The boy moved to the city of Bath to study fine art. There, having decided to update his style, he ventured into the Toni & Guy hair salon with a mood board of Britpop manes. Britpop was less a musical genre than a new marketing phrase for jangly or thrumming guitar rock with catchy melodies. The upbeat patriotism of Britpop was meant to be cutely shambolic, and lyrics invoked national characteristics like listlessness, squalid bedrooms and the class system—a paradox of rock star aspirationalism and not getting ideas above one's station. The hairstyles in the boy's collage were snipped from *Smash Hits* and *Melody Maker*. They belonged to Damon from Blur, Jarvis from Pulp, a guy from Shed Seven and the superior model, Liam from Oasis—uneven fringe, long about the ears, slashed with razor blades. The staff of Toni & Guy were forced to gather round in consultation. None of the hairdressers had done a cut like that before. The result was passable, and subsequently word spread that the boy had become gorgeous.

When a band worth seeing was coming to Bath, the boy bought his ticket at the city's central box office, up a flight of stairs lined with posters advertising plays, run by a skinhead in his fifties named Warwick. Eventually, the boy went even when there was no upcoming gig, just to sit around listening to Warwick hold forth through cigarette smoke. Warwick had a thing for men in combat boots. He peppered his speech with darlings and the royal we. The teakettle would be switched on as Warwick recalled his London nights: the A&B and the Apollo were next door to each other on Wardour Street, the former nearly posh, the latter a pickup spot for trade. The Regency Club was *the last chance corral—where one rubbed shoulders with transvestites, members of the House of Lords, the Kray twins and a nice selection of rent boys....* His lexicon was arcane.

It wasn't long before Warwick took the boy to the closest Bath had to a gay bar, the Garricks Head, which adjoined the Theatre Royal. The pub was divided in half, and one side had been unofficially homosexual since the Second World War—the Green Room, although it was painted red. While the crowd opposite thinned when the play was about to begin, those in the Green Room carried on, poofs and lezzers of varied ages flirting and camping it up. They followed a tradition of theaters as coded destinations that stretches back to something like the sixteenth century.

One night, Warwick rounded up the boy and another two lads, Rob and Ray. They drove to the nearby city of Bristol, to a proper gay bar in a detached building with blacked-out windows. Like the Kaaba in Mecca, the boy thought. On the speakers was handbag house: four-on-the-floor rhythm, hi-hat on the upbeat, diva vocals, with a heartbroken piano line in a minor key threaded through and the requisite drop before a triumphant climax. The boy could barely distinguish one man from the next. Cologne seemed to stick to the fug of smoke, which was rendered neon by the lights. The boy recognized a classmate from his school days, who was clearly annoyed by their reunion. He gave the impression of being long familiar with the place, and it became clear to the boy where he was always slipping off to back then.

Upon returning to Bath, the group wound up at a lock-in at yet another pub. It was there, upstairs in an unused function room lined with stacked chairs, that he was first kissed by another boy—by Rob, who'd been with him all the way to another city and back but had waited until the end of the night. Rob lived with his parents, so they couldn't go to his. At the boy's flat, a temperamental ex-girlfriend had not budged since his coming out, so that wasn't an option either. But they could go to Warwick's. It looked as though Warwick intended to stay at the pub himself, but Rob had his own set of keys, and the two lads adjourned there as if it had all been arranged.

The boy buzzed his hair soon after that. Now he looked like a gay from the decade before, like he was in Bronski Beat. The girls he hung out with, lamenting the loss of his shaggy locks, warned him not to become a cliché. The gays overdid it, were overmoisturized and desperate, listened to handbag house. The boy found he did share a sense of humor with his new gay friends—inexplicably, a line of dialogue on TV would send them shrieking. It was as if he'd just been let in on the fact that all popular culture was subversively designed to amuse gay men. The boy took to saying *fab*, and guffawed at his own affectation. He held a Silk Cut cigarette with a turned-out wrist. He attended a *Rocky Horror Picture Show* party at the theater bar, wearing a blond wig and bandages wrapped around his narrow bare chest, where the crowd did the 'Time Warp' over and over again. But whether this behavior was the true him he wasn't sure. The others were into nighttime park cruising. They outlandishly ogled passing men.

He plucked up the courage to buy a softcore magazine. The models were only slightly fluffed, images of full erections weren't yet legal. They had copious amounts of gel in their hair and were nearly bald everywhere else. Their bodies were too perfect, lacking character and warmth. But they were there. (The boy was not alone in settling for any image of maleness that happened to be available to him. Young homos everywhere were masturbating over the generic models in mail-order catalogues; the chin-to-thigh shot on underwear packaging; certain interpretations of Jesus Christ crucified in a loincloth.) Once the bodies in the softcore magazine had served their intended purpose, the boy cut the pages up and pasted the disembodied torsos, now like ancient busts with lost heads, onto his own paintings of stark rooms. It was a half-knowing critique. He was granting these sex objects agency as he liberated them from the porn, or conversely draining them of power by banishing them to the lonely spaces of his imagination. Like a child who gazes at a doll in adoration before proceeding to destroy it, he identified, dis-identified and counteridentified with a wank, cut and paste.

It was Carolyn, the stubborn ex-girlfriend, who told him about a new club night in London that held a solution to the boy's mild identity crisis. Carolyn showed him the Popstarz write-up in *i-D* magazine: 'a new gay night shakes off hands-in-the-air stereotypes to play top tunes by the latest hot shot Britpop poet laureates,' it read. 'Popstarz offers a credible alternative to muscled-up gay club culture. Pale and interesting types queue here.' There, he could be both Britpop *and* homosexual.

———

In London, the gay bar was undergoing a shift. For decades, proto-gay bars operated on the down-low. Posh homos secreted away in rarefied environs. The rest sought out old pubs and coffeehouses with a wink-nudge reputation. They were undesignated, a bar within a bar. Some central nightclubs were like dazzle ships—homosexuals hid in plain sight amid the spectacular cosmopolitanism. Eventually there were queer-run private clubs, but they were spaces of self-effacement, discreet to the point of dull. Later, dedicated gay bars were unequivocal but clandestine, designed defensively with covered windows and unmarked entries. (The urbanist Johan Andersson noted they were given names like 'Substation, Backstreet and the Fort.') But after AIDS, the seedy underworld vibe was outmoded. A dank club or soiled pub put contamination in mind. Gay (*Got AIDS Yet?*) was inextricable from disease. It was, to crib Susan Sontag citing Erving Goffman, a 'spoiled identity.' To be gay was to be a menace—or a sitting target. In the eighties and early nineties, three different serial killers stalked London gay men; each was reported to have picked up victims at the Coleherne Arms, a pub popular with a leather crowd. The most recent of these murderers, nicknamed the Gay Slayer, is thought to have met all five of his victims there. To his mind, the hankie code—the color fabric in a back pocket flags a sexual predilection, the side it's worn on the preferred position—marked out potential victims: black on the right (heavy sadomasochism, passive) revealed a vulnerability. A Conservative politician called for the pub's closure, conflating the act of predation with its affected community.

A new type of gay bar began to appear in London's Soho in the nineties—airy, glossy, continental. The design sent a clear message: In here you won't catch a disease. The new establishments were not circumspect, nor did they toy with their orientation gradually. These gay bars were born that way. They were conceived specifically to take gay men's money. What's more, the spaces affirmed that gay means chichi (defined by Johan Andersson as 'a failed attempt at stylishness that ends up being merely pretentious').

First, in 1991, there was Village Soho—like 'the Village' in Manhattan, Andersson points out, or Le Village, the bar that commenced the gayification of Le Marais in Paris in 1978. Andersson makes note of how Rupert Street Bar, with its large plate-glass corner windows, had the audacity to adopt the name of its location, as if it defined the street—where, in fact, in the forties and fifties, pubs were raided by police for allowing flagrant homos (*screamers*) to congregate. The spotless new gay bars were fitted with slick surfaces and smooth bartenders. Though gay sex was now seen as high risk, it could still be commodified. (Patrons of such places became accustomed to being served drinks by topless young men.) In the nightclubs around Soho, the muscle mary prevailed, a Hulk-like mutation of the skeezy seventies clone. Where the clones had disco, the muscle marys had house—both, as opposed to the authenticity of rock 'n' roll, evinced the risible artificiality of gay.

It was in this context that the restless nightclubber Simon Hobart launched Popstarz, where 'the emphasis would be on boozing, not cruising, as an antidote to the mainstream gay scene.' Hobart would create a space for the misfits, whereas the promoter of G-A-Y, he spouted, 'factory-farms stereotyped, mindless, blinkered gay people.' He scattered flyers around colleges and record shops—'tapping into a younger, more intellectual crowd.' The flyers promised a weekly night of Britpop and indie, using retro mod graphics to convey a cocky swagger. The gay giveaway was the z in Popstarz, as if spoofing the cheesy bar rag *Boyz*, thereby declaring its own homosexuality.

So this was what the alternative looked like: heterosexual chart rock queered by a misspelling. But Popstarz made some magic out of its banal constituent parts. The paste-up flyers were unlike those of a typical gay club. The men had their shirts on, for starters. Still, the assemblages of magazine cutouts accentuated the homoeroticism of, say, Renton from *Trainspotting* in a soaking wet t-shirt, the Gallagher brothers from Oasis mugging together, Damon from Blur flipping the bird. Why did a finger in the air suddenly look like gay porn? Collage is so gay. Popstarz was an impish resignification, and in its own way it worked.

Hobart succeeded in attracting the type he was aiming for—hot nerds with high cheekbones and snake hips. The crowd at Popstarz was not, as with other clubs, a bunch of gays dressed like regular heterosexual males. It was a crowd of gays dressed like irregular heterosexual males. Specifically, like rock stars. This was in one sense a reclaiming: straight musicians had long taken their aesthetic cues from the fruits. (As a heterosexual music critic wrote in *Attitude*: 'The easiest way to make yourself "strange" is to steal from gay culture.') With Popstarz, Hobart reversed this appropriation, something he wasn't sure he'd pull off. Arriving at the first Popstarz event in May 1995, he was amazed that the line to get in extended down the street.

———

The following year, Xuan and I landed in London to kick off our graduation trip across Europe. Xuan had produced a spreadsheet of museums to visit. I was fixated on getting to Popstarz. It was late March, still cold, and we couldn't bear to hang around until Friday, when Popstarz took place. It would have to wait until we'd toured the continent. We departed south to sunnier climes. In my mind, our travels were simply a tactic to wait out London's rain. From place to place, we were followed by the 'Macarena' and 'The Sign' by Ace of Base, with its whispery interrogation of belonging. In Barcelona, an Ivy League student with an Alvy Singer demeanor gave me head behind a pillar on the Plaça Reial until a man appeared out of the dark and gruffly tried to join in. In Madrid, a tall twink forcefully picked me up in a headache of a nightclub, and I acquiesced just for the excuse to leave. In his bedroom, he removed boots with metal-plated platforms that explained away several inches of his height. The overdesigned shoes made me depressed. He pawed me but I told him I needed sleep.

By Granada, I concluded I was destined for celibacy, like Andy Warhol or Morrissey. Xuan disagreed. Then we have to get to Popstarz, I thought, fidgety from a cocktail of Red Bull and yellow speed. I imagined a pale and interesting boy awaited me there, and didn't want to miss him. On the train to Italy, we befriended a hairdresser from San Francisco who traveled with liquid GHB in a thermos. At a nearly empty nightclub in Rome, the hairdresser and I picked up two friends, mine the less muscled of the two: Piero, a self-identified *cheap model*. (At his place the next morning, he showed me photographs of himself advertising unexceptional clothes.) Piero was pale —*from Turin, the North,* he asserted—but I wasn't sure he was interesting. *What are your interests?* I asked when he accompanied us on our obligatory shuffle through the Sistine Chapel. *I love,* he said, spreading his arms...*my mama.* By Prague, I began to plot ways to tinker Xuan's tour schedule to get us to London faster. We had to be there on a Friday.

The boy moved to London on the first of April. He and Pauley, one of the shrieking gay crew, made the decision to uproot on a whim. The boy's buzz cut had grown out again into a modish thatch, like the cover of the second album by the Beatles. He looked very Popstarz, and the club night played more than a small part in his determination to get to the city. In northeast London, he and Pauley rented a ground-floor flat from an oleaginous landlord who kept a spare room above, fitted with vinyl bench, television set and VHS tapes of male pornography. He was forever muttering to the boy about *arrangements* that *could be made*. Instead, the boy took a job at the front desk of a small hotel in Bloomsbury. He commuted underground. The city was soggy and fumed by black taxis. When he and Pauley went to nightclubs, if one of them pulled, they'd go to the man's place together, an unspoken maneuver of safety. The chaperon would sleep on the couch listening to the other being roughly fucked by the stranger. The boy wondered about some of his friend's choices. Pauley was both myopic and randy. The boy then had second thoughts about some of his own hookups, and considered that he may not be choosing them at all, just allowing himself to be taken. Mundane weekly routines quickly formed. Every Friday night was Popstarz, if there was enough money.

Popstarz was held at the Hanover Grand, just off Regent Street. The queue outside had an expectant air. Now that I was finally there, I found myself serious. Xuan appeared determined, too. I'd cut her hair at a postmodern angle. We arrived just as the place filled. A pretty girl dancing on a platform held her long arms aloft, disco limbs. She reached down and pulled me up. I felt unworthy of being on the stage in such a glamorous room. I scanned the crowd. Everyone seemed to look in my direction. The British kids bounced collectively, with hairstyles brushed forward to the chin. The tall ceilings made the nightclub seem immense, a sickly-smelling cathedral. Atop the wrought-iron stairwell the mezzanine was heaving. The cute boys looked like cartoons of cute boys, like those back in L.A. we thought might be gay until it turned out they weren't—they played in noise bands and were dating Chloë Sevigny. But here they glanced back at me. I swooned over two or three before locking eyes with a boy whose beauty was a few masterful strokes away from ordinary. He twirled his wrists and rolled his eyes skyward sardonically. That was the way to dance to Britpop. The boy moved in a manner at once bashful and blithe. He had a retroussé nose, and a mouth that was small but with pillowy lips. His eyes looked as dark as night.

Then he disappeared from the dance floor, as had Xuan. When I found her at a small table, I saw that the boy and his group were sitting just behind, on a bench along the wall. I made use of the ashtray on the empty table between us, turning back toward him each time I tapped my Gitanes. Soon enough, his companions made a performance out of leaving us alone. *I'm so embarrassed,* the boy mouthed at their departure. He shook his head coquettishly. I took my place next to him, and saw that his eyes were actually blue. He mumbled his name, which I could not catch. *Jeremy,* I shouted back. I could tell we were both trying not to laugh—he did a little, so I did as well, like releasing a thin stream of air from a soda bottle so that it doesn't erupt. I had the sensation of being classmates who'd snuck off together from an insipid lecture, giddy with relief.

I put my tongue in his ear, something I'd never done before. *I love that*, he said, and I was murderous toward any other man who'd licked his canals. I pulled the zip of his orange sweater until it became clear there was no shirt beneath. I left it there at the sternum and slipped my hand in. There was nothing to his chest, no hair or meat. I shoved my other hand down the back of his corduroy trousers and he purred as I pressed down the tip of a finger. Eventually, we flung ourselves through the crowd and upstairs. At the cigarette machine we settled on a pack of Camel Lights to split. *American*, he said. We kissed again halfway over the banister, and a girl shot us a broad smile.

We stayed until it was over. On the street, our ears rushed with the guitar of the Ash song 'Girl from Mars.' We walked through Chinatown underneath red lanterns that scraped against the bright gray sky. He said he'd detected there was something oriental about me. *Oriental is for rugs*, I corrected. He wasn't defensive; like everything else, it just made him grin. I told him I'd studied theater in Los Angeles, but when I returned, I would move to San Francisco, where I would quit writing plays and work in magazines. In the backseat of the night bus, I asked him where we were going. He replied *Walthamstow* with the same diffidence as mouthing *embarrassed*. Our fingers intertwined like a ball of yarn that rolled from lap to lap. Somehow the long journey felt like the afterglow of the sex we were going to have.

In his ground-floor flat, narrow and dark, the ancient

wallpaper was trying to unglue itself from the damp walls. He offered tea, which I accepted only to prove I could wait patiently to touch him. In his bedroom was the same Velvet Underground poster I had back in L.A. (I deduced the pictures of hunky underwear models blu-tacked to the bathroom wall must belong to his housemate, Pauley, who'd managed to travel home with us at a distance as discreet as a security detail.) *I have the same poster,* I told him when he returned with the tea. At first our kissing was more timid than it had been at the club. He moved down my body until his face was on my black underpants. *I love this,* he murmured into my bulge, and stayed there awhile.

Afterward, at my urging, he showed me his paintings. Streaks of paint had run and became part of the form. Figures awoke with mangled expressions in oppressive rooms. *I don't know,* he said, and began an extended caveat I could not comprehend. An artist, I thought, and romanticized him. We snoozed a little, then he was late for work. He still wore a faint smile as he searched the floor of the front room for his missing brown boot. *Where's it gone,* he whispered, as if charmed by its waywardness. I could tell by the way he wasn't mad at the object that he was very patient—lucky me.

Xuan and I had booked tickets to fly back to California two days later. I arranged to meet the boy at Russell Square station on Sunday, the last evening of our trip. We'd travel back to his flat together, where Xuan could sleep on the couch. I imagined our reunion—who would get there first, looking eagerly at each person approaching. But when Xuan and I, wearing our backpacks, arrived at Russell Square, the wide gate was closing. I strained but saw no sign of him. Xuan expressed her disapproval with silence. *I'll pay*, I said, hailing a black cab. *To Walthamstow*, I told the driver. *Whereabouts*, he asked. *I'll know when I see it*, I said. We traveled east and after a spell Xuan commented on the distance. We looked out the windows at the blank stares of gray buildings. The morning we'd left his flat together, the boy had shown me Waltham- stow's street market on the way to the station. He'd taken a pride I didn't quite get in the cheap clothes fluttering from tall rails and the produce sold in shallow plastic tubs. Now as we approached a vacant square, I spotted the skeletons of those market stalls. *This'll do*, I announced. *You two going to be okay?* hollered the driver. Xuan shot me a look.

I found a phone box. The night was inky, seemed to move around us disinterested, as if shuffling with hands in pocket. On the other end of the line, the boy muttered that he'd been forced to take the last train. I fretted that in making that decision he'd felt relieved of me. *Where are you?* he asked. *Near the market*, I said. He went, *Hmmm*, and I wondered again if he wished I hadn't pursued. He gave his address. *Is there a landmark?* he asked, but in my panic I saw nothing. He continued, *From the sounds of it, I would have thought it would be best to head northeast*—all these British qualifying terms trundling toward a compass direction without meaning. I took a deep breath and decided to rely on homing skills. Xuan glared and issued one of her two-word threats: *You'd. Better.*

Xuan instantly calmed, though, when she saw him in his doorway, wearing a v-neck sweater with no shirt underneath, holding a glass in one hand and grinning. He took us into the front room, where side A of *His 'n' Hers* was coming to a finish. *Pulp!* Xuan approved. The room had been tidied. *Gin?* he chirped, pouring two small glasses from the bottle next to the turntable in an alcove. The center of the record had begun to make its spitting noise. He flipped it over. The song 'Happy Endings' sounded overdramatic in that small space.

––––

The boy—I decided to call him the Famous Blue Raincoat— went through a period of sleeping on couches (sometimes sharing beds) so that he could avoid paying rent and save up to visit me in my new sublet in San Francisco. At Pop-starz, Famous met men willing to help him. This was not contingent, not really: some men just like having a boy who looks like that around the house. In the west London home of an accountant who hobnobbed with Britpop musicians, Famous stood in underpants ironing his shirt for the night shift at the hotel. He sensed that the spiky-haired man on the couch, the drummer from Suede, was checking him out. (In an issue of *Attitude,* the drummer aligned himself with his bandmate Brett, the bisexual who'd never had a homosexual experience, by submitting 'I've called myself a bisexual person who's never had a heterosexual experience.') Famous sat among these men in an old tradition of flirtation and fondness across generations but, according to the contrarian zeitgeist, apparently none was actually gay.

Famous made it to San Francisco to stay with me for a month. We proclaimed our love on a park bench after eating magic mushrooms. He returned to London, the second of many farewells. We sent long letters and mix tapes, drew pictures of each other: I was a satyr, he an angel with torn wings. Famous wrote the lyrics to the Velvet Underground song 'I'll Be Your Mirror' on a xeroxed photo of me. I'd always taken the meaning as I'll *hold* your mirror, but those weren't the words. To *be* each other's mirror was what we longed for, and what we mirrored was each other's longing.

He told me to look out for the American release of a British film called *Beautiful Thing*. I saw it in San Francisco that autumn and, as he predicted, wept. In the film, shy Jamie and sporty Ste, neighbors on a London public housing estate, fall adorably in love. There's a set piece in which the two venture into a neighborhood gay pub in the afternoon. It must be a Sunday, because it's bustling. A drag queen in emerald sequins bellows 'Hava Nagila' and the crowd claps along. More men in dresses serve drinks. People greet one another with a kiss on the cheek. Couples on barstools—daddy and twink, two lesbians—are snogging. The boys are blatantly new. They are eyed up by regulars, labeled *chicken*, pulled reluctantly into the drag queen's lascivious banter. ('I think I'll have two of you…and ten of your mate.') The film then cuts to a nearby park after nightfall, where the two are chasing each other through trees. They've escaped into nature, the opposite of the campiness and constriction of the bar. In the woods, the sylvan nymphs run free. When they kiss, they are not only smitten but relieved. They are not only outside of the building, but of category. The song 'Make Your Own Kind of Music' plays. The message must be that our protagonists are too good for the gay bar, where lonely souls fool themselves into a false notion of community. The viewer wishes the boys can stay forever young, never becoming the lecherous, rubicund men in the bar, let alone the drag queen. Famous and I figured we too were destined not for the bars, but the trees.

It must be a gay rite of passage to be intimidated, even

repulsed, by other gays. In 1951, Donald Webster Cory wrote, 'One wanders into the bar in the hope of finding the convivial spirit that comes from being with one's own; but, in the same way, the bar is the frightening specter of a mirror that holds up the image of oneself, which is a true image.' By 1996, *Beautiful Thing* suggested another way, outside of tawdry cliché. Jamie and Ste may be adorably homosexual, but they don't have to be obnoxiously gay. 'I hate it,' Ste says of the pub afterward, though in the final scene they're on their way back there. It's uncertain whether they'll become regulars, change their style, pick up the jargon. They were about to enter the tug between the desire to belong and resistance. One potential reading of this new gay liberation: to be liberated from gay.

———

In February, nearing a year after we met, I returned to London to spend five weeks with Famous there. We were parsimonious through the week and went to Popstarz on Friday nights. I danced dismally. I couldn't really dance to Britpop. A lot of the music was basically chanting. It was so white. Britpop was, among other things, a reaction to the perceived imperialism of the American music industry. (The pivotal cover of *Select* magazine from April 1993: Brett Anderson from Suede, posing in leather, baring a flat but untoned belly, in front of a Union Jack with the headline 'Yanks Go Home!') The politics of Britpop were protectionist. This paralleled the post-gay thesis that vapid gay culture was an import from America, an insidious form of soft power. When Britpop and post-gay melded in Popstarz, the aesthetic was pretty nationalistic. Popstarz advertised itself with red, white and blue—the *o* in its name an air force roundel. It could be that Popstarz unwittingly enacted a new set of borders. The club offered Famous and me a haven, but also put us on display. At Popstarz, the lads cruised one another as straight guys do, as if scouting a good addition to the band. They wanted to lure Famous into their anorectic cliques, and I was envious.

Famous was delighted to report that Popstarz had lent its name to a permanent pub—the Popstarz Bar. Just after I arrived, Famous hosted his twenty-first birthday there. I was proud to be by his side. I looked better in his glow. In the spirit of the club night, Popstarz Bar sold itself as an alternative to what central London gay bars had become, prissy and high maintenance. On the bright red walls were photos of Blondie, Bowie, Iggy Pop, Grace Jones. The sign that swung above the door showed the Popstarz roundel. The bar staff were serving teen angst. They blasted the Buzzcocks and Placebo.

The bar was tucked off the Strand on George Court, a narrow, sloping alley lit by nineteenth-century lamps. In earlier days, it bustled with a greengrocer, tea shop and tailor, but the pub, formerly the George, was the only business remaining on the passageway. The toponym refers to George Villiers, once the private owner of this stretch of land along the Thames. George was the last in a succession of handsome young favorites of King James I. The potentate fancied himself George's 'dear dad and husband.' In 1623, he named George the 1st Duke of Buckingham, and privately addressed him as 'my sweet child and wife.' Others facetiously referred to the duke as Ganymede, the mortal youth abducted by Zeus in the form of an eagle to serve as his cupbearer on Olympus. The duke wrote to King James: 'I naturally so love your person, and upon so good experience and knowledge adore all your other parts, which are more than ever one man had.' The monarch was satirized as being a bottom in global affairs. He is thought to have inspired the epithet *jemmy*, which I suppose one could say is the King James Version of queer.

Incidentally, over time, George Villiers's patch of London turned out to be a sanctum for gay sex. The district is called the Adelphi, although nobody uses the term. It was named for an ambitious Georgian housing development: the Adelphi Estate, completed in 1774, was conceived by the fashionable architect Robert Adam and his siblings—hence the name Adelphi, from *adelphoi*, Greek for *brothers*. Over the years, illustrious residents included Thomas Hardy and George Bernard Shaw. Overlooking the Thames was the estate's centerpiece, the Adelphi Terrace, an impressive row of twenty-four unified neoclassical residences raised on vaults. 'I was fond of wandering about the Adelphi,' says the Dickens character David Copperfield, 'because it was a mysterious place, with those dark arches.'

Eventually, the tenebrous recesses became known as a warren of vagrancy and cruising. The local urinal was especially notorious; a senior judge recommended it be abolished in the interest of the community. One police officer testified that the low-lit areas amounted to a 'resort of persons of the Sodomite class.' Between 1930 and 1932, seventy persons were arrested in the vicinity for importuning and acts of gross indecency. Another ten arrests in the arches occurred through the first half of 1933. That year, Parliament debated the Adelphi Estate Bill, which proposed stopping up narrow footways as well as widening public thoroughfares as part of the area's redevelopment. The Adelphi Terrace was demolished in 1936 and replaced by a single art deco hulk. Gone were those notorious bankside nooks. The historian Matt Houlbrook has proposed that 'the operations of municipal power in redeveloping the modern city were predicated upon the coordinated exclusion of queer men.'

By the fifties, dissolute opportunities persisted in the area. A pair of ancient lesbians on Villiers Street, for example, rented a room for a couple of hours at a time in cahoots with the rent boys of Piccadilly. In 1979, Heaven, the massive nightclub, opened in the arches off Villiers Street. Heaven followed the model of New York City clubs like the Saint—the hi-NRG music, the high-tech light and sound, the mustachioed clones in checked shirts, the celestial name. A couple of years in, Heaven was purchased by Richard Branson's Virgin Group for a reported half million pounds. The young magnate was early to tap into the pink pound. In a 1980 TV documentary called *Gay Life* (produced by the London Minorities Unit of London Weekend Television), the disco is featured in contrast to the working-class drag acts of the Royal Vauxhall Tavern and the hardcore leather scene—two cartoonish worlds in counterpoint to the aspirational ordinariness at Heaven. The jazz singer and surrealism expert George Melly is shown luxuriating at the new club, extolling its uninhibited atmosphere and amazing lights. But ultimately he sees the space as a move toward emancipation from the niche. 'What I hate is rigidity,' he says. 'What I would like to see is no gay scene, because it would be so natural for people to be gay that they wouldn't feel they had to actually form a scene which is really making a shell around themselves to protect them from the censure of other people.' Melly was being prototypically post-gay. (He's actually described by the presenter as 'gay until he was thirty.')

Some of the Adelphi's once insalubrious vaults subsist as the basement of the Royal Society of Arts—rentable for wedding receptions. One original brick tunnel, Lower Robert Street, remains publicly accessible—twisting through an underground garage, a shortcut familiar to cabbies and some cyclists, it is said to be haunted by the ghost of a prostitute called Poor Jenny. The zone is ripe for revenants. In his 1930 satire of private men's clubs, J. M. Barrie, who lived on the top floor of one of the houses, writes that the streets beneath his window comprise 'the only club whose ways I really know, the club of the Adelphi Ghosts.' Barrie imagines the streets to be haunted by giant figures of history, and that if the Adelphi were to be leveled, as indeed it was six years later, all the neighbors would be forced into the river—'a ghost on the back of every one of us.'

My club of Adelphi ghosts, of course, is a gay bar. The land King James gave to George Villiers where, three centuries later, the rent boys slipped down Villiers Street. In the early twentieth century on that same thoroughfare, the fun to be had at the Arena Cinema and the Hotel de France, among other known destinations. Then the disco dancers of Heaven, opened just before the escalation of AIDS. In the nineties, a post-gay bar, perhaps: Popstarz, since renamed Retro Bar, on George Court.

This is why I am telling ghost stories: they open up the city to outlandish possibilities. Gay history is a palimpsest of *what ifs*. Walking city streets in a detective mood—with Famous pointing out the clues I have missed—I'm especially delighted to discover the queer coincidences. But I can't piece them together into a distinct linear meaning. I'm reluctant to, in the words of the historian John D'Emilio, 'read backward in time'—that is, project gay identity onto anterior forms of same-sex companionship—to call *homo*, for instance, the intrinsically unequal dynamic between a powerful king and his dashing subservient, or to romanticize, with a nostalgie de la boue, the rough trade along the riverbank.

I am a participant in an archaeology of looking, of *cruising*. (Cruising was once called haunting, and the men who participated were referred to as ghosts.) What I find may be my projected fantasy—like idealizing a stranger in the dark. But given our history has been erased and revised, I take no issue with inventing a few mythologies. The ruins aid my investigation. Wayne Koestenbaum: 'For gayness to be more than a mere lifestyle or recreational choice—for it to be an encyclopedia, a geography, a wealth of routes and signs—it must acknowledge its own capacious interpretive

mannerisms as more than manner, as matter.' The overlapping histories of the Adelphi may be sketchy in places,
but there is a naughty thrill in making the connections—a
gay bar on an alley named after the *sweet child and wife* of
an adoring king. There's haptic pleasure to be had in the
surviving pieces. I can touch bricks, and for the moment
don't believe gayness is a social construct or stifling inven-
tion, but a legacy. So I overidentify.... Famous and I still
couldn't legally marry, but then look at history: even kings
have been forced to playact.

———

The lesbian couple who ran Popstarz Bar invited Famous to
host a Sunday night party in the upstairs room. I suggested
it be themed on novelty music: Famous was versed in forgotten aerobics instructionals, French pop and old BBC theme
songs. The inaugural night was listed in *Time Out*. I would
still be in town to attend but would depart for the States
later that week. Famous and I had no plan for how to find
our way back to each other again. We spent considerable
energy trying not to argue during our remaining days.

On the night of the debut, we were too wound up to
eat. We nervously sorted CDs into stacks and inspected
the sound board without expertise. Famous played host
by flitting about the place with an opera-length cigarette
holder. A few people attended, which was a relief, but the
lights were never dimmed, and the night never fully gave
into itself. I drank a lot of Grolsch to calm my nerves.
A couple of hours in, I was ill in the attic toilet, then
afterward slumped under a fluorescent bulb on the stairwell.

When I looked up, a pair of men were sitting with me. The older of the two, somewhere around thirty, had a confident, theatrical demeanor. Famous appeared, and the overfamiliar man reported I wasn't feeling my best.

Are you a couple? he asked. His twink remained silent. Famous nodded and sat down beside me, slipping me under his arm. The man arranged himself to kneel two steps below us in a beseeching pose. *You two love each other,* he declared. *You know what you need to do? Tomorrow. You need to go to Birmingham. Take a train. Then lose each other after you arrive. Walk to opposite ends of the town. Then set off toward the center. And eventually you will find each other. Sometime, maybe late in the day. And it will be like seeing each other again for the first time. And you will realize that you love each other.*

This bizarre speech did not stop the spinning. Famous adopted a stoic but scrutinizing air. When the man left, Famous said, *What made that even more strange is, that guy is on a sitcom I used to watch with my family.* Something about the scenario had disproportionately shaken him. I tried to process the actor's scheme for us to rekindle our flame in Birmingham—devised on the presumption that our passion was in doubt.

I wondered whether during the man's speech Famous had, like me, developed a clear image of Birmingham. If so, how different would each version be from the other? I envisioned us ending up in a town square beneath a towering clock. The clock would be ticking away, taunting us about our limited time together.

You know what…, I said.

What, Famous replied.

Oh, nothing. Just. You know. There's no need for us to find each other in Birmingham.

THE WINDOWS

SAN FRANCISCO

But back to when it was thick and glistening and alive. I mean life, never knowing what was going to happen.

—Michelle Tea, 2000

I moved to San Francisco for the windows. The city was a peep show. Before moving there, I visited often. I glimpsed figures in the bay windows of Victorian houses living bohemian, mysterious, randy lives. After one Pride march, I stood at a friend's kitchen sink, and a drag queen waved and laughed across the light well. I'd idle with pals on fire escapes and front stoops, checking out passersby. I got high on the proximity of other people visibly eager to do irresponsible things. I'd come away from San Francisco with not just my own experiences, but the impression of *experience* happening around me. The streets were like advent calendars: I wanted to open each door and reveal a bisexual hippie, leather daddy, elegant transvestite, friendly bull dyke wielding tattoo gun, sleazy yogi, stoned poet, skateboarder too lazy to resist my advances. I wanted to eat it all up.

First, in the summer after I met Famous, I rented a room on 16th Street in the Mission district. The area was a glorious effluvium of nag champa incense and taqueria grease and smoke from crack pipes. The whizz and click of

117

passing skaters brought me to my window every time. I'd skip around the corner to a kooky Wednesday night party called Baby Judy's. I'd drink margaritas at Puerto Allegre with skinny boys who later gave me head with great care and devotion. Even the blow jobs were different from Los Angeles: they were not just a function of mouth and penis, but an experience of the whole body, whole room, whole city. In the evenings, the fog drifted in, and it might as well have been spiked with a philter, the way poppers were once poured into smoke machines in discos. When Famous came to visit, I figured he fell in love with the place as much as with me.

Upon returning from my spell in London, I moved into a new place with three young women who all dyed their hair raven black and indulged my lovelorn state. We hadn't deliberately chosen to live in the Castro district, but an opportunity presented itself to rent an affordable flat in a refurbished Victorian on 17th near Castro Street. The many gay bars surrounding us lined up like a parade of types—leather, jock, queen.... But this being the Castro, the village where upstart homosexuals settled in the wake of the city's seedier gay ghettos, the edges of those archetypes were dulled. There was a softcore leather dive, diner-style tourist trap, pinball joint, place with a cruisy horseshoe-shaped bar frequented by black men, video bar that screened *Ab Fab* episodes weekly, low-ceilinged bungalow with sports on the TV and more than one hole-in-the-wall for old-timers.

Of course, like gays themselves, gay bars can be fickle and go through phases. On Market Street, Detour was a half-assed leather bar with blackened windows, black walls, a red laser that flashed subliminal messages onto clouds of dry ice and chain-link fencing on the go-go platforms. The site had in fact been the first gay bar in the Castro—the Missouri Mule, a lounge opened in 1963 featuring Vivacious (some say Vicious) Vivian playing honky-tonk piano on Sunday afternoons. Across the street from Detour was a Top 40 club for the bridge-and-tunnel crowd called the Café. Apparently it used to be lesbian, but eventually they were only allotted a once-a-month party called Lips. The rest of the time it was taken over by screeching young men from the suburbs and the possessive straight girls they brought with them. They squeezed onto a balcony and hollered down: *Come join us.* I'd roll my eyes and rush home with my takeout tom kha kai and Superstar Video rental. I rarely went into the bars. They were just background noise as I drifted alone pining for Famous.

There was a time in the Castro when cars struggled to get past the throngs of young men in tight jeans. Those crowds had dissipated since AIDS. Here and there, symptoms of the epidemic remained visible on the streets. Emaciated men leaned on canes. It was the first time I'd seen Kaposi's sarcoma lesions. I overheard the words *you AIDS motherfucker* hurled in a domestic dispute between the next-door neighbors while I sat in the bath attempting not to steam the ink on my newest letter from London. 'As for the famous gay life of the city,' wrote Edmund White in 1980, 'I sensed it rippling all around me, just beyond my reach.' By the late nineties, the same could be said for the city's infamous gay death.

The Castro had proven resilient, but was now placid and somewhat steely. Before I moved in, I really went there only for the annual street parties, Pride or Halloween, so witnessed it at its most bacchanalian. Costumed revelers leaned out of upper-floor windows and perched on fire escapes. It seemed then that the Castro was still, as the journalist Frances FitzGerald described the place in the late seventies, 'a carnival where social conventions were turned upside down just for the pleasure of seeing what they looked like the wrong way up.' One Halloween, there was a kerfuffle on the front steps of a center for sober alcoholics, the Castro Country Club. At the first sign of trouble a neighborhood watch pounced, each of its members wearing a leather jacket with a pink triangle on the back: *The Pink Panthers*, someone said. Another year, I was startled to come upon a man being fisted atop a bus shelter.

So it took some adjusting to move into the neighborhood and discover its day-to-day character to be so uptight. Men scuttled between obligations, which often entailed brunching. They sighed with exasperation, leaving their eyebrows aloft judgmentally. On a Market Street sidewalk, I nearly collided with a middle-aged man, each of us moving sideways to let the other pass but in the same direction. I presumed we would laugh together: *Shall we dance?* Instead, he barked imperiously: *Everyone knows when this happens to step to the right.* I was baffled. DOES *everyone know that?* I checked with friends.

I'd imagined that homos moved to the city out of rebellion. I hadn't considered entitlement as a motivating factor. 'I was white, male, and middle class, and I had gone to Harvard,' one gay man confided to Frances FitzGerald in 1978. 'I thought I could do anything I wanted, so I resented having to conceal something as basic as sex.... The solution was to move here.' These newly empowered gay men were territorial creatures. In the Castro, they were in their own way colonialist, displacing Irish Catholic families, who had already begun trickling into the suburbs following industrial decline. Now those Irish factory workers, longshoremen, stevedores and cops were replaced by middle-class gay men wearing variations on those uniforms as fetish. The old families began to refer to them as the invaders; within gay vernacular, the lookalikes among them were the clones.

The term *clone* stuck because it was (according to the *Encyclopedia of Gay Histories and Cultures*) 'as if every individual were an exact copy of some original "liberated gay man"—5'9", 29-inch waist, 29 years old, gay white male (GWM).' The clones slouched on corners, in neat mustache and bulging jeans, like a casting call for a cigarette ad. They swaggered down the street, checking one another out furtively with, as FitzGerald put it, 'a slightly hostile air about them.' Another journalist, Randy Shilts, itemized their wardrobe: used blue jeans, $2; flannel shirt, $1.50; hooded sweatshirt, $1.75. 'The new gay fashion matched a new gay attitude,' he wrote. 'The clothing spoke of strength and working-class machismo, not the gentle bourgeoise effetism of generations past. The politically conscious men of the Castro did not mince or step delicately down the street; they strutted defiantly.' If, in 1978, the corner of 18th and Castro was the crossroads of the gay world, it was an economy of fungible goods: As Shilts recounted, 'drugstore cowboys eyed laundromat loggers winking at barfly jocks.'

As the clones pullulated, the look came to represent not Whitmanesque radical sensualists but self-interested zombies. A 'doped-up, sexed-out Marlboro man,' wrote the sociologist Martin P. Levine, with a '"mefirstism" implicit in the pursuit of unbounded self-gratification.' In a 1978 article in the *San Francisco Sentinel,* the trend was derided as 'a new kind of mindless, wanton consumerism, the purchase of a mass image.' Since forever, it seems, each type of gay has been convinced the other types were *giving gays a bad name.* The wealthy elite disdained clones, who lived for the fleeting moment like a hit of poppers, too scattershot to contribute to the community. The long-haired Trotskyites scoffed at both those populations for their respective forms of conspicuous consumption. The sweater queens in cashmere and preps in Brooks Brothers shirts checked in and out of the scene, too good and yet not good enough to be full-time gays. The drag queens were regarded as giving into the myth that every gay man had a woman's soul. The leathermen donned their own form of drag—'a mask of masculinity,' as the narrator of the 1970 documentary *Gay San Francisco* suggested.

The constant policing of authenticity added another layer to the animus, as well as to the cruising. On weekdays everyone would read Armistead Maupin's newspaper serial *Tales of the City,* published as a novel in 1978. His character Michael 'Mouse' Tolliver, a clone-ish softie himself, laments the experience of meeting men—'nice mustache, Levi's, a starched khaki army shirt...strong...'—and trying to resist visiting their bathrooms lest he encounter 'the giveaway, the fantasy-killer....Face creams and shampoos for *days.*' Mouse was only being wistful, but the underlying effemiphobia was pernicious on the scene. Masculinity can be something that gay men project onto one another, only to snatch it away at the first sign of inauthenticity—that they hadn't rolled out

of bed looking ruggedly handsome, but required a beauty
regime to get that way.

———

For a brief spell, I sold the men of the neighborhood
their face creams and shampoos, in my part-time job at an
organic apothecary at 575 Castro Street. A bubble machine
affixed to the storefront eaves puffed a whimsical froth over
the street. The business was owned by a couple with anti-
thetical personalities, which made it a challenge to impress
either. One of the men had resplendent eyebrows that stood
an inch in front of his face; he did the accounting, was
wired but focused. The other appeared softer at first—the
wife, I thought—but I could tell I made him twitchy. I
had butterfingers in his presence, and he disapproved of
how I apologized for every mistake I made. I deferred to
their right-hand, a redheaded Southern gentleman in his
late twenties who carried himself with unforced alacrity.
He regularly schlepped a ladder out front to top up the
solution in the bubble machine. When he and I noticed a
customer exiting the shop wearing a bandanna in a back
pocket, he showed me the hankie code chart taped to the
wall behind the dispensary, and we used it to assess the
depravity the man was flagging. I was shocked: yellow, on
the right! As much as anything else, it seemed impressively
anachronistic. I tried to envision what color I would wear if
I were uninhibited.

A smiling woman with short gray hair brought groups
of people by nearly every day. Her walking tour was called
Cruisin' the Castro. It turned out the site we occupied was

once the camera shop of the legendary Harvey Milk, who had gone on to serve as an openly gay city supervisor until his assassination in 1978. He and his partner, Scott Smith, took the space—and number 573 upstairs—as their residence five years before that. They put a sign in the shop window that read We Are Very OPEN. Soon that was joined by posters for demonstrations and neighborhood meetings. Young people loitered on the old sofa and salvaged barber chair. But Milk was forced to abandon the space when his landlord raised the monthly rate from three hundred and fifty to twelve hundred dollars. On his way out, Milk posted those figures in the window. According to Randy Shilts, at the shop that took over, three hundred and fifty dollars was the price of a single crystal vase. From 1968 to 1978, real estate transactions in the Castro increased seven hundred percent. 'Business space on Castro Street is tighter than a pair of 29-inch waist Levi's,' a *San Francisco Examiner* journalist cracked in 1979. It was estimated that twenty-five to thirty thousand gay people, mostly men, had moved to the neighborhood and spilled into the surrounding area—as Frances FitzGerald quipped, 'painting and refurbishing as they went.'

By the nineties, a sense of entitlement permeated the street. In the evenings, I traded stories with my roommates, always worded cautiously, about the snippiness we'd encountered that day. Sasha worked at the garden shop across from the apothecary, and came home exhausted by customers' bonsai demands. The occasional free love freak still swept through the neighborhood—one of the Sisters of Perpetual Indulgence on roller skates, a Radical Faerie on a unicycle—but mostly the population was high earners fond of khakis and eggs benedict. (Homonormative, the style would later be labeled.) Life was tranquil, but edgy under the surface. Every time I went to Walgreens, I was braced for someone to flip, at which everyone else would fall foul of one another. It was hard not to perceive the neighborhood as vituperative. I would have preferred to dismiss it as inconsequential, but this was the place where gays were testing out a gay economy and gay etiquette, and I was put off by what they were telegraphing. One day, I arrived at work and spotted on the notice board, between ads for crystal healing and guitar lessons, an FBI wanted poster for the serial killer Andrew Cunanan, who'd made the news for murdering Gianni Versace, and was suspected to be stalking gay men in enclaves like ours. I was convinced he was hiding out in our basement, and told my roommates so. Gay against gay seemed to have reached a grotesque peak. Having dissociated from the identity, I just didn't want to be caught in their crossfire.

————

Nearly every day, I'd pass the large windows wrapping around the corner of Castro and 17th: the Twin Peaks Tavern. Its name was outlined in neon on a jutting sign in the shape of the iconic hills to the west. On either side of the building, long metal box arrows pointed toward the corner door, illuminated by a sequence of flashing colored bulbs in the spectrum of the rainbow. I glimpsed silver-haired men in button-up shirts inside; I had the impression of them as pallid and hunched, and as loners even while I observed their gestures of fraternity. I decided the place was little more than a banal backdrop in the comic strip of my life.

The building was erected in 1883, then stuccoed and detailed in a Mediterranean revival style forty years later. From 1935, it was an Irish dive bar, Gus and Bye; back then its windows were painted on the exterior and blocked with paper inside, presumably so wives didn't glimpse their husbands drinking. When the couple MaryEllen Cunha and Peggy Forster—*the girls*—took over in 1972 and renamed it Twin Peaks, they opened up its facade: it is considered to be the first gay bar in town, some say the nation, to be fronted in large plate glass. The girls insisted this was not a political stance; the windows were uncovered simply because they wanted to look out. But the bar was also unabashedly gay. They later turned the light-up arrows on the facade into rainbows by dipping each individual bulb in paint.

The girls thought they'd make do with one additional employee, but within days it was clear they'd require more help. They hired a group of bartenders—*the boys*—and uniformed them in white aprons. A formidable pre-Prohibition back bar was hauled in while the windows were out. The unique stained-glass lamps suspended throughout the room were custom-made. The girls envisioned an upscale, comfortable place where professionals could mingle; it was the gay version of what was then called a fern bar—straight pickup joints where the stigma of sleaziness was assuaged by potted plants and Tiffany lamps, mismatched Victorian furnishings in the mood of grandma's living room and classy elements like ladies' nights. The first fern bar may have been TGI Fridays in Manhattan, opened in 1965 next door to an apartment building where hundreds of stewardesses resided. San Francisco had Henry Africa's, a saloon of palm trees and mounted taxidermy; its proprietor, a war veteran in tiny running shorts, changed his name to that of the bar. At the Twin Peaks, ferns did hang in the windows, until the boys tired of watering them and they were done away with.

The big windows provided unobstructed views of the street life, but also meant passersby could peer in. At first, lawyers and doctors would head instinctively to the recesses for fear of being spotted and facing reprisal at work, but gradually became accustomed to the exposure. The place immediately attracted an older clientele, survivors who'd emerged from miasmic burrows and plunged into the fishbowl. Their median age gave the bar its morbid nickname, the glass coffin. Elder gays had been doubly invisible, and in the windows of the Twin Peaks, they were a portent the street's perpetual adolescents didn't necessarily want to behold. Then AIDS came, and several of the popular bartenders there died—David, Paulie, Mike, Art and Clint, *the boys*—so the glass coffin took on a wretched second meaning.

The bar's visibility did not so much provoke as normalize. It could be an example of what the critic David Halperin has called 'desexualizing' in order to promote a wholesome, agreeable gay identity. Initially, the girls laid down house rules that banned signs of homo affection at the Twin Peaks: it was a 'no touch' bar. In other cities, such edicts were imposed by the mafiosos who ran gay bars. In San Francisco bars run by queers and allies, it became a form of self-policing. Standards were scrupulously maintained at the Twin Peaks, where the glass meant every move was on display. Had the gay bar been beaten into submission?

The historian John D'Emilio wrote that after the Second World War 'the spread of the gay bar contained the greatest potential for reshaping the consciousness of homosexuals and lesbians. Alone among the expressions of gay life, the bar fostered an identity that was both public and collective.' In effect, the status of the gay bar was declared legal in the verdict of the 1951 California Supreme Court case *Stoumen v. Reilly*. Two years before, Sol Stoumen, the straight proprietor of the Black Cat in North Beach, had lost his license on the grounds that his place was a hangout for homosexuals. 'All was not so gay, gay, gay as usual yesterday at the freethinking Black Cat,' reported the *San Francisco Chronicle*. Stoumen faced the loss of his business; his lawyer, Morris Lowenthal, fought his case on civil rights terms. After a series of appeals, the verdict of the state's highest court finally restored the Black Cat's license, and in doing so established the right of queers to congregate. The ruling was seen as a landmark.

But it was in some ways a pyrrhic victory: the decision qualified that a bar could still be shut down for being disorderly with proof of immoral acts on the premises. In other words, homosexuals had the legal right to hang out together as long as they weren't doing homosexual things. This was seized upon by moralists, or politicians posing as such. In 1955, the California Department of Alcoholic Beverage Control—the ABC—was formed, then given broad authority by a subjectively drafted new code passed unanimously into state law, which stated that providing a resort for sexual perverts was cause for losing a liquor license. The ABC officers dressed in plainclothes and carried firearms (but didn't pack heat while undercover in gay bars, so as not to be found out while being felt up).

In 1956, agents reported they'd been hit on at the Black Cat, and the bar's license was revoked again. In the years-long, costly appeals process that would follow, Lowenthal wielded the Kinsey Report to argue homos aren't categorical pervs. That September, thirty-six women were arrested at a lesbian bar called the Alamo Club and jailed for frequenting a house of ill repute. Only four pleaded not guilty. The newly formed lesbian advocacy group the Daughters of Bilitis prepared a guide, 'What to Do in Case of Arrest,' which instructed readers never to confess to specious accusations. The criteria for what makes a disorderly establishment was debated in courts: Could it, as one ABC agent suggested, include 'swishing movements, high-pitched voices, or limp wrists'? Once again, the greatest transgression appeared to be gender deviance.

In 1959, another appeal over a revoked license was brought before the California Supreme Court—this time, by the Oakland bar Mary's First and Last Chance. At the initial hearing, which had resulted in the bar losing its license, police testimonies were brought up saying women there dressed mannishly, danced together and kissed; that one lesbian told a policewoman 'you're a cute little butch'; that two men, one gray haired, whispered together forehead to forehead before announcing they were 'going steady.' But the ABC didn't cite this evidence in its final decision, instead resting its case on the fact of 'sexual perverts, to wit: Homosexuals' *being there*. It was common knowledge that it was a hangout for homos; the ABC must have figured that was enough. The supreme court, however, decided that while those scandalous scenarios would have indeed made the case for an affront to public morality, the ABC hadn't proven their veracity nor factored them into the basis of the decision. Relying on evidence that homos were merely present wasn't sufficient. Mary's First and Last Chance had its license restored. The verdict reaffirmed the Black Cat decision by reasserting the legal distinction between *status* (being homosexual) and *conduct* (acting on that).

As a result of the ruling, another San Francisco bar, the Handlebar on California Street, also began trading again. Its newly emboldened owner proceeded to report that he'd undergone nearly two years of extortion from police. Other proprietors came forward reporting shakedowns by cops and the ABC. The press dubbed this the gayola scandal. The spotlight backfired on the homos. Officials would be brought to trial, then defend themselves to the jury as moral crusaders battling seedy bar life, and be acquitted. Politicians courted public favor by declaring war on the city's homosexual problem. The police stepped up its tactic of deploying hot cops in tight trousers to ensnare patrons. There'd been no related felony convictions in the first half of 1960; there were seventy-six in the first half of the following year.

In the late summer of 1961, the biggest vice raid of its kind in the city's history took place at the Tay-Bush Inn, when the plug on the jukebox was pulled at a quarter past three in the morning. Eighty-nine men and fourteen women were hauled to jail as seven loads in three paddy wagons. In the end, all but two charges were dropped. The *San Francisco Chronicle* columnist Herb Caen—the eyes and ears and, according to his Pulitzer Prize, conscience of the city—wrote a scathing piece that highlighted how the mayor's office scapegoated these men and women while moneyed queers luxuriated in stylishly decorated homes, not perverted but eccentric. 'The only moral,' Caen wrote, 'if it's a question of morals: Don't be a poor One. Don't be a poor anything.'

In 1963, the Black Cat's license was permanently rescinded on the eve of its annual Halloween party. Halloween was traditionally the one night the police loosened their grip. (Randy Shilts called it the homosexual high holiday.) By the next Halloween, twelve of the city's thirty gay bars had been closed—five of them within one week—and proceedings were under way to bring down another fifteen. But gay bars were learning to play by the state's rules, as vague as they were, by toughening their own policies in anticipation. Customers could be themselves as long as they kept to themselves. Soon enough, gay bars proliferated across the city. From the eighteen remaining in 1964, there were an estimated hundred and eighteen within a decade.

The Twin Peaks aimed to be an establishment above reproach. It long remained one of a network of lesbian-owned 'no touch' bars known for exceptional circumspection. A kiss could get you shown to the door. Such cautious bar owners created a cultural implication from the legalese: since homosexual *status* was acceptable before the eyes of the law, it could make for an upstanding identity; because homosexual *conduct* was enough to get a place shut down, making a show of desire was considered a disgrace to the community. Even as public attitudes liberalized in San Francisco, the terms set by the state had become internalized, so that comportment was treated as a matter of self-respect. As MaryEllen Cunha put it, 'It was for the best. Who wants to sit in a bar and watch people misbehave?' She and Forster envisioned an unimpeachable gay lifestyle: dignified, restrained, professional. What they put on view in those big windows was their standard of decorum.

———

With time, passing that glass monument on the corner, I found myself thinking not only about how it reified the gay liberation narrative of the transparent and visible, but about its opposite—the hidden and opaque. Specifically, I thought about Michel Foucault. Though it would be amusing to imagine him at the Twin Peaks, his intense bald head resting on the glass, it would not have been his scene. Rumor had it that Foucault once spent time in the leather bars, bathhouses and sadomasochistic dungeons around Folsom Street. In his book *Foucault in California*, Simeon Wade quotes his idol: 'I actually liked the scene before gay liberation, when everything was more covert. It was like an underground fraternity, exciting and a bit dangerous. Friendship meant a lot, it meant a lot of trust, we protected each other, we related to each other by secret codes.'

Through the majority of Foucault's lifetime, gay bars maintained a recessive relationship with the street. They had inconspicuous facades and occupied cellars. In her book *Wide-Open Town*, Nan Alamilla Boyd explains how queer-owned San Francisco bars in the postwar period constructed what she calls spatial defenses: back entrance, covered windows, dance floor sequestered in the rear, a discriminating hostess on the door. The owner might opt to tend bar herself, from which her domain could be surveyed. Dimming the lights allowed the staff and patrons to suss out a newcomer before being seen themselves. But such fortified architecture also offered something other than protection: a clandestine thrill.

Three years after the Twin Peaks opened its windows, its spatial inverse, the Catacombs, a private club for sadomasochism and fisting, was established in the basement of a Victorian house on 21st Street. Its founder, Steve McEachern, had run a typing business out of the basement until he began to build the dungeon as a birthday present for his lover. The Catacombs developed into its own kind of institution—a homespun, hardcore version of the gay bathhouses in the city where men gathered not just for sex but to exhibit art and watch movies. Apart from periodic crackdowns, the bathhouses were often left alone. If there were going to be gays, at least they were doing it behind closed doors in the steam. The historian Allan Bérubé contended that sex in establishments that were separated from the general citizenry created 'the first urban zone of privacy, as well as safety, for gay men.' Assembly Bill 489, which permitted sodomy and oral sex between consenting adults in private, became California law at the start of 1976, and destabilized the legal ground on which the state could prosecute homosex on private property.

The Saturday night fisting parties at the Catacombs had an exclusive guest list comprising referrals that grew out of the local chapter of Fist Fuckers of America—sometimes referred to in code as Final Faith of America—which overlapped with the secretive circuit called TAIL—the Total Ass Involvement League. Guests of the Catacombs were required to reserve ahead. They arrived promptly, and relaxed in a front room—smoking weed, greeting friends and touching up their manicures. The two back rooms were the bridal suite, dominated by a four-poster waterbed, and the dungeon, its walls and ceilings mirrored, lit only by Victorian gaslights. 'Just walking into that room,' wrote the critic Gayle Rubin, 'could put a person in a leathery mood.' There was, among other equipment, a seven-foot cage, a suspended hospital gurney and a wooden bondage cross. Cans of Crisco were chained next to each handmade leather sling; on the average Saturday, the Catacombs went through nearly forty pounds of the stuff. The floor was perfectly sanded. The soundtrack moved from lubricious disco to moodier, sometimes menacing tracks, plus the occasional in-joke like the sound of a flushing toilet. The bisexual kink legend Cynthia Slater, a lover of the owner Steve McEachern, brought a few women along, and the men got used to their presence. One of those women, Pat Califia, eventually introduced Friday night women's parties. Now Patrick Califia, he has observed 'a firm sense of balance existed' among the clientele: 'You could be as big a sexual outlaw as you liked on Saturday night, but come Sunday, cooking a fabulous brunch was every bit as important.' But Califia also confides that all the hairs on his body stand up when he recalls the intensity of his first time fisting: 'That illusion of holding another person's beating heart in the palm of my cupped hand.'

In the early hours in late August 1981, Steve McEachern, who had been cavorting on the waterbed, suffered a heart attack and died in the arms of his partner, Fred Heramb. The club was re-created in a smaller location. Then the spread of AIDS threatened to undermine the legality of the bathhouses, glory holes and sex clubs. Health officials, politicians, business groups and gay activists (who variously agitated for total liberty or safety through regulation) collided, often with intense vitriol, over the fate of these sites. Few bathhouse owners could be persuaded to post info about health risks on their premises, lest they spoil the mood. At the Catacombs, though, Heramb maintained impeccable standards, and a sign read Wash Hands after Every Fuck. Shoulder-length veterinary gloves were provided in lieu of condoms. By 1984, the bathhouses were being ordered to close down as a matter of public health, and that year the Catacombs was shut down, too. For such a secret club, it's had an outsize impact on the study of queer social spaces. Gayle Rubin contends that such a sensitively run environment nurtured empathetic relationships as much as any aboveground institution. Covertness was integral to that. To Rubin, the Catacombs was where 'sexual heretics' could be 'insulated, as much as possible, from the curious and the hostile.'

The subculture scenes were not always in shadow; they could provide a polestar. Bill Eppridge's photograph of the South of Market motorcycle bar the Tool Box was printed in *Life* magazine back in 1964, the opening spread of an article entitled 'Homosexuality in America.' (Subtitle: 'A secret world grows open and bolder. Society is forced to look at it—and try to understand it.') In the image, leathermen stand in front of painted avatars in a mural by Chuck Arnett (who arrived in town on his motorcycle and took a job tending bar there). Arnett's figures are strong-jawed, almost Frankenstein-ish. Their black jackets merge until they become the dark room. In one corner, a woman in sunglasses and her male companion appear to be making for the exit. The shot was strategized by Hal Call, president of the homophile organization the Mattachine

Society. The bar owners and regulars may not have quite shared in Call's urge for high visibility, but somehow the remarkable photo shoot happened. The story goes that the men who appear in the picture gave their approval over a shadowy Polaroid similar to the final pick, not anticipating the distinguishability of the image that eventually ran across two pages.

After the *Life* article, men from as far as India wrote to the Mattachine Society for advice. The exposé inadvertently served as a tantalizing promotion for the city. For many readers, homosexuality hadn't previously been named. Now the identity was inextricably tied to a place. According to the historian Martin Meeker, the owners of the Tool Box were forced to sell because they couldn't keep up with the waves of gay tourists. The bar regulars saw imitations of themselves show up, wearing the motorcycle gear but without a hog parked out front. South of Market—the terrain of warehouses abuzz with metal benders and plastic molders by day, and leathermen come nightfall—became synonymous with the homomasculine scene. Ultimately, its gathering spots—nearly thirty, by one count in the early eighties—may have amounted to a string of theaters at which unconvincing plays were performed nightly. Edmund White quipped of another leather bar: 'At the Black and Blue the customers are so butch they swill Perrier water right out of the bottle (the bartenders jam the lime down into it).' But the ruse was beside the point, or was the point exactly—the men didn't come to the city to be who they'd always been, but who they wanted to be. They didn't move to a place they knew as a reality but one inscribed on their imagination.

When the Tool Box was torn down for redevelopment in 1975, its murals remained. This is a very San Francisco story: The leathermen wall stood exposed, some reckon, for another couple of years—near a freeway ramp bringing drivers into the city. One leather columnist, Mr. Marcus, dubbed the South of Market district the Valley of the Kings. He called the old-fashioned Polk Street scene the Valley of the Queens. And the Castro was the Valley of the Dolls....I imagine plastic Kens, on which genitals are nothing more than a mound. The Castro had become the city's acknowledged gay center, and the image it transmitted was upbeat, bright, perhaps castrated. The banal windows of the Twin Peaks Tavern represented this prevailing message of gayness as well adjusted and benign. The panes reflected not the kinky nor the hostile, perhaps the curious, mostly the ambivalent—*me* as I passed daily. I did hear the rumor that a black-painted Victorian on Castro between 18th and 19th included a dungeon, but the notion seemed little more than silly, the way its facade announced itself like a teenager in a satanic t-shirt. Living in the Castro was not, for me, like being a kid in a candy store; gay culture had instead become a shopping mall, with one hackneyed look after another on display for window shopping.

———

The Famous Blue Raincoat came to the city each summer, staying for as many weeks as he could. In San Francisco, he was an intrepid flaneur. He scrambled through the brush along the ocean's edge; once, he chanced upon a cruising area dressed in a Boy Scout shirt he'd found in a thrift store, and beat a hasty retreat when he ignited strong passions. He scampered up the hills south of the city where, urban myth had it, rodents and insects still carried the Black Death. He strolled Valencia Street in the Mission, peering into shop windows at Santeria talismans, art deco antiques, unfamiliar meats, taxidermy. How a city could be so compact and yet so expansive fascinated him. On the third summer, Famous simply stayed.

We'd had enough of the endings. On the morning he was scheduled to fly back to England, at the cusp of his visa's allotted ninety days, Famous did pack his suitcase, a bulky old thing. We let inertia take over: He was not actively, *prosecutably* staying. Rather, he was neglecting to leave. We just let the time slip away, waiting for a cab to the airport that nobody called, acutely aware as the hour arrived for check-in, security, final boarding....We played dumb with time. I invented ridiculous excuses: *We got the date wrong, got stuck in traffic....* We became elated when we imagined his name announced over the intercom—*This is the final call....*

Some confused weeks passed, through which the fugitive continued to live out of his suitcase as if not admitting his crime to himself. My roommates didn't mind him being there for a while. Having Famous around was no more bother than bringing some wildflowers inside. Wanting to send something to his parents to reassure them of his well-being, Famous packaged up leaflets about local heritage sites, just as he used to mail envelopes to me from London stuffed with nightclub flyers and soft pornography. At the post office, we stood in the long line, chatting about moving out of the Castro and into our own place. Everything was nerve-racking. *Oh shut UP,* cried the voice of an incensed man behind us. We turned around but not all the way. We had no desire to test him further. *Oh, I've seen you two before,* he hissed. *Prancing around the neighborhood, jabbering like two queens.*

I knew the queens he spoke of. They caterwauled from the balcony of the Café. I was indignant. Surely I was a phlegmatic observer on these streets. I did all my best mincing indoors among small groups of friends. And Famous *mumbled*—even I couldn't make out a good deal of what he was saying. Moreover, I was still undecided over which kind of gay I wanted to be. I certainly hadn't decided on *queen.* If anything, I was a starling, imitating the calls of other species. I was a fake replicating other fakes, the way a starling can mimic a mockingbird. But mostly we were uncertain and impressionable. We wanted to be better students of gay history. But there was no way to convince a bitter homosexual of all that. We clammed up, once again terrified of gay men.

To get to the post office, we passed Harvey's, named in homage after Milk's assassination (supposedly by a real estate developer who didn't exactly concur with his politics). Before that, it was the Elephant Walk. Opening a couple of years after the Twin Peaks, it took a cue from its predecessor, foisting large picture windows onto the corner of 18th and Castro Streets. On Sundays in the late seventies, the disco diva Sylvester sang in falsetto there, wearing sequin kaftans. Most of the men in the audience were his opposite—more of the same clones. Sylvester's biographer, Joshua Gamson, wrote that the clone culture 'was about gender, and it was about fucking, but it was pretty much the opposite of gender-fucking....Queens didn't fit unless they covered up their nelliness with a mustache and packed it away in jeans.' Yet somehow, Sylvester—black, androgynous, the antithesis of a regular guy, idiosyncratic, *too much*—relieved the clones of the fear of their own femininity. Sylvester was an icon of a neighborhood in which he was otherwise an outcast. He could have represented the fairy that each of those boys had the potential to be, or may have once been. Because he was larger than life, his sissiness so *super,* they weren't actually at risk of becoming Sylvester—they couldn't if they tried. I imagine the sparkles of Sylvester's garments catching the light and dazzling the men's stares, as if refracting their insecurities.

In 1978, Sylvester released 'You Make Me Feel (Mighty Real).' Realness was not only a drag term about passing as a woman, it simultaneously called into question what it is to be an authentic man. Sylvester's *feel* is pointedly not *am*; like the theorist Judith Butler's chosen example of '(You Make Me Feel Like) A Natural Woman,' I take the *feel* as positing our identities always lie in the aspiration. Until his death in 1988, Sylvester was a de facto ambassador within the Castro—not delivering cautious diplomacy between contentious factions, but providing a glimmer of the imagination, as if causing the street an otherworldly leak. Sylvester's look was visionary, and I suspect had some trickle effect: in footage of a Castro street party from 1982, I've detected a few slippages in the clone monolith, my attention drawn to one boy plainly dressed but with a single feather earring.

In 1985, a group of sociologists published the book *Habits of the Heart*, arguing that a real community must be a 'community of memory,' meaning one that remembers its past, including painful stories of shared suffering. Where history is forgotten, they wrote, community degenerates into lifestyle enclaves. Lifestyle 'celebrates the narcissism of similarity,' and elevates private concerns—namely, leisure and consumption—above the common good. The academics announced: 'When we hear phrases such as "the gay community" or "the Japanese-American community," we need to know a great deal before we can decide to which degree they are genuine communities and the degree to which they are lifestyle enclaves.' They could call it whichever they pleased, but if they were talking about the Castro, they risked ignoring how a group of people can rally to deal with duress in the present, as gays and their allies demonstrated during the AIDS crisis before combination therapy. Is it *community enough* that, as Joshua Gamson wrote, 'Living people had their hearts broken many times over, and carried shrapnel stories from one memorial service to another. A woman carried the ashes of a friend around town in a Gucci bag. A man convinced his lover to let go into death by reminding him of what it had once felt like to let his rectum relax around a fist. There was the man who gave douches to a young friend constipated from morphine, and a woman who brushed the teeth of a friend who had gone blind and mute at thirty.'

Those ashes in a Gucci bag make a complicated symbol of the intersection of loss, honor and decadence within a 'community of memory' that's often blatantly unremoved from commerce. Whether some would prefer otherwise, capitalism has been the context, and financial transactions have been used as a mechanism in civil rights. The critic Michael Warner points out that in the lesbian and gay movement, 'the institutions of culture-building have been market-mediated: bars, discos, special services, newspapers, magazines, phone lines, resorts, urban commercial districts.' There will, of course, be compromise when a group's institutions are private concerns. (Gayle Rubin compared gay bars to sports teams—fans may be possessive, but the owner could be tempted away to another city.) And Warner further wrestles with the fact that these sites are dominated by those with capital—namely, middle-class white men. That said, it's the reality that businesses have been consistently present in the advance of gay liberties. Money is part of the story.

Randy Shilts wrote of how Harvey Milk used the civil rights movement in the South as a model—a bus boycott doesn't work unless the bus companies are losing money. Around 1974, a couple of years into his tenure as a shop owner, Milk amended his pet slogan *gays vote gay* into *gays buy gay*. In one of his famed moves, Milk got behind labor leader Allan Baird's boycott of six beer distributors who refused to sign a union contract. Baird already had the support of Middle Eastern and Chinese grocers. Milk's rallying of the gay bars tipped the scales: five of the six beer firms agreed to the pact. Milk and Scott Smith then launched a gay bar boycott of the only holdout—Coors—effectively demonstrating their demographic's spending power. Between 1977 and 1984, according to Milk's protégé Cleve Jones, Coors saw its share of the giant California market drop from forty to fourteen percent. Meanwhile, Allan Baird ensured that gays were getting union jobs driving for each of the other beer distributors. It was Baird who gifted Milk the battered red and white bullhorn that would go on to rouse fed-up gays and survive the wrath of police batons until it earned its place as a protest icon.

The clarion call through the mouthpiece may have been 'out of the bars and into the streets,' but the bars themselves could be staging grounds for resistance. ('The bars were seedbeds for a collective consciousness that might one day flower politically,' John D'Emilio wrote.) The Tavern Guild was founded in the early sixties; it was to some extent a weekly drinking party, but also said to be the country's first gay business association, largely formed to combat harassment and intimidation through solidarity. It began at the Suzy-Q on Polk Street, one of whose bartenders was elected the first leader. Guild members fixed drink prices as a means of discouraging competition. Because the survival of venues was precarious, a loan fund was established for failed bar owners and out-of-work staff. A phone tree allowed members to keep track of the movements of the ABC on a given night, passing along a warning when a raid seemed imminent. The Tavern Guild bars distributed the 'Pocket Lawyer,' a wallet-size guide of what to do in case of arrest published by SIR, the Society for Individual Rights.

In 1973, the Twin Peaks was admitted into the Tavern Guild. That was also the year the guild formed a softball league: eight gay bars would compete against one another, with the winner going on to play the police. At 'the second annual baseball game between the gays and cops of San Francisco,' the former were represented by the boys of the Twin Peaks. According to the gay newspaper *Bay Area Reporter*, the chief of police threw out the first ball, 'lavender and glittered for the occasion.' Drag cheerleaders waved pompoms in front of the large crowd gathered to watch the Fuzz vs. Peaks. Red, white and blue balloons were released. Cops and clones in matching mustaches became friendly rivals in a field under the sun. (The *B.A.R.* detailed: 'A special cheer rose from our throats, deafening, at the introduction of Walter Scott, son of the Chief, who had trouble keeping himself tucked into his cut-offs, necessitating constant re-arrangement, to our amusement.') The Twin Peaks boys were victorious 9–4 over Police Department Central. That night, squad cars parked all over the intersection in front of the Twin Peaks, their sirens flashing. This time, they hadn't arrived to make arrests, but to salute the winning team.

Perhaps it's down to this rapport that the tavern was spared during the White Night riots on 21 May 1979. The Elephant Walk down the street took the beating. That day, the jury had returned their decision in the case of Dan White, the former supervisor who'd shot to death his colleagues Harvey Milk and Mayor George Moscone. The verdict of voluntary manslaughter was shockingly lenient. On the day of the killings, White had entered City Hall through a window with a loaded .38 Smith & Wesson and two more chambers' worth of hollow-point bullets. But his defense attorney presented a string of psychiatrists who reasoned that the defendant, a wholesome former cop, was incapable of premeditation: one reasoned that White, being a considerate man, had chosen to crawl through the window in order not to embarrass the police officer manning the metal detector. It was reported police officers and firemen raised a hundred thousand dollars for Dan White's legal fund. When it was announced that he'd been given the lightest possible conviction, the story circulated that cops could be heard over police radio singing a celebratory rendition of 'Danny Boy.'

That night, an estimated five thousand protesters took to City Hall; some pulled parking meters from the sidewalk to use as battering rams, some made shields of garbage can lids. Others fought with tree branches, chrome prized from buses, slabs of asphalt. One squad car was lit on fire, then another, until a whole block of them burst into flames—'their melting sirens,' Randy Shilts wrote, 'screeching into the cool May night.' The cops, having lost the battle at City Hall, were sure to wage war in the Castro. For whatever reason, their primary target was the Elephant Walk. Officers with hidden badges jumped onto the bar, swinging their truncheons at skulls. They shouted *cocksuckers* and *faggots*. Men were beaten just outside. Up the street, the Twin Peaks battened down the hatches: staff lowered the lights and locked the Dutch door. The patrons lay under tables, and the place went unscathed.

The next day would have been Harvey Milk's forty-ninth birthday. A street disco had been planned, and it went ahead. The regal Sylvester performed. At one point some twenty thousand revelers sang *happy birthday, dear Harvey....* A protest was held that night in New York City across the street from the site of the Stonewall Inn, with placards hoisted into the air, some of which simply read 'We All Live in San Francisco.'

—

Famous could live in San Francisco, but if he were to truly *reside* there, we needed to get gay married. At the time, this was not an actual possibility. We were taken aback to come across the END MARRIAGE stencils on pavements throughout the city. At first we figured it was an anti-gay campaign. But the message was *end marriage altogether*. The activist group behind the campaign, Gay Shame, believed that queers should disrupt and challenge institutions—marriage, military, marketplace—not endeavor to join them. They despaired at gays waving rainbow flags made in sweatshops. They wanted gay people to think critically and follow the money, especially the pink dollar. The objects of their ire included greedy gay landlords, exploitative corporations, discriminatory bar owners, pathetic assimilationists and disingenuously reformed police marching in pride parades.

Gay Shame began as an annual event in Brooklyn in 1998. The acerbic term had been played with previously. In one instance, the critic José Esteban Muñoz proposed a gay shame parade: held in bitter February instead of summer, it would require its participants to wear drab colors, carry signs no bigger than a business card, refrain from chanting and march in single file—not through the center of town but some remote location. Early on, the San Francisco contingent of Gay Shame did organize an event that chimed with Muñoz's poignant joke: a party in an edgeland called Tire Beach. Another event was a Goth Cry-In. It seemed, though, that the group's intent was generally less about introspection and more about being enlightened queers rebuking benighted gays—in which case, shame was not a reclaimed affect, but a verb: a wagging finger.

We'd begun to identify members around town—on Valencia Street in front of Modern Times bookstore, where they held their meetings, as well as at sloppy house parties. They were like muddied lost boys and tank girls, always looking exhausted from sex or a brawl. They wore t-shirts with the sleeves ripped off and could be detected from a distance by the stink. They rode bikes without helmets and swish-swaggered down sidewalks. They were adorned in scrapes and bruises, as well as slogans proclaiming various grievances. Each of them seemed to have a magnificent ass and be writing a book.

They were so fierce and committed I figured they must be right about everything. Yet there was a sticking point: I was open to the idea of gay marriage. If it kept Famous with me, out of jail and not deported, we were willing to be grooms. So when Gay Shame members rode by on their bikes with their agitprop patches, Famous and I lowered our heads. They made us feel so realpolitik. It was as though they could look *through* Famous and me, and detect that if there was a secret ballot, we'd secretly vote for gay marriage. The correct choice among shamers was *against*. They saw marriage as a way for the state to regulate bodies and de-privilege those who fell outside the patriarchal institution. But we just sought relief.

To its opponents, marriage was exclusionary, which would make Famous and me love protectionists. It was private, rendering us love capitalists. But in fact the mess we were in made neither complacent, and both vulnerable. I constantly feared the authorities banging down the door. (We'd moved to a little basement apartment perched at the edge of the city. Damp and shabby, it was well appointed as a hide-away.) But on the question of immigration, Gay Shame could retort: *What about couples where neither member is a citizen?* I was ashamed that my situation was never *the worst*. In the house I grew up in, marriage was seen as a triumph. Mom and Dad got hitched just five years after antimiscegenation laws were banned in the 1967 US Supreme Court case im-probably named *Loving v. Virginia*. For my parents, marriage was redefined as lived—worth fighting for not because it is a complete and flawless institution, but because it has the potential to evolve and change.

Ultimately, *shame* didn't seem to be the right tactic for a debate around hospital visitation rights or partner sepa-rations or child custody. Shame, the psychoanalyst Adam

Phillips wrote, is a 'conversation-stopper.' The cultural theorist Elspeth Probyn ventured, 'I don't think I've ever been shamed for not being a heterosexual, but I have been shamed for not being a good homosexual.' Gay Shame made a powerful statement in calling out bloodsucking landlords and hypocritical corporations. But they were unlikely to listen to a bunch of malodorous misfits. In a sense, that may be all Gay Shame was intending—to ask, rhetorically, *Have you no shame?* To experience shame may require belief in a standard to which one aspires and fails. So the powerful had no shame, while Famous and I burned with it.

One late afternoon in May, we found ourselves back at that familiar intersection of Castro and 17th, between the Twin Peaks Tavern and the Bank of America on Harvey Milk Plaza. The bank had recently closed down, its windows boarded up like they were after being smashed in the White Night riots twenty-three years ago almost to the day. On this afternoon, the shuttered building served as the backdrop to a makeshift stage. A banner announced: *GAY SHAME AWARDS* 2002. The categories included Making More Queers Homeless, Best Target Marketing, Exploiting Our Youth and Helping Right-Wingers Cope. The activists had descended upon the Castro to make a point about complacency and greed within the gay mainstream. I'd concur the rampant consumerism was troubling. Identity had become a commodity. Gays enabled one another's body fascism and luxury. (Soon after that, the Bank of America became a Diesel store, where two twink sales assistants plus a fellow customer gathered round to salaciously convince me to go down a size on low-rise jeans.)

We missed the handing-out of Gay Shame Awards to absent villains. I'd later hear the ceremony culminated in the burning of a rainbow flag. We arrived in time for the afterparty. A 24 Divisadero bus was abandoned where it had been thwarted by the group's makeshift barricade. A sofa and turntables had been dragged into the middle of the street, which was thrumming with dozens of dancing bodies. Cops stood bemused beside the vacated bus, hands on hips. Some of the activist-revelers were dressed in natty sequins and dapper suspenders, while others went for grotesque, including at least one set of joke-shop rotten teeth. There were roller skates, and skateboards ridden by boys wearing only boxers. Animal prints clashed with horizontal stripes underneath torn fake fur. Bras and jockstraps migrated across bodies, now worn as wrist- and headbands. One of our upstairs neighbors was there, resembling a fierce Debbie Harry with faint mustache and thick gold eyelashes. Along with a doppelgänger, she towered above us on stilts. Willowy straight boys cuddled their girlfriends yet managed in context to present queer.

The members of the innermost clique had a palpable intensity about them—they were serious pirates. One of the core members, Mattilda (then Matt) Bernstein Sycamore, was resplendent in makeup applied as if every orifice in her face leaked glitter. Her mottled dress formed tumescent folds at the seams and shoulders, looking very Yayoi Kusama. Her lavender teased wig sprouted American flags, plastic flowers and a doll with a wide knitted skirt—the sort used as a toilet roll cover. Her shoes were constructed of pieces of paper bearing the Prada logo. Someone else's gown was made of shopping bags from The Gap and Abercrombie &

Fitch. An older man wore nothing at all but a backpack; he waved a tiny pennant: 'Queers Against Capitalism.'

The music spat through the speakers: 'Fuck the Pain Away' by Peaches, 'Stars' by Sylvester. The dancing began to include passing tourists and the sort of San Francisco hippies who'll join in anything. It's not your revolution unless they can belly dance. The old white gays in the windows of the Twin Peaks looked on with mild curiosity. They appeared so *conformist*, I was ashamed on their behalf, even as they may have been ashamed of the freaks on the street. The men in the bar were from another era, when the *homo* prefix really meant *same*. Toward that likeness, the Gay Shamers on the street were homophobic. They were aggressively individualistic: fabulous, unsightly, sexy, fat, a total mess. Their street party was not a dialogue but a harangue.

The following year, Gay Shame would protest a fundraiser at the city's new lesbian, gay, bisexual and transgender community center for its association with the mayoral frontrunner, Gavin Newsom, whose policies on homelessness were disdained by the left. The police wound up exerting such force that one demonstrator was hospitalized with a shattered tooth. Reports spread that gala attendees looked on, even cheered, while safely ensconced in the glassy edifice. Those status quo gays found Gay Shame to be at best a nuisance, at worst a scourge on their hard-won respectability. They didn't want their vision of community critiqued; it had just been enshrined in the form of a big, transparent building. Bernstein Sycamore later wrote, 'Those arrested at the Center were held in jail for up to three days and faced charges as ridiculous as assault on a police officer (four counts for me) and felony "lynching," an antiquated term for removing someone from arrest.' It was as though the police skirmishes of previous decades were on the cusp of returning, but with less clear delineations of *us* and *them*.

But on this occasion on Castro Street, I witnessed only the few cops present shaking their heads at the disgraceful display, perhaps raising eyebrows at Gay Shame's appointed mediators. When the remix of 'Deceptacon' by Le Tigre played, Famous and I finally joined in, guided by the bratty, anthemic vocals from curb into street. It was satisfying to dance in public in a disruptive and disorganized way. We smiled at acquaintances. Evening threatened to creep in the way it does in San Francisco—as a bright white haze. We were like characters in a movie who, as a matter of survival, disguise their difference in a crowd in an attempt to blend in. The challenge here was how to look inconspicuous among the conspicuous. (Adam Phillips: 'Shame measures the distance between who we experience ourselves as being, and who we would like to be.') Surely, we were detectable—traitors willing to become gay moderates for a green card. I was certain at least one person present was aware of our position from previous conversations. Still, I relaxed. I found myself wondering what the evening might hold in store, and if it could possibly end in a margarita or threeway.

From what I could tell, the gay men in the windows of the Twin Peaks just carried on with their drinking. The blinds in the huge windows were half drawn like sleepy eyelids. Those men had been around. They'd seen worse vitriol and better parties. Just because they wore chinos now didn't mean they didn't have battle scars beneath. I thought of them as fathers whom we were rebelling against simply because they existed. We were pretending we were orphans, having run away into our own backyard. By participating, I was dancing *against,* but did that mean denying my genealogy? We glanced around, feeling shamelessly pseudo, hoping no one would detect our failure of pure radical spirit.

THE NEIGHBORS

SAN FRANCISCO

I was not thinking about the world. I was not thinking about history. I was thinking about my body's small, precise, limited, hungry movement forward into a future that seemed at every instant on the verge of being shut down.

—Wayne Koestenbaum, 2003

We used to gaze at the fog romantically. Then Famous and I moved up the hills into that fog, only to find it cold and wet. We lived on a dead-end street in the musty basement of a crumbling clapboard house that clung to the edge of a cliff over several lanes of freeway. It didn't only feel like the limit of the city; everyone who visited immediately called it the End of the World. We salvaged chairs from the sidewalk, splurged on houseplants, threw spaghetti on the kitchen wall to test its readiness and basically became lesbians.

The only queer bar in the neighborhood, the Wild Side West, was a lesbian bar in denial. After it was described as a 'super cool dyke bar' in *Betty & Pansy's Severe Queer Review*, a caustic guide to San Francisco, the owners scoffed and corrected them: the Wild Side West was a *neighborhood* bar. Future editions of *Severe Queer Review* read: 'This is a neighborhood bar in Bernal Heights (an area populated by lesbian homeowners). When you come through the door, do not be dismayed to see half a dozen middle-aged women with salt-and-pepper brush cuts smoking cigars and playing cards—they are just neighbors. The interior of the bar is a delight and says much about the history of the neighborhood. The two female owners (apparently good friends and roommates) opened this establishment over forty years ago. If you are a "neighbor," you might like it.'

The Wild Side West was named for the 1962 movie *Walk on the Wild Side*, starring Barbara Stanwyck as a New Orleans madam and woman's woman. The bar was founded in the East Bay, hence the qualifier in the name. It resettled in San Francisco as a frontier-style saloon with a massive antique cash register, fireplace, piano. People said Janis Joplin once made love on the pool table. In the bricolage back garden, at the bottom of a rickety staircase, swing chairs sheltered beneath the trees, glass bottles were buried upside down in the soil and broken toilet bowls served as flowerpots. Later I'd hear those toilets had been dumped on the doorstep (or hurled through the window) in objection to the two women opening for business. Their repurposing was as pragmatic as it was allegorical. Ultimately, the owners' disavowal of the lesbian descriptive spoke to a pioneer mentality—live and let live, just don't slap a label on it.

I, however, adopted an epithet: fag. I started calling myself that after my upstairs neighbors did. There seemed to be a lot of commotion and glamour on the third floor. A revolving cast of genderfuck roommates flung their arms out the windows, hollering down to scruffy friends, like a Muppets production of Tennessee Williams. A boa feather or glitter eyelash would tumble down the fire escape into the backyard. Then at some point, Michelle and Rocco moved in. I met Michelle first; she looked like a cigarette girl and wrote highly acclaimed books under the name Michelle Tea. She introduced me to her boyfriend Rocco, who as a rapper went by Katastrophe. He said right off: *Oh, I've seen you before at the bus stop. I thought, who's the cute fag?* Rocco was still binding before top surgery. He would crack up so heartily it made him crouch. The phrase *Tender Hearted* was inked across his chest. He quipped that Famous and I could provide him sartorial inspiration. We wore old ski jackets, beanies that fell over our brows, corduroys with thrashed hems. Rocco had just tossed that comment out, but it was immensely flattering coming from someone who was transitioning and therefore, I figured, deliberate about such things. We could, in turn, take cues from Rocco. It was like we'd lifted masculinity together in a heist, and now divvied up the booty.

What got me was the way the word moved through Michelle and Rocco's lips: *fag* was a firecracker, not a disorder; neither was it cringeworthy or falsely optimistic. . . . In other words, not *gay*. The word sounded masculine and flaming at the same time. Fag had long been used to indicate a femme, and while that probably hadn't changed, I realized that I had once perceived that femme-ness as a *lack*, something taken away from my masculinity rather than added to it. Now I was loopy with the idea that I could weave effete through the masc. In 2001, a new publication on pink paper launched—*Butt*, billed as a 'fag mag' or 'fagazine.' One cover proclaimed in bold type: 'INTERNATIONAL FAGGOT MAGAZINE FOR INTERESTING HOMOSEXUALS AND THE MEN WHO LOVE THEM.'

I was convinced that meant me. I was giddy with identity. Fag snuck up on me, and I welcomed it. Fag was sexy. It was street. Famous was a scofflaw fag, the way he shirked

159

immigration laws. I quit my editing job in a huff and became a dropout fag. To be a fag was to be a bandit. I liked the way fag looked from the outside. It made me want to fuck myself. For me, identity wasn't about finding something within—a cicada biding time in my underground—but about sensing myself out in the world. Looking at it that way, identity could be, as Famous put it, *photosynthesis*.

To thank us for feeding their cat, Michelle and Rocco took us to dinner at a popular new spot in the Castro called Home. The hostess seemed to weigh the idea of denying Michelle's reservation. We were disheveled and misshapen compared with the preppy gay men there. They were high on cosmopolitans and ceviche. *All these men tuck their shirts in*, I commented. *Yeah*, growled Michelle, like a teenager itching for a brawl. *These motherfucking shirt tuckers*. I was impressed with her finding an internal rhyme on the spot.

It was all about the language. We tried to speak with a sense of place, like bell hooks, with an inflection that told where we'd been. Since at least the fourteenth century, *faggot* meant a bundle of sticks tied together for fuel, used in the Old World to burn heretics alive. A person condemned as such might be forced to carry a thorny faggot for a period as a mark of shame. Now I chose to lug the faggot stigma around with me. I wanted to bestow honorifics on friends, too. *Dyke* had such a cool ring to it. There's conjecture that *dyke* evolved from *deck*—as in a young man decked out in his best clothes. *F-to-M* stood for female-to-male and accounted for the journey between. The terms were imperfect, but fierce.

I didn't use *queer* in conversation—*queer* was academic.

It was convenient, sexless. I used words that were about libido, leaked precum, were a bit handsy. *Queer* was about slipping through categories, whereas I preferred words to firm categories up—*otter, pig, cub, kitchen top, bossy bottom, slut*—denoting the types I wanted to fuck, then write about later using the slang. I doubt any of us actually believed the categories were impermeable or fixed—but they were delectable, puerile, created mutualities, cracked us up. To me, anyway, *queer* seemed serious—somehow adult; it worried.

―――――

Growing up wasn't an option. San Francisco is an immature city. I was under the influence of Michelle's book *Valencia*. The first lines: 'I sloshed away from the bar with my drink, sending little tsunamis of beer onto my hands, soaking into the wrist of my shirt. Don't ask me what I was wearing. Something to impress What's-Her-Name, the girl I wasn't dating.' Named for the Mission district thoroughfare Valencia Street, a promenade for baby dykes and bulldaggers in tool belts, Michelle's book chronicled a certain moment in San Francisco just before I moved there, when she and her pals were caught in a cycle of questionable moves and subsequent overprocessing. By the end, the protagonist is profoundly changed, but it seemed more fun to exist in the book's earlier sections, when she took every substance she was given with a rascally grace.

In a quieter passage, the narrator discovers the writer Eileen Myles, then recites a favorite poem to two friends who stand outside her house in the wet night—'a kind of reverse serenade, calling the words out my window, and

Laurel cried and George smoked a damp cigarette and then Laurel hung by her knees from the bottlebrush tree.' Like Michelle, Myles had given up booze and found clarity, but I wanted to dwell in the inebriate passages, like 'we felt so much better drinking and smoking and seeing a future.' I ignored the fact of both writers getting sober. I went out to bars to be literary. I drank to create content. If I earned a reputation for making trouble, it was so that I could write about it the following morning: making a pass at a twink in a bathroom, who then hit his head on the towel dispenser; being told I looked depressing by a British girl who encountered me alone reading *Factotum;* going home with the boy we called Raised by Wolves, who proceeded to rip apart my American Apparel t-shirt from the v neck. I found myself taking more risks, because failure had a second life—it could spin a yarn. There was an agency in the retelling, in the self-deprecation and of course self-mythologizing. Memoir is how you groom yourself. Memoir is drag.

The writing scene in San Francisco was vivified by events like open mic nights for lezzies at the Bearded Lady café and a literary series held at Eros, a gay men's sauna, but in the lobby so that it was open to trans people and everyone else. These continued a long albeit jumbled tradition. I'd always heard about the city's dual reputations as a muse for writers (lots of hyperbolic men) and a magnet for homos (lots of drama queens). But they were told as two discrete stories. Of course, gay and bohemian are porous states of being, as are the boundaries of their terrains. In 1953, the poet Peggy Tolk-Watkins, 'queen of the dykes,' established the Tin Angel in North Beach. The folk singer Odetta recorded her first album there. The next year, Miss Smith's Tea Room opened on Grant Avenue, a lesbian pickup spot with sawdust on the floor and beat poetry on Wednesdays. In 1955, two of Tolk-Watkins's fellow Black Mountain College alumni set up The Place on Grant Street, where the gay poet Jack Spicer would host Blabbermouth, a weekly open mic. Also that year, Allen Ginsberg read the first part of *Howl* at the Six Gallery on Fillmore Street. Later that night (at the 'big happy orgies') Ginsberg thought, 'at last a community.'

The national media collapsed the city's various new literary strands into the beat generation. In order to stir up outrage about San Francisco hedonists and oddballs—'a pack of unleashed zazous who like to describe themselves as Zen Hipsters,' as put by one magazine—an emphasis was placed on the freaky sex. One journalist pointed to homos as the hardcore of the movement. The 1957 obscenity trial over *Howl and Other Poems* made the book a best seller. Through the next year, national newspapers and magazines furiously tsk-tsked and cast scorn upon the permissive city, incidentally enticing more curious gays to visit. One reason San Francisco became so gay is down to the bad press.

The historian Nan Alamilla Boyd is careful to differentiate between the *kooky* and the *queer* in the North Beach scene. While the two may have overlapped, maybe just for a night, the beatnik and gay communities might be considered distinct, especially if we're talking about the gender transgressions of femmes—a very different pose from the mystic masc of the beats. Male homosexuality was more likely to be considered hip when it was gruff and riotous, earthy in the tradition of Whitman, screamed in lupine lines like Ginsberg's one about being sodomized by motorcycle saints.

163

Then there's Robert Duncan, gay and a poet, who would have scoffed at being called a gay poet. In his 1944 essay 'The Homosexual in Society,' he teased at disclosing his own sexuality, then interrogated the validity of identity altogether. This was very pre-post-gay of him. To Duncan's mind, claiming minority status is evil because it splinters a higher good, the universal. 'Almost coincident with the first declarations for homosexual rights,' he wrote, 'was the growth of a cult of homosexual superiority to heterosexual values; the cultivation of a secret language, the *camp*, a tone and a vocabulary that are loaded with contempt for the uninitiated.' Duncan was fatigued by too many salons 'where the whole atmosphere was one of suggestion and celebration.' There, homos used an argot built on ridicule. He'd found himself nearly indoctrinated (as if in a 'rehearsal of unfeeling'), his own voice 'taking on the modulations which tell of the capitulation to snobbery.' But Duncan decided not to speak that way. The lexicon was 'a wave surging forward, breaking into laughter and then receding, leaving a wake of disillusionment.' My impression is that he considered language to be wasted when it conformed to type.

―――――

My little sister once reported that she had described me in her high school sociology class as living in San Francisco, working for a magazine, having studied theater at a university in Los Angeles. *You see,* her teacher announced into a microphone, *Jenny's brother is a typical gay.* With friends, I joked in portmanteau—about things that were *clichgay,* about how we spoke with *gaydences.* When I was still living in the Castro, Jenny came to visit and remarked on the trios of men strolling past: *Why do gays have to come in threes?* I supposed because they were one another's security. They all looked squeaky clean. I took her to the Pilsner Inn—low-key, for a gay bar, with pinball machines and a pool table. The men inside were reasonably fuss-free. Still, it reeked of cloying cologne. Jenny stumbled onto the sidewalk. *I think I'm allergic to gays,* she groaned before vomiting.

I knew what she meant. Some of us were allergic to ourselves—or had an intolerance to the construction of gay, to its trappings. We'd witnessed the generation just before us react to a plague by morphing into invulnerable cyborgs: hairless, perfumed like bubblegum, with overdeveloped muscles displayed in tight clothes—what Famous called a sack of melons. I beheld the bathroom counters of gay men lined with dozens of bottles of potions, as if attempting to sterilize themselves with grooming. But those who resisted—the anti-gay authors and Gay Shamers—seemed unsporting. I wanted to be *pro-* something. Now that I was happily self-identifying as fag, I needed a new fragrance.

I stopped wearing deodorant. Famous, with relief, followed suit. His odor is celery and mine is pencil shavings. It was a revelation to discover that we came with an aroma we didn't have to pay for. *Why do people use 'the armpit of America' as a pejorative?* demanded a handsome young jerk we took on a camping trip to Big Sur. His Sea and Cake t-shirt smelled of marijuana smoke and salty sweat. We drank Sierra Nevada under tall red trees and arrived home scented with bonfire. We made pheromonal friends who wanted to reside in the armpit of America, in one another's. When a boy only just past nineteen pursued me and I took him to bed, I automatically pushed him into my pit. He resisted. I lost my erection. *I can tell you don't like me,* he said. It was actually a question of pheromones—specifically, that he didn't want to bury his face in mine. I could no longer hang with boys who weren't after a skunky, veiny, furry tussle. I'd come to realize what kind of fag I was. Dirty.

We got in touch with our bodies, and wished to dwell in the era of our birth. We turned to the next best thing: seventies pornography. Our stinky friend Stuvey lent us the DVDs of the Joe Gage trilogy, starting with *Kansas City Trucking Co.,* released the year Famous was born, 1976. The films were skunky, veiny, furry—with sex scenes in the sagebrush, rest stop toilets, roadside bars, auto repair shops, shacks. Men watched one another, licking a palm insatiably before moving it down to the mushroom head on the upward curved tool protruding from the fly of their grubby jeans. The men had shaggy chest rugs and their hairlines were receding. They spoke slowly like they were stoned yet urgently like they were horny. I caught wind that dykes also watched the Joe Gage films. They liked the grit and, so some claimed, the dicks, too. Men externalize pornographically, one sex-positive lesbian commentator explained, and if that was the case I was pleased to share the phallus for their scopophilia. The Joe Gage trilogy added up to a love story—aggressive, but tender. The films also featured extended scenes of driving big rigs in the crepuscular hours, imbued with a deep violet melancholy. Being a fag, it turned out, could be close to the earth—it could be about not the glossy advertisements of our chimerical selves, but a wide-open expanse. For the first time, I saw the possibility of faggotry to be sublime.

Edmund White characterized San Francisco in the late seventies as 'a sort of gay finishing school, a place where neophytes can confirm their gay identity.' This was pretty much unchanged. My default classroom was the Phone Booth, a noncommittal gay bar—one local paper categorized it as a 'gray bar'—in the Mission. There was a Barbie doll chandelier, but no rainbow flag. Historically gay, its mix now included scruffy straight boys (*mountain goats*) and girls in ironic secretary blouses (*feathered fancies*). White also observed San Franciscans in the late seventies who held PhDs in art history but took jobs stocking shelves in supermarkets. (He wrote: 'Just before I left San Francisco someone drew me aside and said, "You know, you have a habit that's considered rude out here: you always ask people what they do. When they realize you don't mean what they do in bed, or which drugs, they're offended."') This was also still the case. People worked retail, odd jobs, part-time. Nine-to-five had little meaning. When boys wanted to get in touch, I told them I'd be at the Phone Booth.

I would stare into the chalkboard above the urinal. There was occasionally a stick of chalk to hand; otherwise, a message could be written with a licked fingertip. The surface was gradually accumulating a varnish from layers of marker graffiti. I would piss out the five-dollar offer—Pabst Blue Ribbon plus Jack Daniel's shot—while decoding the scribbled palimpsest: I contemplated that chalkboard as if it were laden with meaning like a Cy Twombly painting. I needed the bar to be rife with significance in order to justify being in it again.

I could tell what the night had in store by the number of bicycles out front. The bouncer gave a look of recognition and, I detected, faint disapproval. The double doors featured a pair of trompe l'oeil red British phone boxes (K6 model). If he was in a mood, Famous would point out the inaccuracies. The K6 was designed by Sir Giles Gilbert Scott, an architect of cathedrals. Its design is classical in proportions. In England, there may be no smaller architecture that's as revered: certain kiosks have Grade II status — the only listed buildings I'm aware of that smell of piss and are decorated with flyers for prostitutes.

The bar was once the watering hole for the gay men who worked as switchboard operators at the AT&T building across 25th Street. The Phone Booth opened in 1951; under new ownership in 1974, it was promoted in the *B.A.R.*, the gay weekly. The ad featured the slogan *We've got your number…* and an illustration of a man with *GQ* feathered hair, unbuttoned shirt, jacket flung over shoulder and skintight flares, one foot in a phone booth. For years, the back pages of the *B.A.R.* were a gallery of ads for bars and clubs, featuring drawings of stars, sunsets, desertscapes, sailors, cowboys, lions seducing handsome nude men. After the onset of AIDS, these were almost wholly replaced by promos for phone sex. The Phone Booth's name was an incidental portent of how gay men would come to cruise.

Around the time we started hanging out there, pay phones began to head toward extinction. I was preoccupied with the relationship between people and places, and noted the realms I inhabited were conspicuously mortal. My local bar was named after an endangered object, and moreover was situated in a neighborhood being gentrified beyond recognition. I'd taken a job in a video store, where people would ask all the time how soon we'd go out of business. This was my domain: I loitered in the fading-away.

At the Phone Booth, we dressed like seventies clones. Not in a kitschy way, it's just that the uniform (hoodie, jeans, checked shirt, Converse)—what the artist Hal Fischer, in his 1977 photo project *Gay Semiotics*, identifies as 'basic gay'—had become the default style for hipsters in the aughts, gay or straight. The boys at the Phone Booth wore jeans with a low rise, their flannel shirts inching up as they gesticulated, revealing the fuzz on their bellies and the smalls of their backs. (Roland Barthes: 'Is not the most erotic portion of a body *where the garment gapes?*') Cyclists rolled up the right leg of their jeans to avoid catching in the chain, their calves swiped with black grease. The hoods of sweatshirts were up, thick cotton foreskin. A quintessential item was the foam-front, mesh-backed trucker cap, like the one on the head of the musician Arthur Russell, our fag patron saint. He couldn't give a fuck about genre—experimental composition, country, disco—and was ahead of his time that way.

We grew beards. The initial days itched. It was amusing to watch each other's facial hair bloom, like curious new werewolves. Mine was asymmetrical and partly red. Our shaggy faces reminded me not just of seventies porn but of the painting by Gustave Courbet in which he depicts himself meeting his wealthy patron on the road to Montpellier. Courbet doffs his hat, but then so does his wealthy benefactor. While the patron's ginger beard is pilose and groomed, Courbet's wiry thicket stands several inches in front of his face, as if semierect. Our beards were not just uppity like that—they were perverted, their bristles perfumed with the sudor of scrotum.

ZIPPERED SWEAT SHIRT

FLANNEL SHIRT

BRACELET

LEVIS

CONVERSE SNEAKERS

STREET FASHION
BASIC GAY

The majority of the Phone Booth clientele was probably straight, yet somehow the atmosphere was predominantly gay. This was an advantageous situation; the straight boys respectfully gave the impression they might capitulate. Ostensibly straight boys whom I kissed there included a construction site foreman, a professional skateboarder and an acrobat. Somebody would always put 'Family Affair' by Mary J. Blige on the jukebox, with its message about leaving one's *situations* behind at the door. As much as gay, the bar identified as late twenties. The 2003 edition of the *Severe Queer Review* quotes graffiti observed on a wall at the Phone Booth: 'I'm 28 and I can still get a boner.' Sometime after midnight, I'd glance at the bar's clock, and reality would hit. The clock face was stamped *1974*, the year of my birth. Thirty years old approaching, I'd become an old barfly already. I was finally a regular at a gay bar. And yet, what kind of gay bar? A *kind of* gay bar.

An honest account of the gay bar must include bisexual, pansexual, confused, questioning, transitioning bars. As a matter of fact, the Black Cat, whose 1951 victory at the state supreme court established the right of homosexuals to congregate, was one of those that flitted about the spectrum. In the forties and fifties, the spot on Montgomery Street was, in the words of Allen Ginsberg, the 'greatest gay bar in America'—but precisely because of the fact that it was 'totally open, bohemian, San Francisco...and everybody went there, heterosexual and homosexual.' He elaborated: 'All the gay screaming queens would come, the heterosexual gray flannel suit types, longshoremen. All the poets went there.'

The Black Cat's resident performer, José Sarria, had begun going there with his sister in the forties; they made a bet over who'd win the affections of their favorite waiter, and José won. He covered shifts for this lover, and was ultimately hired on himself. José started singing there in the early fifties, wearing a bit of makeup and his mother's earrings to accentuate his allure. The story goes that one night, a woman in the crowd suggested he try on her heels. They fit, and she told José to keep them. He performed in those shoes four nights a week on a stage of pushed-together tables to a crowd of two or three hundred. This transformed the Black Cat: José *became* the Black Cat, as he put it himself.

He switched to red high heels and became iconic. José was known to travel around town in the sidecar of a motorcycle driven by his propman. On Sundays, he performed satirical operas at the Black Cat. In his staging of Bizet's *Carmen*, the heroine was out cruising in a city square, dodging vice cops. He would alert the crowd to the current movements of the police—the 'blue fungus.' To José's mind, patrons of the Black Cat were leading a double life—uninhibited in the bar, conforming everywhere else. He gave pep talks: 'There's nothing wrong with being gay—the crime is getting caught.' At the end of his opera, he commanded the audience to stand and, with arms around each other, sing 'God Save Us Nelly Queens.' This sometimes spilled out into the night air, as he serenaded the walls of the vicinal city jail for the sake of any gays who happened to be in custody. In the early sixties, José ran for San Francisco city supervisor. He lost, but garnered enough support that after his campaign nobody in town ran for office without courting the gay vote.

In 1964, the best-named gay activist of the era, Guy Strait, self-published an article entitled 'What Is a Gay Bar' (and laid out with the headline in French—'Qu'est-ce Que C'est? Gay Bar'). According to Strait, while homosexual men had long sniffed out hotel lobbies, public squares, dive bars and gentleman's clubs with a tacit reputation, a true gay bar was something different. His first rule for a gay bar was its 'freedom of speech'—the use of idioms and unguarded sex talk. (Anyone who wanted to be schooled could order Strait's own *Lavender Lexicon: A Dictionary of Gay Terms and Phrases* for two dollars.) Strait contended that while a cruisy hangout could fly under the radar, a gay bar might be forced to shut down based on the conversations. 'Gay bars are not the best pickup spots,' he wrote, 'but they are the safest; they are not the worst thing that has happened to society and may well be one of the best.'

The poet Aaron Shurin has told of his first gay bar, the Rendezvous in the Tenderloin, in the mid-sixties, also using the framework of linguistics: 'They had long hair and misty eyes, they had lean stomachs and tender kisses, they had hard-ons in company and interlocked smiles; they were made of silly gestures and dramatic arches and too-muchness and high language, of alliteration and sibilance and "sensibility."' We wanted to *go there*—the Rendezvous may have been closed by then, but back to what remained of the old school (Hole in the Wall, Cinch Saloon, Gangway, Ginger's Trois, Aunt Charlie's Lounge, the Stud, the Eagle) in the ghettos of the Tenderloin, Polk Gulch, South of Market. Other scrappy young fags descended upon these spaces along with us. The daddies must have noticed this with mixed feelings, but we preferred their company to our prissier peers. We'd hitherto known gay bars architected as aspiration and escape; they were neutered. These rougher spots could be raunchy or campy, neighborly or lugubrious, but what they shared in common was the sense of being built from the bottom up. We went to sex clubs and saunas, where we were frequently obliging. We went to clothing-optional beaches. (Naked on the sand, we picked up a boy while the guy he was dating had his nose in *The Ethical Slut*.)

We made friends with gay boys who were not hostile. They were frisky and nice. They were stoned. They were allies, not mere competition or a potential fuck, though possibly the latter. They did not have six-packs. They flashed tattoos at picnics. We sat in the grass at Dolores Park hoping to track a case of chlamydia that had infiltrated our circle by drawing a tree of who'd slept with whom, and it turned out that nobody was separated by more than two degrees. I thought I must be liberated. We'd go dancing and at the end of the night our pal Jesse would say, *Jeremy, that guy you were making out with on the dance floor?* I'd nod. *Just so you know: NOT cute.*

It wasn't supposed to be about lowering standards, but reassessing the standardized image of sexy. Gay liberation in the seventies had helped replace the fetish for servicing straight guys with a mutual eroticism between gay men. After AIDS hit hard and stigmatized that very generation, 'gay' sexuality often privileged straight dudes again. The city's gay video stores were filled with DVDs of broke straight boys, amateur military men, cocky skaterboyz.... We watched as many of these as we could, and were thereby informed that straight guys were hotter—scruffier, and yet cleaner when it came to disease. A bulk of the M4M hookup listings on Craigslist included the winning adjective 'straight-acting.' I think a lot of us had grown tired of all that, and were eager to see one another as multidimensional beings—handsome, funny, literate, flaming. HIV-positive status was something to work with, not recoil from. And homosexuality could be *homo* again—as in being attracted to somebody who reflected and affirmed aspects of your own faggoty self.

We knew other fags around town to say hello to, to flirt with aimlessly, which seemed very San Francisco in the seventies. At Dore Alley, the most anything goes of the leather street fairs, we hung out with new acquaintances like Matthew and Ricky. Matthew, tall and curly haired, was always just arriving back from a survival weekend, still in some of the gear (waterproof trousers, muddy boots). I climbed onto his shoulders like girls used to at stadium concerts. Ricky's shoulders were slighter, and exceptionally hirsute. He had a bayou accent, and smelled of patchouli. They both grinned constantly—a sharp turnaround after years of gays holding their lips tightly like they'd just received bad news.

Sunday was the beer bust at the Eagle. A ten-dollar plastic cup was refillable out of the kegs until the afternoon turned to evening. On our first visit, we handed cash to a man in a leather vest with frizzy ginger chest hair, then pulled back a hide curtain to enter into the armpit. The place was a miasma of male odor. It smelled of all the places where a man's body folds. The admixture of booze, cigars and barbecue made a heady blend. I was astonished to enter a zone of such obscene stink.

The leathermen put up with us; perhaps it pushed them to perform. There was a lot of nipple-tweaking and slapping. The large patio was like the anarchic deck of a pirate ship. The troughs were an intense scene for the undinists. Being pee-shy next to a piss fiend was irksome, but then again I was on their terrain. Cock and ass fell out of chaps. The older men were at ease, a little gruff, nobody unfriendly, the bartenders hunks. The social circles kept to generations, so that we were segregated in proximity, but the grown-ups, even if they ignored us kids mostly, were pressed so close that the fur on their backs brushed us, and I was convinced we were ultimately united.

Daytime drinking was somniferous—like afternoon sex, lazy and sunkissed. I'd look at Famous, detect a slight unease on his countenance, and understood. This was it: the wild west, pioneer town, edge of the continent. There was a faint disenchantment to each day. The city was an overcast Oz. The denizens fought against the ennui with emphatic weirdness and genuine goodwill. But I thought I detected a desperation lurking beneath the way people pushed boundaries. Such were the downcast thoughts of the third or fourth beer.

We picked up a beautiful young man with blond curls in a sleeveless top, smiley but laconic. I decided we must be in *his* story—surely he was the lead. I struggled all the way down Harrison Street with him on the back of my bike. We toppled at least twice. He stood on our bed in small briefs, his furry thighs apart, looking like the Greatest American Hero, his hand on the ceiling, and we learned the distinctive scent of blond males. We saw him on a subsequent night picking up somebody else at the Cinch, a long, narrow cowboy saloon on Polk Street; generations had begun to overlap there, too. One man, wearing bulging jeans, mirrored shades and a blank expression, always assumed the same position against the wall between the toilets and the smoking deck, looking like a cardboard cutout of gay cruising. I finally got that he was *posing*. Whether or not he made contact was not the point; he got off on his stance and all its raunchy potential.

By then, Famous and I had moved into an apartment above El Rio, the most kindhearted bar in the city, another *gray* bar, I guess: the slogan was '...*your dive.*' The top half of the Dutch door was kept flirtatiously open during business hours. A shuffleboard ran the length of the front half of the bar. In the capacious back garden: lemon trees, romantic pergola, giant Carmen Miranda, tropical plants, oysters on the barbecue every Friday evening. The bar staff was like an earthy Star Trek crew: baby dykes working toward a PhD; *maricones*; Tracy Chapman types; grungy F-to-Ms; Josh, the doughy straight boy. (Famous adored him to the point he's referred to cute boys as *Josh* ever since.) El Rio was run by a handsome blonde woman who gave us carte blanche when we threw an occasional party there. We'd task Josh with moving speakers and chairs.

Mr. M, the landlord, opened El Rio back in 1978 as a Brazilian leather gay bar. He was a stoic giant. He'd moved to the woods north of the city, and it was easy to picture him there. When he first showed us the apartment, he resembled a big black bear trapped indoors; I began to have doubts about taking the place because it shrank in his massive presence. But Mr. M charged cheap rent in exchange for the compromise of living above the din. I did my best to ignore the bass reverberating through the floor and juddering across our bathwater, the cacophony of bottles dumped late at night, the stench of stale beer and bleach in the morning.

Sunday afternoons were the legendary salsa party. The whole patio throbbed with the dance, and if I wasn't at the Eagle, I sat and watched from the fire escape. It was a bohemian status symbol to party on Mondays: there was a one-dollar well drinks special, and some DJs with impressive record collections hitched on so that it became the hippest night of the week. We ambled downstairs. I'd call out, *If you can't beat 'em, join 'em*—as if it were a chore to join in. We skipped to the front of the line, but the gossiping, preening crowd at the bar would be five or six deep. I ordered gin so cheap I didn't recognize the label, two at a time, double-fisting. To get into a bathroom was such an ordeal people adopted the strategy of ducking into the sketchy dive bar next door until eventually it gave in and became a gay bar, too. Our pals ran upstairs to our place to pee. The crowd was a mix, but the fags sensed one another through the blur of everyone else, so that we had our own bar within the bar, as I'm sure the baby dykes and heterosexual hipsters also did.

On Thursdays, like a wolf pack, we took over Aunt Charlie's, a poky dive bar in the Tenderloin with a single covered-up window, blocked from the inside by a claw crane machine called Ye Olde Gift Shoppe. The geriatric drag queens delivered classic glamour: the Hot Boxxx Girls. But the new Thursday night party was something different. We were first invited to Tubesteak Connection by Spider, who manned the door. The DJ, Bus Station John, played ecstatic sets of arcane disco, hi-NRG, Italo and boogie. He was in his forties, and wore a thick mustache, muttonchops, flat cap. Bus Station John gave the appearance he might be prickly, but he called us *child*. He was there to bear witness, to testify, using rare tracks from what he called 'the golden age of gay,' the period between Stonewall and AIDS. The music was our time machine. We were conscious the discs he put on the turntable may have come from the collections of deceased gay men.

Each Tubesteak flyer design was pasted together with a glue stick and scissors. A guileless young jock from a skin flick might feature, but so could a caricature of an aging queen with ascot and blubbery lips. At the heart of the oeuvre were the divas: Joan Crawford, Candy Darling and, most often, Grace Jones. On the night of Tubesteak, all the bulbs in the place would be replaced with red ones. Sleazy movies and drag ball footage played on television screens covered with red film. Blowups from seventies porn mags of hairy, sweaty men were taped onto the mirrored walls and scattered on the bar. Their erections set expectations high. The place surged with faggy testosterone; it was as though all of that porn-in-public stripped us of our inhibitions. Bus Station John knew what he was doing.

Between eleven and midnight, the neon sign above the bar—spelling out Aunt Charlie's—would be turned off, and eventually a strobe light shattered the tiny dance floor into pieces. The maximum number of randy young fags who could possibly fit squeezed their way in. Somehow, we still made the space to dance expressively. There was Matthew, back from another trek through the wilds, his arms spread wide as if proselytizing. There was Ricky, you could smell his patchouli. The carpet was going threadbare underfoot. Our enthusiasm threatened to make the records jump and skid. *I have never heard this song before,* I said to Famous repeatedly. Bus Station John would politely decline to divulge the name of the track. The mix was far from seamless: it halted and lurched. There were lots of vocals—so many sisterly, triumphant, empowered, positive messages. Piano lines rolled through the room like illuminated ships pulling into a city harbor.

Bus Station John told a local paper: 'There's not just a gap, but a chasm between generations that AIDS created. Their absence is felt by those of us who are old enough to feel it. But the younger ones are never going to know about them unless we tell them.' We went out to be told. We went out to feel it. We went out to experience how it used to be, and Bus Station John was happy to be our gay liberation daddy. A mature writer for a gay newspaper reported that the seventies bathhouse vibe at Tubesteak Connection was 'so authentic, people were actually cruising!' For years, checking one another out meant *scrutinizing*—a potential rival, possibly diseased, the type of gay who gives gay a bad name. Here, we *recognized* instead—saw the others' strength and sense of humor. The dancing was not posturing; it was celebration and foreplay—finally, like Aaron Shurin reminisced of his gay bar, we too knew 'hard-ons in company.' Some boy would pull me into a deep kiss after midnight. I was aware I did not look untouchable: anything remotely expensive-looking about me was on discount by that late hour. So I got used to the attention—boys handling my damaged goods. Once, when I had just arrived, already blind drunk, someone locked his mouth over mine, depriving me of air to the point where I thought I might pass out or vomit. On another occasion, an inebriated skateboarder—new to town—decided to come home with Famous and me, and then *did* throw up, behind a dumpster on the street. He shook his long burgundy hair, wiped his mouth with the back of his hand and continued to our place to have a glass of water and give head.

My impression was that young fags were less fearful of catching HIV. We were safer-sex natives, and now better edified about what truly constituted risk. We understood that the word *risk* had become moralistically equated with doom—that life *is* risk, you don't give up living. Some among us were positive already. I caught wind of others who were reckless or didn't seem to care, as if HIV was too outdated to catch. But for whatever combination of reasons, San Francisco felt sexy again. San FranDisco. At another party, thrown in the basement of a club on Larkin Street, I pulled back a heavy curtain to reveal a dozen or so young men with their erections out, some standing to be serviced and others on their knees. They were hip, slender boys with sideburns and falling-open lambskin-lined jackets and un-buttoned Dickies. I thought I was jaded but the high quality of males in this dark room was surprising. We looked at the pals we'd arrived with. They shook their heads broadly. *No way*, one mouthed. *All such huge dicks*, the other whispered. Famous and I waded in, touching the tops of heads like mossy stones as we went. We pulled ourselves out of our pants and dropped to our knees. At some point, I was lifted out by a lanky lad with an Irish accent. I thought he wanted me to go down on him, but he was *rescuing* me.

In his hotel room, he said, *I knew you were too good for that.* Yet he'd been telling Famous and me about how back in London, where he lived, he hailed taxis with the explicit intent of servicing the drivers. In his heroic act of saving me from the orgy, he'd dragged me back to a very nineties style of casual hookup that was furtive, even hostile. He yanked me out from a scene he found distasteful in order to have unsensual, awkward, somehow socially acceptable, *private* sex. The young man was in the city on business. The hotel furniture had underlit ledges; at the press of a button, bland electronica piped in. The blinds were drawn. We could have been anywhere. I wished I'd stayed at that party. I didn't want to be in this room, cut off from the city. San Francisco was a beautiful problem that wasn't meant to be solved. I wanted to get back into it.

———

We'd go hiking in the sunburnt hills to the east. *To dry out* was how we put it, referring to the fog in our lungs, not the booze. I'd scout ahead to find a suburban gay bar we could visit on our way back. We'd find ourselves the only customers in a windowless barroom, gazing at the ghost-town dance floor. With nothing else to do, we read the listings in the bar rags about other gay places in the region.

We took a couple of younger fags up to the woods along the Russian River, following the tradition of daddy bears who'd made a gay resort of a town called Guerneville. In the parking lot of the Rainbow Cattle Co., a rustic saloon—very seventies porn—a lone man with dark stoned energy shared his potent joint with us, then lifted me up to crack my back. I guess he could tell I'd been the day's driver. I wriggled away and we walked off, very paranoid, through the empty streets under the redwoods. Back at the motel, I went out for a cigarette on the porch, and a middle-aged man stepped out from his room next door. *Magical,* he said. *My dream came true this weekend: I had my first threeway.* I expressed my approval and didn't tell him about mine. The forest around us buzzed, but with more than a hint of menace. Much later, I'd learn that the proprietor of the Rainbow Cattle Co., who also owned other bars in the area and in San Francisco, had been shot dead on his secluded property, along with one of his young employees.

One Valentine's Day, Famous and I traveled to Oakland to see a Wolfgang Tillmans video installation at the California College of Arts and Crafts. When we entered the dark gallery space, the video wasn't playing. We picked up a remote control and walked around pressing the Play button aimed in all directions. Eventually a mature woman, hunched, wearing a Christmas sweater, arrived in the lobby. *Oh,* she said. *Raymond took us all to lunch. The video isn't playing? It's supposed to be. Oh, I can do that. I think I can. Do you know Raymond? He's a very famous artist.* Then she walked around the room pushing Play as we had, but with two different remote controls, one in each hand.

Finally, the video played. *Lights (Body)* depicts the rigging above the floor of a nightclub. A deep house remix whaps and hisses. The lights rotate and flash. Tillmans locates the viewer in the rafters, omnipotent over the communal experience below. The mechanical sequencing of the lights does not spoil the magic, but adds to it. The mirrored squares of a disco ball reflect the alternating colors. There is no evidence of the clubbers below, the sweaty throng of bodies, except the specks of dust that dance in an oscillating light beam. In the exhibition notes, Tillmans pointed out that dust is mostly human skin. Famous and I watched the video several times over. We'd come all that way. We thought about the dust, how we were inconsequential yet expansive, mortal yet transcendent—not so much in a spiritual way, just that we are constantly escaping ourselves. The flecks intermingled, having fleeting affairs. I believed the interactions to be homosexual, but this was dust—literally posthuman. The video made me consider the nightclub as a site of loss—losing inhibitions, your friends, your possessions, yourself. It's a place to find something through abandonment.

On the way back, we stopped for a beer at the White Horse on the border of Oakland and Berkeley, which may be the oldest continuously operating gay bar in the country, if that's not Café Lafitte in Exile in New Orleans, both opened sometime around 1933. A few wisecracking lesbians in baseball caps perched at the bar. The warm, lived-in vibe was at odds with the glass box dividing the center of the place. It had been constructed for smokers, and left standing after that was deemed a bad idea. The glass formed an interloping waiting room, housing a pool table and a mural of a carousel, with a large mirrored horse at its center. The band Erase Errata recorded an eighty-second song about it: 'The White Horse is bucking. It smashes you with its hoof. It wants you to go for a night of gay dancing. So picture yourself at the White Horse. And picture yourself among the beautiful. And picture yourself alive.' The lyrics may be ironic, but they assert something many queer people know well: an unshakable fondness for the only gay bar in town. It's not about holding out for a good night, but rather a letting go—accepting the gay bar's unconvincing promise of escape.

———

Famous and I entertained ourselves with the final stage in our infiltration of the city's gay terrains: we would reclaim the Castro. Over the years, the neighborhood seemed determined to make itself unlikable. Its rows of self-improvement businesses—vitamin shops, gyms, waxing, pet grooming—were like acts of denial: of AIDS, of different states of ableness, of character and grit. I heard reports of racism at the door of the bar with the best pinball machines. It was the same old trick of forcing people of color to show multiple forms of identification. The situation was made doubly unsavory by word the owner was in the process of buying up the bar opposite, which catered to a black crowd.

But the Castro could also endear. At the Faerie Queene chocolate shop, a man who looked like Santa Claus shoveled fudge. Feathery pixies dangled in the window display. The grand movie theater was designed in the style of a Mexican cathedral, and an organist played 'San Francisco (Open Your Golden Gate)' on a mighty Wurlitzer which descended as the film began. Such elements, at once campy and earnest, and the area's storied, problematic history made us want to see the district anew. It seemed wrong to consider ourselves too good for the enclave when what it stood for was much bigger than our two small bodies. Perhaps I'd never really given it a chance.

We weren't sure where to start: the bars on 18th Street off Castro (the Mix, Midnight Sun, Men's Room, Moby Dick) each seemed the same as the next. We settled on Moby Dick. We liked it in the afternoons, when sunlight streamed through the windows over the pinball machines. A massive fish tank offered phallic coral as a conversation starter. The bar's whale logo, easily mistaken for a splashy cock and balls, was another talking point. Suspended from the ceiling in the center of the bar were back-to-back monitors playing a loop of music videos—anonymous Europop deemed appropriate for any gay bar anywhere. The videos involved trench coats and sports cars and trysts in hotel rooms lit in ice blue. Often, the singer would rotate toward the camera in a slick white Eero Aarnio ball chair.

We did not go to Moby Dick to cruise. The dimly lit bathroom did have mirrors over the troughs, but they were mounted too low for fruitful glancing. On a windowsill were small blank cards on which to write a message for another customer. This I learned when a man handed me one with a vehement proposal on it. Everyone else was looking at Famous, or Stuvey when he was along with us; both of them held a torch for the bartender, Stanley, with his sandy-colored mustache and hint of a paunch. Famous kept losing at pinball and would trot to the bar to ask Stanley to trade a dollar bill for quarters. Stanley's friend Dane was an embarrassingly handsome brunette who worked at Harvey's, two blocks down. We clocked that Dane would saunter over after his shift for interbar gossip. One night, he leaned in close to Famous between the pinball machines. Famous was draped in the gypsy scarf he bought at a cabinlike thrift store in Malibu Canyon. It was printed with roses and edged in gold fringe. We were convinced it once belonged to Joni Mitchell. Famous wore it over his boy clothes—jeans, hoodie—like it was a no-big-deal juxtaposition. Adoration came over Dane's matinee idol face. He whispered through cupid's bow lips, millimeters away from Famous: *I keep seeing you. Everything you do is perfect.*

Moby Dick was established in 1977 by Victor Swedosh using money inherited from his family's panty hose fortune.

The bar was wood and brass, the clientele collegiate types. Moby Dick was also briefly—for some four years from 1980—the primary disco label in San Francisco. This was headquartered at 573 Castro Street—where Harvey Milk once lived above his camera shop. The label's output includes the thirteen-minute clone anthem 'Cruisin' the Streets' by Boys Town Gang, a filthy late-night narrative that mentions the potential effects of 'a big ol' boy nine inches or more': He 'might make you sore,' but 'absolutely guaranteed it won't be a bore.' The song becomes audio pornography, climaxing in an orgiastic police raid. The label's dance floor filler 'Jump Shout,' by Lisa, name-checks Los Angeles clubs Studio One and Probe, of which it makes a couplet with the action in the strobe. The next song on Lisa's album was 'Sex Dance.'

In David Diebold's oral history of the Moby Dick label, one producer summed up the company culture: 'Too many bosses, too many queens, a lot of jealousy.' A former employee recalled, 'I thought I was at home working with my own kind. . . . Let me tell you there is more jealousy, backbiting, dishonesty and corruption in our own ranks than any other group I've ever seen.' More than one interviewee details the copious amounts of drugs. Party favors trickled in from the weekends at the Trocadero Transfer nightclub, the bender only leveling off midweek before heating up again. According to *Time* magazine, Moby Dick Records folded in 1984 when seven of its ten core employees died of AIDS.

I would try to get everyone to finish their drinks so that we could move on to someplace else. *You're always looking for something better*, Stuvey's latest boyfriend said. I thought that was the whole point. If nobody could be bothered, there was Orphan Andy's, the diner with hunky waiters, open all night long. It was like a seventies time warp, an old C-print by William Eggleston. I couldn't decide if it was a cozy sit-com diner or amphetamine den; it seemed to slip between, to transmogrify as if by some greasy alchemy.

If Famous and I had the energy to dance, we did so at a large, newish place called the Bar on Castro. *Betty & Pansy's Severe Queer Review* reminds me that the site was formerly the Castro Station, 'hangout for the most grizzled queens imaginable.' Betty & Pansy continue: 'The whole front was open, not unlike the "fourth wall" in a surrealistic scene of tired decadence. Grandpappies in leather chaps with sagging asses, pierced dicks and/or visible cock rings would face the sunny street from their darkened corners. They beckoned you closer with a nod of their head, since one hand was filled with a cocktail and the other a smoldering cigarette or cigar.' Transformed into the Bar on Castro, it became the slick opposite. (Betty & Pansy: 'The reeking mystery smell was replaced by the gentle waft of faint cologne.')

I would have despised it at one point in time. And yet we always seemed to luck out and be there on hip-hop and R&B night, when one floor-filler played after another: 'Magic Stick.' 'Milkshake.' Thin black homos danced using a broad range of levels—arms upheld like malfunctioning windshield wipers, then crouched low like gliding toward a ski jump. '1, 2 Step.' Girls pushed their palms out from their chest, doing *the uh-oh*. They threw their heads to the side as if being told a secret. 'Drop It Like It's Hot.' Extensions and hoop earrings whipped across the floor. 'Get Busy.' On the benches, in front of pink padded vinyl walls, boys with sideburns that tapered to a fine point would pop and vogue.

One night there, a pale boy with brown hair and small bones danced nervously near me. He was dressed in a crisp white shirt unbuttoned twice like a waiter just off duty. His neat black trousers had a sheen that made them look inexpensive, yet managed to fit his taut thighs as if bespoke. I wanted to relieve him of his well-behaved clothes. It was obvious he was new in town. *I've dropped out of seminary*, he confided. *Welcome to San Francisco*, I replied. We attempted to discuss questioning one's faith and migrating from the East Coast while dancing to 'Naughty Girl' and 'Pon de Replay.'

Get this. I updated Famous by the bathrooms. He was looking pallid under the fluorescents. Back on the dance floor, Famous greeted the failed priest with his usual courtesy, though he'd begun to sway. I had plenty of questions for the priest. I tried to tease him with badinage that I was too gin-soaked to sustain. *Wait, where's your friend?* the priest inquired several songs later. I looked around. Something like 'It Wasn't Me' by Shaggy was playing. It was true that Famous was nowhere to be seen. The priest and I searched. We patrolled the edges of the dance floor, looking like two undercover ABC agents back in the day. We left the bar, speculating Famous may have gone for fresh air. We glanced this way and that. *There he is*, the priest pointed.

Famous was in a fetal position on the sidewalk, several shop fronts away. *Jesus*, I said. *Are you ok?* asked the priest. Famous rose weakly, then glared at me with as much resentment as he could muster. *Where WERE you?* he shot. *Lost in the music*, I protested. Why was he so far away? Famous explained that the bouncer had ordered him to move along because the sight of him was bad for business. He took a deep breath. *Tonight…*, he said, *I briefly had the experience of being homeless on the streets, and I've seen the full gamut of humanity.* Famous centered himself. *Somebody spit on me*, he reported. *And somebody gave me ten dollars.* He handed me the crumpled bill he'd been clutching in his fist.

It didn't seem likely the priest would phone, but he did. By then, we were living in yet another place, a converted store-front halfway up a red-hued hill. We'd adopted the routine of seducing new boys by taking them to the summit. The grid of streets below hummed and crackled. The twinkling city was bounded by fog and the deep, cold bay, which was bedded with decomposing suicides. There is nothing like it, we all agreed. I recalled how when Famous first visited the city, we took psilocybin and sat atop another hill, overlooking the rooftops. He'd said, *I'm sure I've seen this exact view in a dream.* We kissed and believed in fate for five minutes, then he went pale and let me know he'd better go back to my place to barf. Now we were growing restless with the town. I was beginning to perceive the city as an island.

I looked over at the boy. He was so unexpected. He hadn't come here to be an experimental artist like other new arrivals we took up the hill, who discussed Anne Carson or arcane disco producers, did cartwheels, picked us up and twirled us around. Some had lived in New York. They were insubordinate and avant-garde already. This boy, in the calm upheaval of his tentative apostasy, was wise and guileless at the same time, as if fallen to earth and landed in a weird city, but he must have chosen it with the notion that he too could belong.

Back at ours, Famous kissed the priest for the first time, like he'd hurt him if he didn't go gently. We undressed him and, as I'd imagined, his well-behaved clothing looked out of place on our cracked concrete bedroom floor, with its clashing, overlapping rugs and Famous's hippie scarves and my smelly t-shirts that our tortoiseshell cat embarrassingly drooled over as she nuzzled into the steaming pits. We took him into our bed fumblingly. I pulled down his boxer briefs. Even his erection seemed polite and amenable. I moved back up from it, and we all took turns going down—one on two, two on one, but always returning to one another's faces, an act of reassurance, a reciprocal confession.

Oh, he murmured. He'd cum already. I recalled another new boy in town who had done the same thing—even quicker, shot in his underpants one minute in. This point of comparison made me realize I'd become *that guy*: the creep who stalks fresh meat. You see them at it in the bars, with a susceptible new twink each time. You want to warn the boy, but figure it's a rite of passage for him to go through. Later, the boy will see that man with another initiate and think the same thing. Famous petted the priest's chest reassuringly. *You must have a lot built up*, Famous said. I know Famous to be confident and egalitarian when he is naked in bed after a threeway. He thrives in that tender hour, when the boy can't bring himself to get out of the bed and leave, so we prolong the hoarse-voiced conversation, while the possibility hovers of it all starting up again.

THE APPRENTICE

LONDON

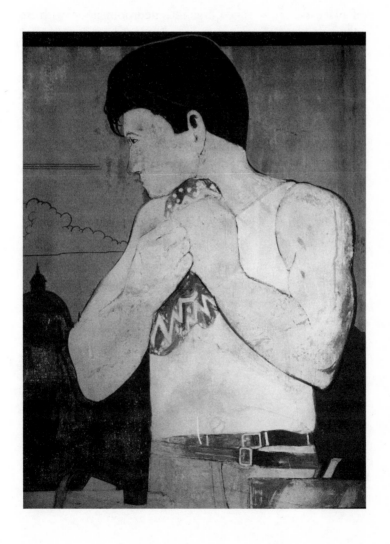

Because there was such a thing as drunkenness, I aspired to it. I took it, it was there. Moderate friends would wince and even suggest I was 'self-destructive' but that didn't sound right to me. Things would happen, that's all.

—Eileen Myles, 2008

It nearly escaped our notice, but the United Kingdom implemented civil partnerships for same-sex couples at the end of 2005. This allowed me, as the foreign partner of a British citizen, to settle in the UK. A year and a half later, Famous and I completed the paperwork, packed two of the largest suitcases allowed on the plane and migrated. We wound up in London, renting a one-bedroom, third-floor flat on an estate that backed onto Hoxton Square, skirting the district of Shoreditch. The territory was no longer *the East End*, a pejorative invoked from the Victorian pulpit and in the halfpenny press to indicate slums, vice-ridden and seeping with cholera. It was simply, authoritatively *East*. By the time we moved there, the working-class area was on the cusp of extreme upscaling. The bland intersection above Old Street station would come to be nicknamed the Silicon Roundabout, epicenter of the nation's tech industry. A penthouse residence would cost over four million pounds. The private members' club Shoreditch House, with rooftop pool, opened in 2007. A Versace store would follow. A generic inn was taken over by the American boutique chain Ace Hotel, its restaurant given the name Hoi Polloi. Gentrification was an unabashed part of the branding—a joke.

In Shoreditch, the narrow passages we took were lined in the brickwork of former furniture warehouses and small factories converted into nightclubs and boutiques. Waves of immigration had settled over three centuries—Huguenot weavers, who brought with them the word *refugee*, Irish Catholics, Ashkenazi Jews, Sylheti-Bangladeshis. In the nineties, many of the hyped Young British Artists had studios in the area. (Much of their output revalued white working-class taste.) By the aughts, a noncitizenry proliferated, youthful and hungry, displaced by persecution of a subtle yet acute kind, misunderstood elsewhere, infidels, individualists, whose only allegiance was to the vague federation of fashion, and who saw East London as the place to land because it too was constantly on the move.

This arriviste was unlike bohemian or slacker. They created corporate content, conceived pop-ups, fired off emails. They networked in a bar that went by an amalgam of the two wholesalers previously occupying the adjoining spaces it knocked through: Dream Bags Jaguar Shoes. They were evidently made of considerable gumption, and were to most observers frankly annoying. Some mimicked the laboring roots of the area, donning flat caps, blue work jackets and fingerless gloves. But the dominant style was more obstreperous, and began with bottle blond hair. Neon plastic was big, as was unnatural animal print: dalmatian on purple, zebra on lime yellow. When Famous's father came to visit, he informed us that everyone he'd passed on our street looked like Boy George. In fact, Boy George did own a flat in Shoreditch. But we'd heard he'd chained a male escort to a radiator there, so was for the time being incarcerated. I exhaled cigarette smoke out our window, squinting at pass-ersby to determine who was a post-electroclash pop star (M.I.A., La Roux, the XX) and who just dressed like them.

The media loved to deride the frippery. (The whole nation seemed to use the masculinist slur *Shoreditch twat* as a metonym for pretentiousness.) But I found it refresh-ing. The sartorial pizzazz amounted to a kind of dazzle camouflage for androgynous gay kids who would have once felt vulnerable on these streets. Gender and sexual trans-gression were decreed universally hip by hetero-oriented media like *Vice*, who took up its UK offices in the area. Now that the conventions had been upended, it was some-times unclear if public displays of same-sex affection were homos enjoying the new tolerance, or straights getting up to homo shenanigans as mischief and shock value. Was gay the new cocaine? When Famous glimpsed two lads dressed in what appeared to be school uniforms kissing passionately in the men's bathroom of a straight pub, he returned to me astonished. *I don't know what I've just seen.* To us, that brazen act was not something young homosexuals would ever do in a heterosexual establishment. Were they gay boys liberated by the new permissiveness, or straight boys free to experi-ment when the mood struck? Either way, I regretted I hadn't seen it myself.

There were a few gay bars in the area, too, and they happened to be the best in town. In 2007, the *New York Times* ran a story called 'Where the Club Boys Are.' It was illustrated by a photograph of Hoxton Square, our de facto backyard. In the picture, young people sit on the short grass in small groups, forearms idling on knees. The high-profile White Cube art gallery makes a stately backdrop; on the horizon, new skyscrapers encroach. The article proclaimed that, in contrast to the Soho and Vauxhall muscle scenes, Shoreditch 'has emerged as a grittier, fashion-forward and often outrageous hotbed of gay nightlife.' Such hype hinged on three bars we called the Triangle, with each point indicating a different disposition or time of night: jolly George and Dragon, sordid Joiners Arms and laid-back Nelsons Head—a respective five-, ten- and fifteen-minute walk from our building.

We first chanced upon the George and Dragon on a late afternoon shortly after our arrival. It jutted into an alley, looking scuzzy compared with the Palladian architecture of St. Leonard's Church opposite. The pub was closed but made the right impression on us with the DIY posters in its windows, so we returned at opening time. Inside, all available space was stuffed with zany bric-a-brac: plastic fruit, animal masks, unfolded fans, an alligator carcass escaping from the heap. There were cut-out cardboard figures of Cher, Elvira and Divine—the type once displayed in video stores or cinema lobbies—and one I thought was Kim Basinger from *Batman* but turned out to be Kim Wilde, singer of 'Kids in America.' A massive animatronic mule head chewed on a carrot hypnotically. The cellar could be seen through the slots between the thick floorboards. With our half-pints of Murphy's, drawn for us by a skinny young bartender, we sat gazing at the motes of dust in the few shafts of sunlight penetrating the room. I realized it wasn't a gay bar but a gay *pub*. I lived in London now, and hung out at a place with a name like George and Dragon, very Byzantine. The pub's musty cheer would have been unfathomable in the London of the nineties that Famous left behind. It was unlike the slick Soho gay bars, with their look of the penthouse suite, but neither did it retreat to the seedy basement; it was more like an overstuffed attic. But somehow in the new London, its existence was unsurprising. It was totally of its moment by giving the impression of having been there all along.

Within a week, we returned at night, and it was crowded then. The boys looked like sailors, in matelots and kerchiefs, with tattoos of galleons and anchors revealed by the deep v of their tees. Some were more like swashbucklers—but hungover ones, in baggy pirate pyjamas and battered Vivienne Westwood buckle boots. More than a few had the gaunt, mocking faces of an Isherwood fop, updated with sinople-red hair plastered around their pale skin. Late enough in the night, a few club kids would be in the mix, towering above the rest in fright wigs or gimp hoods or both.

I learned that the G&D had only opened in 2002, its barrage of cluttered decor not so much accumulated as installed readymade. In fact, despite its creaky, dusty ambience, the premises had most recently been occupied by a shoe wholesaler. Going further back, the pub dates to at least the mid-nineteenth century. One of the new owners moved to London from somewhere up north, and imported a homely sensibility by way of the tchotchkes and the unpretentious lagers. In 2005, the bar's interior was reconstructed at the Institute of Contemporary Arts—the replica of a simulacrum. The pub then opened its own gallery in the fetid toilets—the White Cubicle. Even Wolfgang Tillmans exhibited in the White Cubicle, hanging a huge, glossy framed portrait of Richard Branson over the toilet. The only time I've wielded power over that tycoon is when he looked on as I flushed at the G&D.

I came to recognize the regular DJs. Svelte, unencumbered Cozette, wearing a tuxedo jacket, was said to be of Freud lineage. She DJed with an angular male counterpart, and eventually a twink joined in their sets like an adopted son, donning mesh tops, poised and serious-faced at the decks. An ageless milliner, looking like someone's auntie, placidly selected tunes from Dr. Buzzard's Original Savannah Band. Princess Julia wiggled in wearing a tidy forties dress and jet-black hair. It was rumored she had gone out every night since the Blitz Kids days of the early eighties. She spoke like a Cockney sparrow—born, as the saying goes, within the sound of Bow bells (more precisely, in transit in an ambulance somewhere along the street of the George and Dragon). The handsome Prince Nelly, new gay bar royalty, lip-synced along to his power ballad selections with a crooner's passion, both his fists at his sternum. He announced the next song into a microphone, imparting copious factoids. In general, the music was eighties pop—Dead or Alive, Bananarama, Belinda Carlisle, the Human League—and stuff irresistible after imbibing cheap beer: 'Fantasy' by Mariah Carey. '9 to 5.' Crystal Castles. CSS. Janet Jackson's 'When I Think of You.' 'Just Can't Get Enough' by Depeche Mode. 'That's Not My Name.' MGMT. 'D.A.N.C.E.' 'Last Dance.' I recognized the Lovely Jonjo from his appearance on the cover of *Butt* magazine. In that image, he was nude and cherubic, looking over his shoulder, blond curls licking his forehead. I used a mutual friend as an excuse to introduce myself. He put his headphones down and 'Ready for the Floor' began to play. He grinned broadly. The Lovely Jonjo was another Londoner born and raised, but dressed like a California teenager in sea-foam blue and hot pink. I could easily summon his bare bum to mind. One by one my images of London were materializing. Famous plucked up the nerve to say hello to Konstantin just as he was leaving. Konstantin, villainously handsome, was a star on Flickr, the photo-sharing website through which the two were linked along with dozens of international fags who admired one another's intimate snapshots obsessively. Soon enough, we appeared in Konstantin's pictures ourselves. We are naked and supine on rumpled sheets, photographed from above. Between our shoulders you can spot Konstantin's socked feet.

Famous and I began to travel with the crew I met at my new job for a fashion designer—especially with Robbie, who had a square jaw and long brown hair and had been brought out from New York City with the company. As our group entered the G&D, I was aware we were acceptable, even afforded a certain status. I'd been branded by my asso-ciation with the label. The fashion industry regulars clocked us like cats raising their brows then dropping back into a snooze, assured of familiar company. We became a different kind of wallflower—not shrinking violets but judgmental pansies. In this way, we contributed to the worst element at the G&D: an insiderness wherein anonymity could not be sustained—a place for *networking*. London's fashion scene thrived on a provincial urbanity: people surveyed the room the way they do at art openings, fully aware of one another's currency.

Gays have nine lives, I thought, and I was on maybe four or five. Having decided we would finally behave like grown-ups upon moving to London, we instead regressed as soon as we figured out we still scanned as young enough to play the new boys in town. For the first time, I had an *accent*. Early on, I brashly quizzed the skinny bartender at the G&D where we should go out dancing when the pub closed. Sundays meant a club kid night called Boombox, but he warned us that it got so crowded it was hard to get in. Otherwise, everyone just decamped down the road to the Joiners Arms, but he advised us not to expect too much—it was just the sort of place people would *end up* because it was there and open late. We bore that in mind, little suspecting it would become our routine.

We'd hang out at the G&D until around a half hour before closing, then traipse down Hackney Road to the Joiners. This was timed to narrowly avoid the masses as they were ejected from the G&D, when the pub staff pulled down noisy metal shutters and barked at punters to finish up their drinks. The bartenders wanted to go to the Joiners, too. Between the venues, we slipped into a cramped off-license and bought Polish beers, ten cigarettes and Buzz Fizzy Mix, and then sucked it all down in the cold yellow light cast by a lonely cyber café. En route to the Joiners, we'd pass a few club kids huddled under a tree; an epicene with one dangling earring rushing back to the G&D for whatever or whoever they'd left behind; someone vomiting onto a wall.

The Joiners Arms, an unprepossessing shack across from

an office furniture wholesaler slash parking lot, is said to have existed in some form since at least 1869. The proprietor was a disheveled dandy wearing a soiled jacket and neckerchief, leaning on a cane, cigarette between teeth, his lips curled into a sly smile. David Pollard had taken over the place in 1997, hoisting a rainbow flag without apology, a dyed-in-the-wool leftie catering to working-class gay men who lived locally. People said there used to be a dark room upstairs. Something of the ribald atmosphere remained under Pollard's laissez-faire stewardship. He brought to mind a haggard innkeeper catering to smugglers and ship wreckers. It was said he was unconcerned with money, just effortless at hosting. The cachet of the place was not the result of a brand strategy, but down to its shambolic character. Everyone wanted to be a part of that. We gossiped about the latest celebrity to arrive by chauffeured car and dash in.

Any restraint maintained at the G&D was abandoned at the Joiners. *Let go*, Famous demanded of a cheeky boy at the bar who immediately cupped my groin with his palm. We'd watch it fill up within the hour. It looked better with bodies. Empty, it could be any forlorn gay bar on the edge of any town. At the same time, perversely, it might pass for a preschool, with its yellow walls, low ceiling and world map. Visitors marked their place of origin: San Francisco, Tokyo, Melbourne. That was the map of our cosmopolitan London—in those days, we were always being introduced to a hunk called Rafael from São Paulo, or bonding over a cigarette with a comely Andalusian rabble-rouser named Paz.

If Wolfgang Tillmans was there taking pictures, it made everything doubly exciting, as if he were a satellite beaming us to the rest of the world. I once watched him photo-graph a crumpled napkin on the bar. He caught my eye and grinned. Then there was the time a few rough-looking old geezers took their semierect cocks out on the dance floor. The British call them willies, and that seemed exactly the right word for their pale uncut meat. They smirked and laughed, having asserted this was still their territory. A good-looking teenager prowled around collecting glasses or playing games of pool, so that I was never sure if he was employed there. He was always topless, a hoop through one nipple. His sweaty thick skin would nearly make contact as he squeezed past. It was as though the humidity of his flesh generated the ambience of the whole place.

We danced to whatever—Rihanna, Lady Gaga, 'Finally' by CeCe Peniston. On Thursdays, a DJ collective played esoteric house, which Famous complained was too serious. Our ongoing joke was how miserable it would be if we ended up dying there: the Joiners Harms, we called it, as Robbie passed around shots of sambuca, the syrup coating my tobacco-stained fingertips. The dingy unisex bathroom was the bar's climax, so habitually commandeered for drugs and sex it was eventually assigned its own bouncer. Appar-ently, it used to be worse, permanently flooded, and when the toilets were remodeled, some regulars took home the cubicle dividing walls as souvenirs. Now the line snaked halfway through the bar. When I finally got to the front, I'd make a beeline for the next vacated toilet, where I'd squint as I pissed, trying not to see what floated near my feet. Once, a man came from behind like vapor and barricaded the stall door. I was only liberated when the guard knocked furiously. The next time this happened, it was in the disabled stall, and by two men. I was backing into the corner when once again saved by security, though I was spared no harsh words, presumed to be in on it. On other occasions, I was. The Joiners Harms sobriquet was less amusing the morning after we took home a handsome daddy who topped me so recklessly we ended up in the emergency room, where both Famous and I were prescribed a course of PEP once the nurse heard tell of how events had played out in our bedroom.

After a few years, the novelty of the neighborhood wore off, but it was loud out the window so I'd use my old line on Famous—*can't beat 'em, join 'em*—and we'd go out into the night. With time, we took to approaching the Joiners from the opposite direction—farther east, from the Nelsons Head. Maybe we'd outgrown the overaccessorized and colorful G&D, what young Londoners called try-hard. At the Nelsons, we tried hard not to try hard. The men were plain and attractive. They'd once modeled for Prada or acted in porn or played in indie bands or some combination thereof. The style was understated: five o'clock shadow, spritz of sandalwood, A.P.C. jeans. The Nelsons Head has been around since the 1820s. In the early aughts, it was run by an elusive character, said to be a legless queer man nicknamed Peggy—as in pegleg. The Nelsons was reopened by Farika and Patrick in July 2007, the weekend the ban on smoking inside bars went into effect. This may explain the message on the chalkboard just outside the door: No Screeching.

Farika and Patrick didn't will the place into being any more gay than it already was. The East End, as Farika surmises, has just always been that way inclined. (In London, drag has been as much working class as gay. It's said that around the corner at the flower market pub the Royal Oak, for instance, a cross-dressing couple named Lil and Maisie performed while bombs fell in the Second World War.) Anyway, once Farika and Patrick hired an especially cute bartender, that did it: the Nelsons was a gay bar. (Guy Strait once described the conversion of a struggling venue into a gay bar by way of hiring the right staff as turning it on.)

Tucked away between a cobbled street leading to the flower market and a towering Soviet-style public housing estate, the Nelsons was well appointed as a low-key option for those in the know. Upon entering, we'd scan the row of antique cinema seats against the wall; each seemed to be occupied by a dishy young man. Those wanting to avoid ending up at the Joiners brought along their terrier or greyhound as an excuse to get back home. Like the G&D, the Nelsons was filled with objects, but the scheme seemed more cerebral: vintage white ceramic vessels lined the high shelves running around the room in elegant counterpoint to the teal paneling. An impressive panoply of flea-market painted portraits gazed back at us. None was more iconic than the blond nurse with the haunted stare. On occasion, the walls would be rehung—all flower paintings, all nudes. The carpet was florid and untattered. The jukebox routinely returned to 'Tusk' by Fleetwood Mac. With friends, we ordered house red wine by the bottle in rounds. We'd egg one another on to the Joiners—*for just one dance*. Once, as we gathered ourselves to get over there, a bartender gamely poured our remaining wine into large waxed Coca-Cola cups. We sloshed our way across the grounds of the forbidding eleven-story apartment block, managing to spill with nearly every step. The cold night was a sea—and as much a part of the revelry as the ports. That was our Triangle. I didn't realize then that some people called it the Bermuda Triangle, but of course they did.

———

In one knock-on effect of the smoking ban, large numbers of gays were now visible on the street in front of gay bars. On balmy nights at the George and Dragon, the babbling crowd spilled into the alley between the pub and the church graveyard opposite, a fragrance bomb of lager, unisex Comme des Garçons perfume and cigarette smoke. The boys boasted the very signifiers that would have been disdained in clean-cut Soho: hairy chests, scrappy beards, hoop earrings. Black jeans were as tight as leggings, and once white plimsolls were fashionably grayed from base- ment dance floors and gutters. Singly and in pairs we nipped behind dumpsters to pee.

If this was an attempt at marking territory, we were surely too late. We took the same routes already trodden by local Bengali lads. Some were intimidating, seemed a little too interested in our presence, a curiosity I saw as menacing. Some were developing an allegiance to Islam more scriptural and political than the contemplative faith of their fathers. In 2006, *The Telegraph*, a right-leaning British newspaper, wielded a poll showing that four out of ten British Muslims would prefer sharia law to prevail in areas they considered their terrain, fueling the image of the demographic as un- integrated. It was more complex than that, but from a fag's perspective it could seem that, despised just for being there, we were guilty of not merely sin, but the one that made them most squeamish.

In retrospect, of course it was going to escalate. When populations that have been marginalized for very different reasons intersect in the same location, everyone walks on an edge. Some on the bar scene griped about South Asian men spitting on the streets. To the minds of some local youth, the gays pranced around in repellent attire, not acting our age. We may have concluded these local boys, who lived on council estates yet purchased flashy cars, were driving themselves into dead ends. But our aims to be global visionaries—the next Alexander McQueen—must have made it seem to them like we were only ever visiting. They drove those cars down *their* streets. We posed on that same concrete for international magazines. Maybe we appeared to be an abomination not so much because we were disbelievers, but because we were so full of belief in ourselves.

From what I understand, in 2008, a twenty-one-year-old fashion student named Oliver, his hair dyed copper red, was walking with a female friend toward the George and Dragon. It was early in the evening toward the end of summer. Oliver had moved to London two years before, and was making the most of the long days before graduating from Central Saint Martins. A friend later described it as one of those periods when they went out every night. This time, though, they did not make it past St. Leonard's churchyard. The group of juveniles who attacked Oliver did so over a period of four and a half minutes. The knife was first stabbed through Oliver's back and into his lung. Then they went for his neck, chest and heart. According to a report in *The Independent*, as he lay motionless, one of the assailants returned and jumped on his head. Oliver arrived at the hospital clinically dead. His chest was cut open, ribs lifted and lungs parted. A doctor took Oliver's heart from his body, held it in his hands and resuscitated it on a tray. Oliver had only a small chance of surviving and did. He's been in a wheelchair since. I am loath to tell Oliver's story because it's the narrative that gets told time and again about him. But it was important to us who went out locally. Word spread. Before I learned the details, I pictured the incident occurring at a late hour—on the way home, drunk, four a.m.—not at dusk, when the night was still a vague plan.

From his hospital bed, Oliver helped his friends plan a fund-raiser in which fellow students would sell their art. This grew into something much bigger. Their new charity, Art Against Knives, held an auction at Shoreditch House, with work by Tracey Emin and Antony Gormley on the block. Daniel Radcliffe reportedly bid seven thousand pounds on a Banksy. It's difficult to fathom how the *Independent* headline got signed off on: 'A Brush with Death: Why Britain's Coolest Art and Fashion Names Have Rallied Around a Victim of Random Knife Crime.' The 'brush with death' pun. The 'coolest' superlative. What finally gnaws at my mind is the word *random*. This may be so, but it was also possible that the attack was a hate crime. It did not seem to be an isolated incident. After one of Oliver's assailants, a fifteen-year-old, was sentenced to ten years in prison for harm with intent, the George and Dragon was stormed by a band of some thirty youths; it was reported they struck out at customers and left the doorman beaten. Sometime around then the windows were smashed, incising a brittle, sharp spiderweb. Again, we couldn't be sure whether it was coincidental—*random*—but when we smoked outside, we took it personally to glance over and see the pub cracked. I was sure that more cars had begun to take the alley where we clustered, and at high speed—parting us like a bully in a high school corridor. In at least one case, the driver obviously swerved toward the crowd on purpose. The differences between locals suddenly felt mighty. My naive take on the neighborhood as a melting pot ignored its potential to reach a boiling point.

Awareness posters were put up in the bars. The messages were about community safety and vigilance. A dedicated Facebook page posted descriptions of harassment by groups of 'Asian guys.' Sides were being delineated, leaving me more than a little conflicted. I wanted to understand the local teenagers; to know how they were seen by their families, one another, their mosque, the police; to make sense of how they saw me. When chatter about the string of incidents started up, I'd anticipate someone might say something racist, so I'd change the subject. Yet my own posture was defensive on local streets. I knew that gays were often blamed for gentrification. We always seem to be on the scene just before the Swedish bakeries or Japanese bicycle shops, followed by the glass high rises and oligarchs. This was nothing new. In Antonioni's 1966 film *Blow-Up*, one sighting of a male couple in a London neighborhood prompts a tip to buy quick: 'The area's already crawling with queers and their poodles.'

A few years later, posters and stickers appeared in the vicinal district of Whitechapel. They read 'Gay Free Zone' and were, almost comically, illustrated with a slash through a rainbow. 'Arise and Warn. And Fear Allah. Verily Allah Is Severe in Punishment.' The BBC reported that the Metropolitan Police was out to find the *culprits* who were distributing this blight. Not so long ago, it was the sodomites who were the *culprits* they pursued. A nineteen-year-old boy was fined one hundred pounds for stickering lampposts. The next year he was jailed for possessing Al Qaeda literature. The powerful East London Mosque was held to task. Word spread that a speaker at the venue had given a lecture including a 'Spot the Fag' split-screen slide show (an example: 'Spot the Fag—Elton John, or 2-Pac?'). Community organizers solicited statements against gay bashing from the East London Mosque, which were duly given.

An opinion piece about Muslim homophobia was published in *Attitude*: 'East London has seen the highest increase in homophobic attacks anywhere in Britain. Everybody knows why, and nobody wants to say it,' the journalist Johann Hari proposed. 'It is because East London has the highest Muslim population in Britain, and we have allowed a fanatically intolerant attitude towards gay people to incubate among them, in the name of "tolerance."' Hari put forth valid points against bigotry, and expressed solidarity with an intersectional identity at especially high risk—Muslim gay kids—but elsewhere his logic seemed rash. 'When gay people were cruelly oppressed in Britain,' he wrote, 'we didn't form gangs to beat up other minorities.' This isn't strictly true; it just exempts homosexual perpetrators, repressed or otherwise, whose attacks are not carried out under a gay banner. Hari argued, 'Where people choose to behave in a bigoted way towards gay people, we need to act. We need to require them to change this aspect of their culture.' (It would seem that when the article was republished by the

Huffington Post, that condescending 'require them' line was deleted.)

Others contended this was not a strictly Muslim issue, but spoke to economic inequality more broadly. British people of Bangladeshi and Pakistani origin are something like three times more likely to live in poverty. And all kinds of disenfranchised young men hang around giving the impression of being up to no good. That's down to a jumble of factors, not least of which how they've been preconceived. Disenfranchisement moves across populations and mutates. A couple of decades back, factions of local white skinheads made very clear their hatred of both *Pakis* and *poofs.* In 2011, just as the 'Gay Free Zone' campaign proliferated, an event called East End Gay Pride was cancelled because one of its organizers was accused of past ties with the far-right English Defence League. We were forced to confront the uncomfortable reality of Islamophobia eliding with gay pride.

Still now, when people say of East London *It's not like it used to be...,* I think: It was never one thing. It's possible that as often as it was about distinct identities colliding, it's been about the slippages within each identity—and mistaken identity. Amid the stacks of local hate crimes that I've forced myself to look through, an incident from 1980 stands out to me: on the tube under East London, a Pakistani mechanic in his forties named Kavumarz Anklesaria was beaten to death for his smile. Anklesaria's perpetual grin had resulted from an accident when the rickshaw he was riding crashed into a tram. On the Bromley-by-Bow station platform and then on the tube carriage, a twenty-year-old named John Till thought that Anklesaria was smiling at him 'like a homosexual.' So Till delivered a fatal karate-style kick. 'Even if this unfortunate man who was killed was a homosexual he hadn't done anything more than smile—and smiling is not a capital offence,' stated the judge in the case. 'There are some people whose features show a perpetual smile, and there are those who smile innocently at passengers in a train.' Still now, when people say of East London *It's not like it used to be…*, I think: One could never really know what that means.

———

We rented our place from a friend of a friend of a friend who'd moved to New York City. It had been steadily stripped back by a succession of tenants with Donald Judd taste, leaving concrete floors splattered with paint stains. There was no heat. The street was noisy. We were happy to be there, in the center of things. We'd lived there some five years before Famous lugged out the artifact. We knew it was there all along—the previous tenant had mentioned it—buried in a storage cupboard along with other stuff the landlord hadn't gotten around to moving out: his Macintosh Classic, the locked filing cabinet without its key. Now I arrived home to see, as Famous apprised me by text, that it was resplendent: the London Apprentice pub sign, leaning on its wrought-iron bracket.

Famous had removed the cobwebs from the filigree, and the sign instantly took pride of place. An illustration is crudely but evocatively hand-painted on the metal, depicting a young carpenter in a sleeveless t-shirt laying down tools and wiping his hands on a lavender-crimson ombré hankie. He looks westward at a vespertine skyline. His skin is only slightly less pale than his top, which is as white as photocopier paper. His biceps are butch, but the tone is wistful. The image of the young man turned toward the city is a potent one: there's a hopefulness to it—if only the trifling kind that accompanies the start of the evening. He looks ready to unwind, willing to take his chances—horny. A series of horizontal strokes among the clouds are like adumbrations of the night's possibilities.

The venue that the sign was wrenched from was a few minutes' walk away at 333 Old Street. In the eighties and nineties, the London Apprentice earned a reputation as a rough but convivial gay bar for skinheads and leathermen. As the clientele expanded, art fags made a dash from Old Street station through what was then a notoriously sketchy terrain. Supposedly Freddie Mercury once arrived at the London Apprentice by landing a helicopter on its roof. When I mentioned the sign to the historian Adrian Rifkin, he said he'd been wondering where it was all that time. He remembers basically running from the tube into the fuggy embrace of the hi-NRG. On one occasion, he brought along a prominent gallerist. *To inspect the fauna,* Rifkin clucked, momentarily transported back to the snarling skinhead in tight jeans who leaned against the wall as they entered. I told a curator friend we had the sign. *That's the holy grail of Shoreditch,* he affirmed. (On holiday in distant Cornwall, a former Londoner in a rustic pub used that same phrase; the straight salesman regaled us with a fruitless tale of his one night as a sleaze tourist there.) Sam Ashby, who published the film journal *Little Joe* at the time, stood before it in awe, looking not unlike the lad depicted on the sign—with his Roman profile and mouth downturned at the corners. Too young to remember the place himself, his was a borrowed nostalgia. He pointed out the apprentice's sartorial eccentricity of looping his jeans with two thin belts. The septuagenarian artist David Medalla wound up at our flat one evening and stood in front of the sign attentively. *Somebody painted this...*, he muttered. He drew attention to the dots and zigzags of the handkerchief. *Not just a sign painter. An artist. Somebody....*

The sign took over from our undated world map as the room's conversation starter, as guests tried to ascertain when it would have been painted. In its cityscape, the dome of St. Paul's dominates. A hastily drawn Post Office Tower dates the sign to after 1964, when that cylindrical beacon was constructed. The apprentice's hair is combed up and back, a lilt of Americana perhaps indicative of the rockabilly revival favored by some British gay men in the early eighties. (*Gay Times* called them 'clone-a-billies.') In general, London club fashion had truculently turned from the frills of the new romantic look to faded t-shirts and torn jeans, an antistyle dubbed 'hard times' by Robert Elms in the September 1982 issue of *The Face*: 'Somehow the atmosphere when you walk into a club today is different; gay abandon has evolved into a clenched teeth determination where precious lager cans are cradled to stop them disappearing and sweat has replaced cool as the mark of a face.' I'd date the sign to sometime around 1983—when it was chic, according to the scene maker Sue Tilley, 'to flaunt your newfound poverty,' and 'no one was properly dressed without at least one belt slung around their hips.'

I emailed our landlord, John, about it, and his reply brimmed with nostalgia. He told me that he frequented the London Apprentice—the LA—weekly in the early nineties, before moving into the immediate vicinity. *It was a bar for its time—it was men only and had a distinct edge of anything goes. It had a macho feeling. Leather was very popular but there was no dress code. On Friday nights they had a maze upstairs where people had sex…although quite discreetly. But people were having sex in the toilets as well. There was a dance floor in the basement that played great music. Upstairs on Saturday became a drug den. There were two tables, each with its own dealer. One sold speed and acid, and the other hash. People would line up. It was completely open. Speed and acid were very popular then…and lots of pints of beer.* An LED sign behind the bar cautioned against drugs on the premises, even while they were being blatantly exchanged and consumed all over the place. The women's toilets were repurposed as a dark room. Men came from all over London, and much farther afield. Jean-Paul Gaultier arrived from Paris on the weekends. Marc Almond would attend, as well as Boy George, who seemed to John like he'd arrived from a different era.

The London Apprentice would have been our closest gay bar if it hadn't gone straight again by the time we moved in. We passed by on most days; it was operating as a live music club called 333 Mother. It was located on a narrow, snaking stretch of Old Street, which is indeed very old, already called Ealdestrate in the year 1200 and le Oldestrete by the end of the following century. The London Apprentice is thought to have existed since at least 1767. Around 1894, it was entirely rebuilt as an elaborate three-floor pub with billiards in the basement and an upstairs dining room. On the ground floor, some thirteen separate public and private parlors radiated from the same large bar, suggesting the clientele was minutely segregated by class. It's possible, though, that the pub was named in a spirit of solidarity with the 1595 riot at Tower Hill by London apprentices incensed by the social imbalance between have-nots and elite. Five of those rioters were hanged, drawn and quartered; the pub's moniker may have been selected to make a martyr of them.

This particular apprentice, I'd surmise, worked with wood: Shoreditch had been the country's locus of the furniture trade since the eighteenth century. Eventually, production was broken down into stages between different small-scale manufacturers so that, as the urbanist Peter Hall put it, a kind of dispersed 'assembly line ran through the streets.' The zone became dotted with piles of unpolished furniture and frames stacked high on barrows. The population of the parish more than tripled in the first half of the nineteenth century, nearing one hundred thirty thousand in 1861. Ancillary trades flourished—raw materials, accessories, tools, finishing—and necessitated a service sector. The new low-wage, less skilled jobs were taken by immigrants, particularly Eastern European Jews. Other industries moved into the district: tobacco, printing, boot making. In the twentieth century, factories were constructed outside of London, and by the forties, the furniture industry in Shoreditch had largely dissolved. According to the 1984 city directory, though, the neighbors of the London Apprentice at that time still included a furniture carver, potters' supplier, tool dealer and machinery merchant.

It must have been about that time when the London Apprentice was taken over by its new publican, Michael Glover, and the place earned its homosexual reputation. From the 1983 edition of the *East London & City Beer Guide:*

217

'Has discos, fairly pricey.' The 1986 edition is more explicit: 'Used by gays.' Glover is understood to have been influenced by his experiences on the New York City scene, which likely places him at the hedonistic disco palace the Saint and the meatpacking district leather bar Mineshaft where, as the British artist and filmmaker Derek Jarman once recalled, guests were sniffed at the door to ensure they weren't covering their natural musk with aftershave: 'In fact, so dark were the recesses of The Mineshaft all you could really do was touch and smell.' Glover turned the basement of the London Apprentice into a dungeonlike disco—the Tool Box. Wall to wall, men posed in leather jackets, steelcapped boots, cropped hair, tattoos.

Two centuries on from its inception, the London Apprentice name proved conveniently pliant, suggesting a lusty nubility. On the sign, the young laborer was reinterpreted as a bit of rough trade. For most of the twentieth century, London's gay subculture was dominated by cruising grounds and unmarked pubs frequented by rent boys and the gay men who picked them up, the latter sharing between them, as the historian Rictor Norton put it to me, an uneasy camaraderie. Middle-class homosexuals would boast of their encounters with *a real man*, meaning not one another. The British diarist J. R. Ackerley searched for his perfect companion (the 'Ideal Friend') not among fellow gentlemen of privilege, but errand boys and soldiers. His criteria: young, normal, working class, obedient. Hooking up with a bit of rough was not merely a matter of taste, but a way of playing by class-conscious rules: it could always be a dalliance, not a commitment to an aberrant existence.

Rough trade was imagined as instinctive, dangerous. His

alluring brawn was also a potential threat—all the more exciting. (The archetype is so commanding it overshadows the true range of gender expression in men of lower social status. Poor femmes—*queens*—have been consistently targeted by police or erased by other gay men. If the pub sign was revised as a different apprentice—a mincing hairdresser's assistant, a giggling dressmaker's trainee—it would be read as a derisive caricature.) Rough trade self-perpetuated the brutish image, and cultivated it in one another's company. They egged each other on. The historian Matt Houlbrook noted that tapping wealthy older men was seen as street smarts. Trade instigated and pursued transactions themselves. Sometimes the money exchanged was so negligible it amounted to little more than an excuse. The London Apprentice pinup—with his large hands, small lips, hammer—embodies this mutually devised ideal. He looks like he smells of sawdust and sweat, his biceps earned by cabinetry, not a gym membership. But he has agency: he is not merely gazed at, but gazing.

The narrative of wealthier homo as predator has had plot twists over the years: in 1891, for instance, the well-to-do English socialist Edward Carpenter spotted George Merrill on a train from the platform. Merrill, who'd drifted between manual jobs since the age of thirteen, more than returned his circumspect glance: he jumped off the train. Merrill liked dirty jokes, was a resourceful craftsperson, had bedded several aristocratic men. The two of them became a thing while continuing amative relations with others. Eventually, they created a domestic life—one darning socks, the other mending a shirt—which struck admiring acquaintances as utopian; for them, it was a matter of splitting the chores. They'd found a way to live. Such luck in love contained the potential to destabilize a whole class system. In 1954, one worried magistrate issued a statement—coincidentally from the Old Street court just across from the London Apprentice—in which he condemned homosexuality as morally wrong, physically dirty and degrading. And: 'Is not this conduct even more anti-social where the participants are not of equal status…?' His examples of such offensive trysts were 'the artistic genius and the younger man needing his professional help' and 'the man of wealth or title and the friend from a simpler walk of life.'

In the seventies, the import of American clone style into London discos unseated the entrenched cross-class tropes and introduced a cowboy-hatted egalitarianism. Social roles became harder to read, became roleplay. Gay liberation sold itself as a story of equality among men, a sexy democracy. In doing so, it revised historical class systems as fallacious in the first place. The apprentice himself gently evades clear-cut social status. With that faraway look and strands of hair dangling foppishly forward, not to mention the handkerchief, he serves an alluring ambiguity. Who's to say if the apprentice is trade who doesn't think of himself as homosexual, or trade who *does*, or a middle-class gay fronting as rough, or a straight model posing for gays, or something slipping between.

Nearby, at 56 Hoxton Square, a group of neo-transvestites (they dressed in women's clothes without necessarily adopting a female persona), led by one Greg Slingback, squatted a shop front previously occupied by the leather gear retailer Expectations. In the hands of

the neotransvestites, it was turned into Gl'amour, a sec-
ondhand boutique for cross-dressers. Apparently, straight
guys—burly Irish builders, footballers—would arrive to
get oiled down and 'trannied up' in lingerie before having
a wank in the basement—or being encouraged along by
the staff to the London Apprentice, where they could strut
their stuff.

In 1990, the landlady of the Young British Artist hangout the Bricklayers Arms took over the license of the
London Apprentice. She largely maintained its lawlessness
and kept the men-only policy, exempting herself. The next
year, Rupert Haselden's bleak article 'Gay Abandon,' almost
wholly set inside the LA, appeared in *The Guardian*. The
scene is established as smoke-filled, 'with shafts of coloured
light piercing the gloom.' At the LA, Haselden writes, 'AIDS
dangles like a flashing neon sign.' He speculates that the
destructive behavior was proof of an inbuilt fatalism, which
he attributes to gay men being 'biologically maladaptive'
and unable to reproduce. He regards these men as resigned
to HIV infection, even viewing it as a form of graduation.
The bar manager pronounces the casual sex a game of
Russian roulette. Haselden concludes the risks amount to a
spiral of denial and recklessness. He despairs at the futile
act of 'falling into each other's sweaty arms at the London
Apprentice.'

The article elicited a week's worth of debate in the *Guardian* letters page. Gay men wrote in to assert their custom
of practicing safer sex. David Bridle, an editor at *Pink Paper*
and *Boyz*, faulted Haselden for neglecting to mention how
customers and staff raised funds to convert the upper floor

of the pub into a drop-in center for people living with HIV and AIDS. The *Guardian* offices were picketed for allowing such a pernicious angle on homosexuality; the editor called meetings to ensure the paper maintained credibility with the gays. Haselden himself died from the disease three years after his article was published. His partner, Nigel Finch, passed away the following year, while a movie he directed about Stonewall was in postproduction.

Around 1993, our landlord, John, had moved into the flat, from which he could walk to the LA and to the gay karaoke bar the Spiral Staircase. John characterizes the area as low-key and local yet cosmopolitan, with artists not yet priced out, and the image of Cool Britannia netting international attention. *It was a great place to be gay,* as John puts it, *because it was kind of post-gay.* But when I pressed John later, he also recalled fractures and simmering tension, including otherwise liberal queers making comments about homophobic black people, while gays and lesbians of color made known they felt unwelcome on the scene. People were not only freaked out by reports of London's latest gay serial killer, the Gay Slayer, but were under constant stress over AIDS. It was a time of surging violence against gay people, yet this did not always inspire unity.

———

By chance, I came across a photo of the sign in its original context. I was scrolling through annual reports from GALOP, the Gay London Police Monitoring Group, learning that the summer of 1986 through the next year marked a concentrated increase of gay bashing in the city. GALOP was especially troubled by what appeared to be premeditated attacks near London gay bars. The digital scan I was reviewing was fuzzy, but still I discerned a familiar form in a small photograph: *the apprentice*. The sign was at that point mounted high on the pub's exterior.

It turns out a remarkable number of this spate of hate crimes took place outside the London Apprentice. According to the GALOP report, in August 1986, over twenty men were attacked by a band of youths with bricks and bottles. Two men were hospitalized. That month, another gay man was kicked and beaten, sending him into the hospital. In September, a party of four was attacked on Hackney Road on their way home. The group of ten or fifteen attackers wielded bricks, bottles and blunt instruments. One of the victims had his jaw wired for two months. Only one assailant was arrested, and was the first to be charged in any of these incidents. In February 1987, another man outside the pub was attacked by four or five youths. In March, two gay men were punched and kicked in the face. Later that month, another two men were attacked after leaving the pub, thought to be by the same gang. They were cut about the face with broken glass. Police officers arrived within seconds, but failed to make any arrests, though the perpetrators loitered only yards away. Instead, an officer cautioned one of the victims to stop spitting blood, or he'd be arrested himself. The second victim was told *Shut up you queer bastard* by another cop.

That was the summer the young author Neil Bartlett was beginning to conceive what would become his novel *Ready to Catch Him Should He Fall*. As the story (an intergenerational romance set in a somewhat surreal unnamed gay bar overseen by a matron reminiscent of a Genet madam) took shape, Bartlett was hanging out in two East London spots in particular—the Backstreet, the city's first dedicated leather bar, and the London Apprentice. Bartlett began to sketch the book out in his head on his late night perambulations from the LA through the deserted city. 'Those nights out were inspiring—but the solitary walks home were foolish,' Bartlett writes in a foreword to the book's reissue. 'London, in 1986, was not a safe place for a visibly gay man like my twenty-eight-year-old self to be out alone after dark—or even by daylight, for that matter. The cresting of the first wave of the British AIDS epidemic had been accompanied by an extraordinary outpouring of hostility towards us both in the media and on the streets.'

Boy, the nineteen-year-old at the heart of *Ready to Catch Him Should He Fall*, is a walker, too. A precariousness hangs over Boy and his cohorts, even as they are discovering rare, intimate joys. The book's narrator, one of the bar's regulars, interjects news of the attacks: 'I know there's not always blood, it's just that each time I hear this, that's what I see, a knife coming down. Sometimes it's not that at all, but a metal bar across the legs. Or a single word thrown out of a car window, tossed at you like a bottle, so like a bottle that you involuntarily duck to avoid it, or look down to see the broken glass at your feet.'

An East London bashing also features in Alan Hollinghurst's 1988 novel *The Swimming-Pool Library*, when a gay man is set upon by a group of skinheads. The blond, Oxford-educated homosexual protagonist, Will, calls skinheads 'a challenge.' While the first iterations of skinhead looked outward—namely to Jamaican ska music and rude boy style—an agitated white contingent enveloped the hard look of bare scalp and military surplus into their aggressive stance against outsiders. In the eyes of the horny and privileged character Will, the skinheads loitered on city streets and estates 'magnetising the attention they aimed to repel. Cretinously simplified to booted feet, bum and bullet head, they had some, if not all, of the things one was looking for.' Having ventured to Stratford East, a landscape of gasometers and warehouses, Will is encircled by a group of skins, who call him poof. He tries to get the tone of his comeback right—a high-wire speech act familiar to many gay men. 'I acted out a weary sigh, and said, tight-lipped: "Actually, poof is not a word that I would use."' He fails at the adverb. '"Isn't it, *actually?*" said the leader, again with a smile that seemed to say he knew my game, he knew what I liked.' Will is rebuffed with a broken bottle and boots.

It's a persistent trope: upper-class homosexual desires contemptuous thug, hot for the brute as likely to kick his ass as fuck it. Now gay men wanted to not just copulate with but *be* that bully. (As Rupert Haselden wrote, 'For 20 years we have been mimicking the traditional force of oppression, the macho male. By sidling up close, by taking it home and fucking it we, in pantomime, had been destroying its power over us.') With skinhead style, British men could transpose the American clone archetype into their own nationalistic fetish. Gay skins hung out at the Union Tavern and the Coleherne, a discreet upstairs nest called the Craven Club, the Anvil, the Block, an exclusive club called Skins '95, as well as at the London Apprentice. Steve, a skinhead and regular of the LA, remarked: 'People look at me on the Tube like I'm trouble, like I might be about to kick their face in. I wonder what they'd say if they knew I was a poof.'

Interviews with gay skins in the zine *Square Peg* turned up a range of motivations. Peter was rebelling against who he used to be: a nice middle-class boy at university. By going hard, he figured he could no longer be called 'not a man.' Dave had been a skin for six years—two years longer than he'd been an out gay. Tom chose to become a skin because it turned him on. The uniform was erotic predilection and protective shield. In his book *Gay Skins*, Murray Healy posited that you were less likely to be bashed if you looked like a basher. That is, until the skinhead aesthetic—especially late at night, in London, near a gay bar—began to look like chinked armor. The final interview in Healy's book is with a gay member of the neo-Nazi skin group Blood & Honour: 'For me, the gays have fucked up the Nazi skinhead image.' People on the street in London used to shout *Nazi bastard* at him. Now, due to the proliferation of gay men with skin style, they'd begun to hurl *batty man*—the Jamaican patois slur for obvious gays—instead.

In Britain by the nineties, elements of skin style infiltrated a generic gay look: rolled jeans, flight jacket, boots, a buzz cut of grade four or below. What appeared like an obvious case of appropriation—as *The Guardian* put it in 1992, an anti-gay image mirrored by a gay group—didn't just operate in one direction. The common perception would be that in order to *become gay*, a snarl and heavy boots require *purloining*, to be then adorned like a sheep in wolf's clothing. But there have probably been gay skinheads as long as any other skinhead. As Murray Healy put forward, 'Who's copying who here? Who owns the copyright? Were skinheads ever the property of heterosexuality?' He gives the example of a man known as Wolf, signed by the Ugly modeling agency in the late sixties for his convincing skinhead authenticity. In 1973, his corpse washed up on a shore of the Thames, reported by *The Sun* to be a suspected gangland hit. Wolf's apparently duplicitous personality confounded the media. He was an actor, drag artist, criminal with several aliases: Michael St John, Bernard Cogan, Anthony Cohen. And if his birth name really was Wolfgang von Jurgen, who was that exactly? A well-spoken German man, he lived alone in a room with walls painted red and covered in pictures of Steve McQueen and other men in motorcycle gear. He wore expensive leathers himself. His landlady had never known him to have a girlfriend, though he was often seen with two close male friends. These apparently contradictory aspects were irre-solvable to the tabloid press of the early seventies. As Healy put it, Wolf would always 'remain an unidentifiable body.'

In the eighties skinhead revival, homos again provided some of the most iconic imagery. The homosexual neo-Nazi Nicky Crane, with his tall, taut frame, bald head and mean mug, became a skin poster boy. In one image, Crane is shown stomping, photographed from the sole of his boot. One hand makes a fist, the other foists an upturned index finger at the viewer. Used as the cover of an Oi! compilation album, it was then printed on t-shirts sold at the East London skinhead shop the Last Resort. The poster was tacked onto bedroom walls by teenage boys around the nation. This craze was vividly captured by fifteen-year-old photographer Gavin Watson when he snapped his little brother emulating Crane's bellicose posture in front of the poster at Oxford Circus.

As a ringleader in the far-right group the British Movement, Crane recruited young members and organized attacks. With a gang of over a hundred skins armed with iron bars, knives and pickaxe handles, he ambushed a queue of mostly black filmgoers at a cinema in southeast London. It's said he led a mob of two hundred in attacking Asians on Brick Lane, turning over market stalls and punching and kicking Pakistanis; beat a black family at a bus stop; struck Jews at a Remembrance Day event; stomped on a young leftist's head until it was unclear whether he was alive. He was in and out of jail. Even after Crane began working as a bouncer at Heaven, he remained a fascist, helping found Blood & Honour. There were raised eyebrows about his proclivities, but because he was brutal, he was left alone. In 1987, Crane was reported to be organizing a gay skins movement—meeting Friday nights at the London Apprentice. Eventually Crane became so nonchalant he turned up in gay porn—demanding men lick his boots as he shouted racial epithets. Finally he renounced fascism, and changed his look. ('I saw him riding around Soho in Day-Glo Lycra shorts,' Gavin Watson told the BBC. 'I thought, good for you.') Crane died of AIDS-related illness at the age of thirty-five in 1993, in a hospital in West London, a young man named Craig by his side.

Earlier that year, a black man had been set upon by three racist gay skinheads inside the LA. This exacerbated an impression that bar management was turning a blind eye to swastika armbands worn by customers, though at least one fascist skinhead claimed that they were expressly verboten. (Disturbingly, the custom of gay men aiming for authenticity meant that a punter with a fascist tattoo could pass as merely *passing for* a hooligan.) A boycott was called. The Lesbian and Gay Campaign Against Racism and Fascism picketed the club. A meeting was held between activists, landlady and customers, and a consensus reached that the venue wasn't liable for its fringe element. In John's words, *In such an anarchic clubhouse, it was hard to police anything.* Violence can lurk not only outside a gay bar's boundaries, but within.

———

Around 1998, the landlady of the London Apprentice changed the pub's name to its street number, 333, remaking it as a live music venue in a ten-day refit. *It was being turned into a straight club,* John explained. *They had pulled the sign down and left it on the footpath. This was during the day—workmen were inside. I remember walking past the sign and I thought…just have to grab it.*

So I went back and just picked it up and brought it back. It was very heavy. It was an impulse action that felt very right at that moment.

When it was hanging off the side of the building, swinging only in the strongest gusts, the apprentice was solitary. (Unless you count his double on the flip side—his clone. One is drawn in a much more rudimentary manner, either the rushed copy or the practice run.) Bracketed to the wall, the apprentice was a captive in some sense, like a bartender who is forced to listen to patrons as they fill up with drink. Finally, the apprentice was kidnapped—brought home by John, who intuited he needed to be spirited away to his people.

Famous and I have lived with the apprentice for more than a decade. (He leans against the wall, his better side facing out.) Recently, Famous mused: *There's something camp about him.* I balked. The sign is not priapic and overblown like Tom of Finland, or parodic like the Village People. If anything, it understates, and because of that could appear on the street simultaneously as code to a queer observer and banal to another passerby. I hadn't really considered that this is camp's methodology. A few days later, I happened upon Eve Kosofsky Sedgwick's definitions of *camp* and *kitsch*. I read aloud to Famous: the latter, Sedgwick says, is either designed by the unenlightened, or made to cynically manipulate the sentimentality of an unenlightened audience. 'Camp, on the other hand,' Sedgwick wrote, 'seems to involve a gayer and more spacious angle of view.' *That's it—spacious*, Famous enthused. To Sedgwick, a camp object asks 'what if the right audience for this were exactly *me?*...And what if, furthermore, others whom I don't know or recognize can see it from the same "perverse" angle?' Camp is an open secret.

Susan Sontag confirms—in number 17 of her canonical essay 'Notes on Camp': 'Behind the "straight" public sense in which something can be taken, one has found a private zany experience of the thing.' In note 51, Sontag proffers that homosexuals constitute the most articulate audience of camp. She adds parenthetically in her note 53: '(The Camp insistence on not being "serious," on playing, also connects with the homosexual's desire to remain youthful.)' Then there's the apprentice's hairstyle. In his book *Camp: The Lie That Tells the Truth*, Philip Core includes 'quiff' in his alphabetical list of things so camp they need no further explanation, alongside *'Querelle de Brest'* and 'quickie.'

The critic Susan Stewart writes, 'In all their uses, both *kitsch* and *camp* imply the imitation, the inauthentic, the impersonation.' The apprentice is making furniture, but what of himself is he *constructing*? The image casts doubt over authenticity itself. Authenticity attaches itself to working-class and rock-'n'-roll and skinhead identities and, so the narrative goes, inherently evades gay men, who, from the first indication that their flair is considered abhorrent, become lifelong impersonators of *real men*. Gay men are capable of not only unsettling gender roles, but exaggerating traditional masculinity unsettlingly. Sontag contrasts camp sensibility with the preciousness of the dandy, the nineteenth-century man of leisure whose engagement with urban life tends toward disaffected or snobbish. It's almost as though she had the crowd at the LA in mind when she wrote, 'Where the dandy would be continually offended or bored, the connoisseur of Camp is continually amused, delighted. The dandy held a perfumed handkerchief to his nostrils and was liable to swoon; the connoisseur of Camp sniffs the stink and prides himself on his strong nerves.' I take from Sontag that camp can be dangerous and raunchy.

Homophobia is instilled by not only gay as an absolute, a known quantity, but the capability of gay to subvert and surprise, to fool and to blur. It must be no coincidence that all those beatings occurred outside the London gay bar whose signage and clientele willfully twisted the iconography of the working male. No longer an invisibility cloak, masculine had become ostentatious. The *real man* had been perverted, by way of the sign and the bodies passing beneath. Each bashing outside the London Apprentice was an attack on the pretenses and failures of maleness—including, of course, the pretenses and failures of the attackers themselves.

———

When I think of the word *poseur,* the person who comes to mind is Walt Whitman. The American poet loved to lay down with farm boys but wasn't a homosexual, exactly. ('No, no, no,' in his words, plus the word *homosexual* wasn't used in English until 1892, the year of his death.) Eve Kosofsky Sedgwick called him a 'louche and pungent bouquet of the sheepish and the shrewd.' (He referred to himself as a furtive hen.) Whitman had a thing for sending his portrait along to correspondents and companions—'hang up my picture as that of the tenderest lover' goes one of the *Calamus* poems—so that he became a pinup on the walls of other men. His lust for laborers extended to a longing to inhabit their rough, loamy look, as in the frontispiece to the 1855 edition of *Leaves of Grass,* wherein he is depicted wearing coarse trousers and an open-collared, rumpled shirt. Whitman's friend William Roscoe Thayer called him 'a poseur of truly colossal proportions, one to whom playing a part had long before become so habitual that he ceased to be conscious that he was doing it.'

Then I think of how the word *poseur* was hurled at me when I was thirteen years old, on my first day of high school. When I heard it, *and it felt true*, I was led to believe that there must be some genuine thing I was failing at being. Whether the accusation was pointedly homophobic, to come up short of realness was tied up with the impression of homosexual chicanery. I was seen as inauthentic by this guy who'd elected himself border patrol. To be perceived as pretentious may be the greatest offense, and whatever I was pretending to be, his objection was about my presumed middle classness as much as my homosexuality. My crime: I was wearing an army-green, plain, but brand-new shirt with a label sewn into the cuff. My accuser made a show of pointing this out: my department store extravagance was clearly inferior compared with his stolid thrift store clothing. I covered the telltale label with my fingertips.

After school, I sat in the park across from campus, tearing at grass with two girls my age. An older crowd clumped under a nearby tree, a cloud of clove-scented smoke and fumes of Manic Panic hair dye wafting around them. Then the sole skinhead of the group approached. It took a moment to realize it was me he was addressing. He was tall and broad-shouldered, square-headed and amped-up, wearing a white t-shirt I could almost see through and cherry red Doc Martens boots, probably fourteen-eyelet. *I've been offered ten dollars to beat you up*, he announced. I looked over to the group. Laughing hardest was the boy who'd called me a poseur earlier that day, and I knew it was his idea. I thought I'd soon be pulp. I did nothing, glanced up at the skinhead, who inspected me like he couldn't decide what to do.

I considered how the boy under the tree who'd judged me to be an imposter held a view of the skinhead as a henchman. He presumed the skin could be hired to destroy me with his brutal working-class fist. It was quietly momentous for me, not only because I was scared I was about to be hurt, but because I was astonished by the financial transaction involved. The girls I was with had strong words to give, and they directed them to the decision makers under the tree. They went to the top. The skinhead walked away. He wore his thin elastic suspenders hanging down, so that they framed his butt like a jockstrap. As I watched him go, it struck me that of everyone, we two were somehow on the same level. I considered him to be, as much as a threat, in his own way humiliated. He was meant to puncture my inauthenticity with his realness, thereby cementing each position. Instead, in the end, he left both unresolved.

———

Famous and I resided in that flat in Shoreditch for seven years or so, longer than anywhere either of us had lived previously. Around 2015, the club at 333 Old Street restored the London Apprentice name. But it wasn't reverting to gay. It was now just some whatever bridge-and-tunnel place. The windows were opened up after all those years of concealment, revealing sports projected onto the wall and Ping-Pong tables. Staff would be stationed outside offering Jägerbombs to the punters arriving into the area on Essex trains.

The George and Dragon was remodeled, adding a loft from which the DJ would spin, and this had the unintentional effect of dulling the bonhomie in the room. The Joiners became known as a late night option for straight students on drugs and out-of-towners with an intense drive to have the best night of their lives, which is never going to end well. (The historian Seth Koven has uncovered midnight omnibus tours of the East End as far back as the 1880s. By 1893, *English Illustrated Magazine* ran an article on the question 'Is Slumming Played Out?,' its author outraged by rich people with literary preconceptions who complained the environs weren't slummy enough. East London has long elicited speculation over the profane and passé.) On the pavement in front of the Joiners, the Heineken-branded metal barrier was replaced by a red velvet rope, and a cover charge was introduced. The management issued some kind of card to people who could prove they lived locally. I never got one myself, because we just explained ourselves each time at the door and were generally waved through out of vague recognition. We had stayed too long at the party.

John was selling the flat, which was hardly surprising considering the property boom. We'd begun to give up on Shoreditch anyway: The pissoirs were rolled into Hoxton Square on Friday nights as large groups arrived for the weekend. The riled-up men wore button-up shirts with jeans and leather shoes. More than once I was awoken by a group of girls shouting Adele's 'Someone Like You' on the street after the clubs shut. By Sunday morning, Shoreditch was a soggy ashtray, the curbs littered with nitrous canisters. Vomit pooled at the base of historical brick walls.

We moved south of the river, where the lay of London is defined by a spectral quality, the neighborhoods strung together by large, wild graveyards. Undergraduates study Derridean hauntology at Goldsmiths University. We rented a flat near a cemetery in Brockley, an area as leafy and wholesome as its homonym. I emailed John and told him we were happy to remain caretakers of the sign—*for safekeeping*.

We rarely returned to Shoreditch. We did find ourselves there one late afternoon in November 2015, at the Ace Hotel for the launch party of the final issue of Sam Ashby's journal *Little Joe*. In the basement bar, I found Francis, whose eyes twinkle like Walt Whitman's, and interrogated him as to whether they were going someplace afterward. Francis informed me with a shrug that it was the last night before the George and Dragon closed for good, and everyone would head there soon. Though it probably shouldn't have, it came as a shock that the G&D was closing. It was the last remaining point in the Triangle. A while back we'd chanced upon the Nelsons Head with its windows shuttered like gay bars used to be to protect their patrons. The closure of the Joiners I caught wind of in the press. It became a big stink: the building was being razed, and a highly mobilized coalition formed to fight for it to be replaced by a community-led queer venue. Finally, the G&D had been slapped with an unaffordable rent increase. It seemed such a stalwart that it was unnerving to think it was only ever renting.

It rained. In the doorway at the G&D, we ran into Prince Nelly, who looked shell-shocked, and pulled him into an embrace. The G&D was always the night's amuse-bouche.

It was seldom salacious. However, there would inevitably be one pair of fresh-faced geeks having a big sloppy snog in a corner, elated to pair up so early in the night. And there they were: tonight's two boys clinging—the last of such couples, I figured, who I'd witness getting off there under the carrot-munching mule. One wore spectacles: he momentarily prized himself from the embrace in order to remove and desteam them.

The barroom was becoming crowded. We jostled against one another. Several of the sticky decorations had been taken down already. We thought we'd just have the one nostalgic beer with the tumbleweeds, but things were heating up—*like it used to be*, someone said. Everyone had come out of the woodwork. *I mean look at us*, I said to Famous, *two termites*. We chatted with an acquaintance who said he hadn't been there in ages, either, and that he'd texted Robbie, who might come later. But, I thought, we really should leave shortly. I couldn't stand the situation, like seeing a gay bar in hospice. I already had a headache from the lager. We were far removed from the boys we used to be.

It dawned on me that many of the people we used to know to say hello to we never really *knew*. We just enjoyed recognizing faces. *There's that tribal gypsy*, I pointed out. *He's finally cut off his dreads.* Famous said, *I'm glad he still looks like he lives in a squat, though.* There was the teutonic-looking woman with violently chopped hair, the husky fashion blogger in his belted trench coat, the silver fox with his newest twink. Later, the club kids would arrive, wearing inflatable collars and vinyl platform boots, along with the drag queens, dressed to set the scene of other people's experience. What was being lost as all the gay bars folded was that particular satisfaction of the company of strangers. The atmosphere relies on the presence of brand-new gays. Over the years, they'd continued to come—the freshly arrived, in a tailspin from pre-drinking, turning around like whippets trying to locate the bathroom. I knew when they finally found it, they'd encounter the juxtaposition of putrid toilet and high art, and also that they maybe wouldn't really process that as noteworthy. After all, I can't even recall my first gay bar. But I can remember being new to the scene.

And there's Jonjo. He was still blond and cherubic, still lovely. *You're leaving?* the Lovely Jonjo asked incredulously. He'd just arrived and was scheduled to DJ. *I want to get the place dancing,* he said plaintively. He said, *I remember when I first met you guys here. You came up and talked to me. I can't believe it: we have no place left. Where are we going to go?*

I was thinking: back to our flat in Zone 2, nearly Zone 3, where we cook vegetables procured at the Saturday market and comment on their intense reds and vivid greens. Our randiest neighbors are foxes, literally *Vulpes vulgaris*. They mate with ungodly wailing. I am intimately aware of the goings-on in a magpie nest I can watch from our bed; the daddy magpie defends his eggs with stentorian warnings delivered to local house cats. We've surmised that some-one living near us throws chemsex parties—according to Grindr, he's as close as twenty meters away—but we haven't determined exactly where the place is, and the one time we recognized the host in the street we were spooked. Basically, it's the neighborhood where gays go to retire.

From the swelling throng of the G&D, I posted a snapshot to Instagram. In it, a young man can be seen putting his fingers to forehead, a random gesture but it looks appropriately despondent. I saw that a friend who'd moved back to New York had already reposted somebody else's picture of the cardboard Divine effigy, now packed in bubble wrap. Several dozen *likes* within minutes, and one comment read: *It used to be our home.* We rode the Overground back to Brockley, itchy with sugary beer. *It used to be our home:* the comment stayed with me. *Was* it my home—did it *used to be?*

The next day, I happened to read some lines from Proust, in which the narrator opined that being among strangers on holiday compelled him to care again about making an impression, reignited his desire to see and be seen, made him want 'to please others and to possess them.' He pitied those holidaymakers who, by insisting on not mingling between classes, denied themselves 'the disquieting delights of mixing with unknown company.' I reconsidered how people are wont to call their regular gay bar a home. To me a good gay bar is a vacation, promising the novelty of a resort full of strangers, making me want 'to please others and to possess them.'

Several weeks later, early in the new year, we stayed on a large forested property in northern California—a former commune that had been purchased by an artist. He had turned it into a living art project and informal residency. One night at dinner, the closure of the George and Dragon came up in conversation. The artist was familiar with it: *Such a shame,* he said. *It was such a community.* I could sense Famous shifting like I did. The artist said, *In London you have such a great queer community.* The G&D was so familiar to us, and made a brilliant footnote in the area's history. But I couldn't relate to this widely held notion of community. We hear the word *community* all the time. Often it sounds like wishful thinking. *Queer community* is just as vague—just piling a confusing identity onto an elusive concept. *Maybe community*, as Famous says, *excludes inherently*. At the word *community*, both of us are prone to hear *clique*. And here, in densely wooded headlands at the edge of the Pacific, the term was being thrown around to describe a London gay bar, several thousand miles away. Imagining London, I saw not one big queer coterie, but different people moving in different directions, entropic. I thought of amiable moments I shared with nurses or people who worked in local shops. They came to mind clearly. A queer community I couldn't picture.

The day before, the Irish social historian Iain Boal had arrived to tour the property. He'd said something that stuck with me—that language is doomed to fail, but metaphor can help explain things. *Community* was the word that had consistently failed for me. So: Could I solve it through metaphor? If the word *community* is indeed a failure of vocabulary—too broad, too utopian—perhaps the metaphor to best replace it is *metaphor itself*. Disparate objects are brought together, alike in some, but not all, respects; in fact, metaphor edifies and amuses when things are vastly dissimilar in all ways but one. I'd like to think we can be different together—even *homos*, ostensibly the *same*.

The commonality I experienced in the G&D, or in any given bar, is tenuous and fleeting. The staff will be intimately familiar with one another, of course, but what they serve to the rest of us, even the barflies, is the opposite of routine. Gay bars require strangers, a constant influx of immigrants, whose presence foreshadows the next morning's regret. A gay bar is the idea that you may end up going home with the first hot guy you see. Then every drink is dopamine, as you determine whether it is him or the next guy you'll see. Gays can relax in a gay bar, people will say, but I went out for the tension in the room. Perhaps you could call a gay bar a galaxy: we are held together but kept from colliding by a fine balance of momentum and gravity. I miss, more than any notion of community, the orbiting.

THE BORDERS

I was so nervous walking into this nightclub. I'd never been to a nightclub before. And what I thought would happen, this is quite naive maybe, but I thought I was this new guy in town, and somebody, at least one person, would approach me and tell me who I am.

—Simon Amstell, 2019

Somewhere along the line I became a daddy. I'm pretty sure that no longer means daddy issues. It has been re-defined as men exploring one another, and not necessarily across wide age gaps. Daddiness still denotes masc, but now that's more open to interpretation. Instagram tells me you can be a teenage cheerleader and get called daddy. I can definitely be one. Maybe *daddy* smashes the patriarchy.

For a while, a pale young man in our neighborhood liked to text the emoji of two dads with one son to us. If he's polymorphously perverse, it's in a low-maintenance way. He is clever and droll, and each time he came over he'd lose his millennial nose ring in the cauliflower furrows of our renters' carpet. He wouldn't let me top him because, in his words, anal sex requires *too much admin*. More theoretically, he inter-rogates the overemphasis on anal sex, and the myth of the transformational nature of losing one's prostate virginity. *Anal sex*, he sighs, *is so heteronormative*. To demonstrate esprit de corps, I shared with him how another young man made me pull out before informing me: *Your penis is lovely, but it's not without its flaws*. The admin twink cackled and, pulling on a pair of wide pale jeans, snapped, *That's so true*. These boys don't need my wisdom. Camaraderie, perhaps; it's not guidance they're after. I texted him the link to a 1987 essay by Leo Bersani, 'Is the Rectum a Grave?' He texted back: *Ooooh. Don't tell me how it ends.*

'In the queer world, memory is very fragile,' Michael Warner once stated. 'You don't learn from your parents how the gay world is structured. So there's not a whole lot of intergenerational transfer.' That's one argument for preserving gay bars. In a *Guardian* article published as UK closures were peaking in 2015, Ben Walters quoted a twenty-year-old student and North London gay bar regular: 'You can end up talking to a gay man in his sixties and learn so much about gay history and culture. It's like your nan passing on wisdom.' To the British, pubs can be like a town hall or church, so the social value of a gay version doesn't require a big leap.

Americans may be less cozy about their sins. Where I grew up in the suburbs, bars were shunned locations. Therefore, bars stigmatize gay as much as the reverse. In 2016, after the massacre at Pulse, a college student from Louisiana penned an editorial in the *Huffington Post* titled 'Gay Bars Were Never a Safe Space.' Young people, he contended, aren't allowed into such venues in the first place, and once they are mature enough, they encounter, let's face it, a *bar*, not a sanctuary: 'they're thrown into a pen where the majority of older, queer individuals they meet want to simply get them drunk and fuck them. Because gay bars are idolized as places of acceptance and love, these queer youth flock towards these spaces that are more dangerous for the unsuspecting than we admit.' Though that doesn't mirror my own experience (of being desperate for someone to get me drunk and fuck me) I take his point. The young see the gay world's structures, including the flaws, and are not necessarily inclined to maintain the old gay ways. They're not apprentices, but upsetters.

If a twink were to ask about my first gay bar, I'd confess it may be a confabulation. I'd muse that I'm unsure what qualifies as a gay bar. They were never one thing. But whichever it was—the ex–gay bar, gossipy coffeehouse, past-its-glory nightclub—I can testify it was disappointing. Gradually, I learned to give in to the experience for what it is: tacky but effervescent, artificial, cutthroat, *cringe*. I discovered that gay bars are about potentiality, not resolution. Gay bars are not about arriving. The best ones were always a departure.

The last time I saw that wicked son of ours we ran into him at a screening of African films at the South London Gallery. He'd had an afterwork drink already at an old pub in town I'd never heard of—*not but kind of gay*. He joined us for dinner. I paid the bill, and he offered to get us a drink across the street at the Chateau, a feisty little 'pop-up gay bar' that was operating in a cellar fitted with stained-glass light boxes imported from Italy. (It was formerly a wine bar with a holy communion theme—each order came with a wafer.) The ceilings are so low it forced the drag queens to slouch, and the voguing invariably went horizontal on the floor. This gave the place an atmosphere.

When we got to the door, they were charging a cover to support the queers, and we hesitated. Our son took a call from his new boyfriend. They made a quick plan to meet at his house, he relayed, because the boyfriend's phone was low on battery. He hugged us goodbye, whispering, *Let's get together we have an open relationship I'll text you*. Famous and I went to the straight pub across the street, rammed with young skaters and old geezers, and were momentarily remorseful about not supporting the queers. My phone lit up: it was the boy texting the two dads emoji. I wondered to myself how often he went to gay bars, if at all. Surely it wasn't formative to him the way it was for me. Then again, there was the young man I kissed in the corner of the marquee at a middle-aged wedding. (*We'd better stop, the straight people won't understand,* he said.) I'd mentioned my inquiry into whether gay bars are still necessary. *Of course they are,* he'd snapped affably. He worked at one.

The caustic son we'd met on Grindr, of course. He is, as he puts it, one of the many sickly-looking twinks living in our mellow neighborhood. Around the time Famous and I settled down in South London, it seemed the whole image of homosexuality had chilled out. *Cozy queer,* Famous would joke when yet another biography of a notable gay from history came on BBC radio. (They never mention the dark rooms, just their knack for gardening.) In the first year we moved to the area, on some summer nights, Famous and I would sit in the grass of our park and contemplate going to a gay bar. But we'd just take a stroll instead. When ride-hailing apps became a thing, we got into the habit of going out on occasion knowing we could get home cheap. We went out to be a part of the world again. We went out seeking release.

Hannah and Rosie live around the corner. The two artists have probably been to more gay bars in the nation than anyone. They made a name for themselves setting up one-night gay bars in their studio under the name *@gaybar*, replete with stainless-steel fixtures, custom light boxes and real-glass glasses—plus the tatty rainbow flag from the Joiners Arms. For their project *UK Gay Bar Directory*, completed in 2016, the pair visited over one hundred venues and filmed them while empty. Of course as a young female couple they faced skepticism; sometimes they'd go in wanting to celebrate a place only to be rejected by its gatekeepers. What they did document accumulated in a nearly five-hour video montage. Hannah and Rosie have spoken about how identity is not just inscribed on our bodies, but articulated in the places we inhabit. If our habitats are extensions of ourselves, these empty gay bars are cast-off exoskeletons. The footage draws attention to how a room is both more and less itself when unpeopled. Most of the interiors look cold—glowing purple, with roving lights that make the barroom ripple like an aquarium, fitted with pink vinyl couches and legless z-shaped bent plastic stools. The artists film the gayest of things: rainbow flags; metallic curtains; a strobing palm-tree lamp; flyers hectic with information about club nights, hate incidents and safer sex; obscene graffiti; a Sweetie, darling! stencil above a framed menu of shooter cocktails; a backdrop reading Bitch please! on a tiny stage under sequenced LED lights; a cloud rushing in from a smoke machine.

The barscapes are at once spectral and pathetic. Tracks by Luther Vandross, Alicia Keys, Erasure and ABBA heard in the background warp into echoes and are then enveloped by field recordings of melting icebergs and monsoons. The hyperbolic analogy with global warming suggests it's our shared duty to position the relevance of anything in the context of the climate crisis. As long as humans survive, there will be social spaces, and they will contain hierarchies negotiated in terms of power and exclusion. When Hannah and Rosie score their gay bars with sounds of the end of the earth, it makes me think: Will there be gay bars in outer space? Identity is articulated through the places we occupy, but both are constantly changing.

When I mentioned I was writing about gay bars, they told me right away to go to Blackpool. I knew that the low-rent northern seaside spot had long been a destination for gays to party. Based on their enthusiasm, I figured they found the place to be the real deal, meaning genuine kitsch. They told me that the bars there were filled with older people and women, an unusual mix, unlike anyplace else. When I saw them again and mentioned we'd bought the train tickets, they reminded me that Growlr, the men-only club, was held above Man Bar. Growlr shares the name of the hookup app for bears. I suppose, as with Grindr, dropping the *e* is contemporary gay sexy, the linguistic evolution but aesthetic opposite of that nineties move of spelling plurals with a z.

In Blackpool, nearly everyone was as white as a seagull's belly. Census reports indicate less than five percent of Blackpool residents are not. Some are actually burnished red, or gray from nicotine. An emaciated woman who stumbled toward us along the concrete steps of the north shore was alarmingly green. At first I thought she'd painted herself that way, like a Kathakali dancer, then wondered what cheap drugs she'd been taking. It was a Saturday at the end of September and a rare occasion of unclouded sky. A sunbather with skin as bright pink as her hair spilled a premixed cocktail out of a plastic bottle in the shape of a palm tree. The puddle she straddled was preternaturally blue. *Toxic,* she pronounced. When she discovered it had saturated her spliff, she added, *I've nothing to live for. Throw me into the sea.* This was delivered to a mannish woman I took to be her partner, who chortled.

The population of Blackpool has been declining since 2001. There are high rates of depression, obesity, smoking and liver disease. In the city's poorest ward, men have the lowest life expectancy of any in the country. The week we were there, the BBC announced that eight of the nation's ten most deprived neighborhoods were in Blackpool. In 2016, over sixty-seven percent of its voters cast their ballots to leave the European Union, returning the largest majority in the North West region. In Blackpool, the line seemed to be: there may be nothing to live for, but at least you can always hurl yourself into the sea. It wasn't up to me to determine if the intention is to drown or prove you can swim. There, I glimpsed an Anglo national identity articulated on the esplanade and in karaoke bars—a dignity in mess, resilience, a binge-drinking stiff upper lip, the art of salting the chip on your shoulder. What I hadn't anticipated was how this identity could also be so gay.

At night, the gulls were lit from below by the signage of nightclubs and arcades, and the humans also took on glints of the town's neon as they darted across streets or stood smoking. On arrival, I pulled our suitcase on wheels from the train station through a residential neighborhood made remarkable only by the signs indicating that many of the terrace houses were actually small hotels, and of those several included some semblance of a gay bar in the lobby. They are called Legends or Chaps or the Prince Albert. Guests may be treated to amenities such as two bags of Haribo on the bed and a bottle of Rush on the adjacent sling. Famous pointed out a hotel called Trades, with a baleful facade and members-only sign. I've read that another local guest house briefly called itself the Viagra ('We will keep you up all night!') until a horrified mother went to the press, the council intervened and the proprietor facetiously switched the name to Niagra ('We will keep you wet all night!').

Peek-a-Booze, our first gay bar in Blackpool, was heaving. I moved through the crowd sideways, new in town and ready to be appreciated. But the few eyes that caught mine were indifferent. Above us was a low grid of flame-resistant tiles, an office ceiling. The barroom floor and stage were fitted in tartan carpet, with a linoleum dance floor between. I ordered two gin and sodas. *Doubles,* the butch bartender assumed. *Singles,* I replied. She shot me a look of mock disapproval. I corrected myself. *Any fruit?* she asked over the giant goblets. I could only think of lime, which further disappointed her. She threw in some juniper berries. Neither could I think of anything to add to meet the credit card minimum. *Shooters!* she proclaimed, gesturing to a display of tiny bottles behind her in an array of shocking hues. We opted to add another gin and soda. On the stage behind us, a man in a metallic top under a denim jacket stood in front of a twinkling curtain, singing a slightly off-key rendition of 'Grace Kelly' by Mika. When the singer went into falsetto to hit the octave jump, the bartender mouthed along spiritedly. I happened to have seen a young drag queen perform the same song onstage at the Royal Vauxhall Tavern not long before. While their avant-garde clown makeup and stunning vocal range was objectively more impressive, it was here that I suddenly, as if for the first time, heard the lyrics. Apparently 'Grace Kelly' is a song about going *identity mad*, which entails the attempt to mimic iconic celebrities, then exploring all the colors one could be: brown or blue or—octave jump—*violet sky*....

Famous and I found a place in a corner, standing at a tall table. I dumped half of the third drink into each of our glasses. *Triples,* I said. Bald men in tight t-shirts stood around us in cliques of three. Less predictably, at large tables along the far wall were groups in a wide range of ages, genders and body types. They faced toward the dance floor and stage wearing expressions like residents at a retirement home, at once unimpressed and content. A variety of people wearing mother-of-the-bride dresses sipped through straws. A diminutive woman in a wheelchair wore a top hat with a glittery skull sash around the brim, while her giant companion donned a ruffled shirt and high black boots. The place seemed to perform multiple functions at once: village hall, working-men's club, trans support group, senior citizens center. Middle-aged cross-dressers moved through in tea party frocks with no attempt to transform their heavy gait. The singer had moved on to Bob Marley, informing the room that everything was going to be all right. When he took a break, a drag queen DJ put on 'Together in Electric Dreams.' Groups of women danced with evangelical arms. A pair of transvestites fell into an embrace at the word *together.* A small guy with a crew cut and cocky swagger, wearing a shiny black tracksuit and black polo buttoned all the way up—a Blackpool tuxedo, maybe—squeezed through. The bartender who'd poured our big drinks walked past collecting glasses. She goosed a woman she knew, and they broke into laughter.

A club around the corner beckoned with a long illuminated sign box reading *it's a gay thing!* It was nearly empty and smelled of stale cleaning solvents. I watched as the teenage bartender attempted to impress his female colleague by hocking a loogie onto the wall over the sink. Down the street, the Flying Handbag was more upbeat. There were wooden tables and booths on either side of the central bar, sprawling like a restaurant in the American suburbs. But it was a distinctly Blackpool trope when the chubby drag queen DJ picked up the microphone midsong to toss out sardonic comments. I couldn't understand anything she said, as her northern idioms rumbled against the grille of the mic. I thought a pair of conferring lads resembled Famous and myself until it dawned we hadn't been that young for ages.

At Man Bar, we ordered a drink from a bartender who stood with pride in front of some eighty different brands of gin. We then gave cash to a boy at the end of the counter, who handed us each a paper wristband granting admission into the cruising club, Growlr, and took the stairs. It was almost a gentlemen's parlor, with its stuffed furniture and wood cabinets, the size of a standard two-bedroom apartment. Objects were suspended from the ceiling: skinhead braces, handcuffs, jockstraps, football shorts, a deck of playing cards. We peeked into a side room with metal gym lockers and walls painted gaffer-tape gray, with hi-vis gear and hard hats dangling overhead. The foyer was fitted with a velvet settee, painted with tree murals and strung with camouflage netting. A rifle case was mounted to the wall; boots, rucksacks and camo overclothes dangled from the ceiling. This was a perverse homage to the homophobic father of Barry, the leatherman who once managed the bar. As Hannah and Rosie had heard it, Barry's father had been imprisoned for attempting to shoot his mother with a hunting gun. Barry had cut the crotches out of his dad's trousers and strung them above the private booths. *Queer talismans*, Hannah and Rosie thought, but Barry explained it as the best revenge he could think of.

It was a very Caucasian room. The Union Jack bunting I found ostracizing; the American flag made me feel no more welcome. On a high shelf, a green wooden sign spelled 'Cocktail Bar' in golden gothic lettering. A pair of black bovver boots with white laces was placed centrally in front of it, leaving only 'Cock Bar' visible. On the far end of the club was the maze. At its threshold, we got the impression of how tiny it was—truncated down to its dead ends. A few men bumped around without much room to maneuver, and we couldn't bring ourselves to enter.

Instead, we took seats on a circular bench facing a porn of beautiful young Slovak men. I wondered how often the locals had anonymous sex here. Tourists surely passed through, but generally the men—already a dozen or so present—were chatting away with a familiarity that made the sex club setup seem more decorative trope than fit for purpose. The delirium meant to fill a cruise bar was acknowledged rather than experienced. A notice prohibited drugs and sex. Growlr was, it asserted, *a cruising and posing club only*. Still, out of habit, I broke a blue pill in two, and we each washed down half with our gin.

Just as we were swallowing, a man swooped onto the bench next to Famous. *Are you two together?* he asked. We nodded. He looked at me. *Can I spend some time alone with him?* He pointed at Famous. *NO*, I snapped vehemently. He began to speak to Famous anyway. He rambled about being from a small town in Yorkshire, and how there was nothing going on there. *And I'm not gay*, he said. *Oh, wait*, he corrected himself. *I actually am. I keep forgetting*. The man alluded to Trades, the sketchy-looking hotel we'd noticed earlier in the evening. According to him, the dark room there was even darker. *You can't see anything at all*, he reported. I pretended to watch the actors rimming each other on the TV.

We wrangled ourselves away, moving through a group of middle-aged men in tight Fred Perry polos. The alpha slipped his hand onto my ass. Famous and I peeked into the locker room again, surprised by a group of passably attractive young men in a confab around a table. None looked up. They seemed to be playing a card game without cards. We landed on the velvet settee under the dangling field sports gear. We'd reached an impasse: I fumed that Famous had blithely led the creep on. Famous explained he hadn't heard the man ask my permission to take him away, and thought him harmless. Couples in gay bars is a tricky thing. Jealousy and envy can entangle so that they can't be told apart.

An attractive young black guy made himself known to the room. He glanced back a couple of times as he slipped out onto the smoking terrace. Through the glass door, the man and I looked at each other, him smoking silently, me in heated discussion with Famous. Back inside, he passed the pack in polo shirts, and the alpha grabbed him. I registered the fact that he and I were the only two nonwhites in the room, and wondered if that coincided with this man's entitlement to our bodies. I thought about what each of us represented to the other. That Union Jack bunting taunted me, and each of the other objects around us appeared totemic of patriarchy, maybe even white supremacy.

We left for some fresh air, moving toward the seafront past a windowless building flying a rainbow flag, with a dull light box proclaiming it a men's sauna. It gave no sign of life, not even steam piped into the air. We took the concrete steps down to the water. The ocean was black in the night. Looking back at the town, I saw the signs advertising fish and chips, and knew we'd have to get some greasy potatoes eventually to absorb the gin. But for now we stood apart on two different levels looking over the inscrutable sea.

At breakfast, the hotel proprietor, a pocket-size septuagenarian, greeted us in waistcoat and tie, as in his portrait over the grand piano. He deftly pulled our dining chairs out for us and brought thick coffee in a silver pot. Famous had chosen a classy place. A grandfather clock ticked reassuringly and the heavy fragrance of a huge bouquet hung in the air. A classical music station played. The commercials broke the calm, and each seemed to mention Brexit. Two middle-aged couples, straight and gay male, were already eating. Each of the men wore a patterned button-up shirt. I was ashamed to be in trackies and a cap. At least I'd pulled off the Growlr wristband. I took off my cap and hung it on the ear of the chair. The cabinet behind Famous was filled with an impressive array of dustless English porcelain, including the classic pair of Staffordshire King Charles Spaniels. They rattled when a paunchy man entered the breakfast room. I thought he could be the troublemaker who'd approached Famous at Growlr. He had that same butternut-squash face shape. *I think I saw you two out last night,* he said. *You,* he pointed at Famous, *you definitely passed me at the Flying Handbag.* He snorted. We affirmed we'd been there. *Didn't get any better,* he grunted. We tried to be chirpy, saying what a nice night we'd had. *Nobody around,* he said. *Maybe it'll be better tonight. But it gets depressing, doesn't it. No young people left. You need young people. They're gone. Moved. Or on their phones. I don't know. You need that energy. You just sit there alone. Nobody to talk to. So you just sit there, staring at the door.*

In Blackpool, we kept missing spectacles. Arriving on Friday night, we were just too late for Ukraine's bid in an international fireworks competition. The next evening, the Blackpool Illuminations dazzled the seafront, but we were in an Italian restaurant under a ceiling painted dark blue and inset with tiny twinkling bulbs like a starry sky. Neither did we ever get far enough south to see the giant disco ball, which balances on a pole like a golf ball on a tee. It's claimed the disco ball was the world's biggest until it was bested by one at a musical festival in 2014. Blackpool's spans twenty feet in diameter, revolving ten feet above the ground, comprising forty-six thousand mirrors and weighing four and a half tons.

There is a more humble disco ball suspended in the center of the grand art deco theater where the cabaret Funny Girls takes place. There are a few more on either side of the stage, which is set high off the ground with a full bar running its length in lieu of an orchestra pit, staffed by drag queens. The reigning queen, Zoe, is compere and DJ, stationed beneath her name in glitter, stage right. Famous and I wound up sitting in a luxurious box in the upper circle. A switch occurred after a middle-aged man made gruffly clear we were unwelcome in our assigned box, which we were meant to share with him and his wife and another heterosexual pair. It's true it would have been a tight squeeze, but we plaintively held aloft the tickets that proved we belonged in the two empty seats. The usher had no time for my complaint that the man was being homophobic. A younger straight couple on the level above noticed the scenario and pointed out the plush chairs across from them had been vacated. We made a big show of settling in there.

The cabaret was a spectacle of energetic musical numbers on elaborate sets. The star attraction is Betty Legs Diamond, whose pirouettes and high kicks are especially impressive given she's been doing them for decades. 'Do Re Mi' was a standout number. Then Betty Legs Diamond did a goose step with index-finger Hitler mustache. *That's an English classic,* Famous explained at my puzzlement. Drag here was less gay, more working class, British, comic. It was drag in the sense of the folk etymology that Shakespeare's marginalia read *Dressed Resembling a Girl.* It was drag as if spoken in Polari—the British cant slang often called the gay language but also a lingua franca among fairground showmen, wrestlers, sailors, criminals. Here, drag was populist. It did not aspire to high fashion like the New York City ball scene, or to the avant-garde as with new Instagram look queens.

In between each number, the audience was on its feet. 'Saturday Night' by Whigfield would play. Behind us, a half-dozen buxom young women in schoolgirl uniforms did the 'Cha Cha Slide.' Friends shimmied together to Tina Turner's 'Proud Mary.' DJ Zoe periodically sent out birthday and engagement wishes to the crowd. Famous marched downstairs through the theater twice to hand her a slip of paper with my name and 'Freedom! '90' by George Michael written on it, but Zoe never honored the dedication request. *This isn't really gay, is it?* I finally asked. Famous gamely pointed out a few gay men here and there in the stalls. *But, no, it isn't*, he agreed.

It was, in a way—just a gay that was no longer mine, or never belonged to me, *gay* as in *gaiety*. After the show, we danced between the bachelorette parties dressed as cheerleaders and vamps, the buxom schoolgirls. (As Bus Station John once put it, 'drag queens are catnip to the "woo" chicks.') Now drag is everyone's escapism—perhaps more like it used to be. Camp is the stuff of wedding receptions. Doing the 'YMCA' is a first-world coping mechanism. Overidentifying with the diva vocals of spurned women is no longer the sole prerogative of gay men. Looking around as I danced to ABBA and the Spice Girls, apparently the ladies were overidentifying with the ladies, too. Gay appropriations coming full circle—a mindfuck. The loot we pillaged has been plundered.

Funny Girls was closing. I was sure the bachelorette parties would be spilling into the bars across the street, my guess was most of them to the one that announced *it's a gay thing!* We went back to Man Bar, as if to go full gay, true man-on-man gay, paying again for the wristbands to go upstairs to Growlr, where we resumed our places on the settee under the woebegone dangling objects. I'd later find out that Hannah and Rosie returned to Blackpool multiple times—to film, but also with the intention of interviewing Barry, whose father's possessions hung above us. But Barry wasn't working at Growlr anymore, and nobody knew of his whereabouts. Eventually, Hannah and Rosie found out that he'd suffered a violent assault after his drink was spiked in one of the hotels. This put him into the hospital for months, then drove him off grid.

I pestered Famous to stop for a nightcap at Peek-a-Booze. The assembled crowd was a hodgepodge like the previous evening. A woman in a Happy 60th sash flashed me a broad, gurninglike grin. When I attempted to smile back, her face dropped. She and her entourage eased into a floor-bound conga line, in which they rocked back and forth on their thighs and asses. Famous and I stood together at a tall table, where I annoyed myself thinking of Theodor Adorno's 1944 Marxist treatise: 'Amusement under late capitalism is the prolongation of work.' It seemed to me that we still partied in that way—Saturday night getting us through the week. 'Pleasure,' Adorno and Max Horkheimer wrote, 'hardens into boredom because, if it is to remain pleasure, it must not demand any effort and therefore moves rigorously in the worn grooves of association.' The group on the floor barely scooched forward to the bass of 'Uptown Funk.'

People do need relief…, I sighed. *When you're in the grind, when you work full-time…* I struggled for the words. *I understand,* Famous said. *It's bread and circuses…and yet, god, who could deny anyone their circus?* And at some point, the circus went gay. Camp is a bright-pink succor amid the grind. Gay is the opium of the people. We once flattered ourselves that all popular culture was subversively designed to amuse gay men. It's become apparent gay men are there to make popular culture amusing to everybody else.

We've been entertaining the people for years. Current iterations include *The Graham Norton Show* in the UK and *RuPaul's Drag Race,* now pretty much everywhere. I was a personal assistant to RuPaul for a few days, back when I was a student in L.A. He was filming a pilot in which he played a superhero drag queen. I walked alongside him, arm stretched to its limit, holding a parasol to shade RuPaul as he headed onto set. *Work the sidewalk, sweetie,* he'd say. In his trailer, he handed me his video camera and asked me to interview him. I didn't know the rules of interviewing: that you start with a compliment and a softball. I asked: *What would you say to people who accuse you of selling out?* RuPaul inhaled in surprise. *Honey, if you're buying, I'm selling,* he retorted. His expression returned to its usual detached appraisal. *Now give me the camera, sweetie.* This comes back to me because of how he kept to his line: RuPaul is very entrepreneurial. The success of *Drag Race* has given a lift to gay bars in cities globally because performances by former contestants draw big crowds. In this sense, he's put back into *the community.* It must also be one of the reasons that gay bars are now a domain of young women. They're fans of the show. Audience sympathy for the struggle of the contestants, thanks to deft editing, is strong. A couple of years back, when we were headed to Brighton for the weekend and I checked ahead for gay bars that might appeal to us, I kept thinking they were all lesbian until I realized the crowd photos were of young *Drag Race* fans.

At Peek-a-Booze, people were letting loose through secondary gayness. The act of crashing the gay party — latching on to another culture's mode of escapism—is easy to critique as appropriation and exploitation. We earned our rainbow stripes by putting up with hard rain. Famous and I often return to a conversation about lived experience. It must mean something to share similar memories of being treated as *less than*, the specific humiliation of having limp wrist and lisp corrected, the constant threats by bullies, the hope there will always be somebody gayer in the room to take the heat. When a straight person says *I'm basically a gay man*, my first thought is *But you didn't go through the hazing*.

The act of latching on to other people's escapism *is* appropriation and exploitation. It is *othering*, even and especially when it thinks that it's not. I know this well; it infiltrates the minutiae of all kinds of ordinary interactions, like when straight acquaintances speak to me *in a gay way* to demonstrate we are having fun and on the same page about it. Whenever they cry *Yasss, queen*, it's hard not to take it as mocking. But affectation has also been, in many cases, precisely what gay men are peddling. We anoint one another *queen*, say *sister* and *girl* in endearment. The reality is, people speak in other people's terms. People let off steam vicariously. At what point does 'YMCA' not belong to the gays anymore? We took the lyrics to mean YMCA as the place for gay men to seek refuge and cruise one another in the big city of the seventies. Now it's just a catchy initialism. It trips off the tongue and lends itself to arm poses. We each submit in our own way to narratives of emergence and triumph over adversity. Gays don't have the patent on butterflies and rainbows. (Though some, with the latter, have tried.) The connection to a lyric may be no less meaningful to another pining listener. There's a visceral catharsis that comes with shouting along to 'I'm Coming Out' by Diana Ross, no matter where you're coming from. (Think of how it's common parlance to call Diana Ross a gay icon, meaning she's an icon *for the gays;* we can't put that kind of claim on a person and not let different kinds of people sing along to our stories, too.)

For some reason, Blackpool is an epicenter of these cross-connections. It seems like everybody goes to the gay bars there, bringing along their own personal strife to release. There's something about the place that propagates not just cross-dressing but cross-identification. The DJ Ian Levine, born in Blackpool to casino owners, made an extraordinary career based on such joys. At the Blackpool Mecca in the seventies, Levine helped cultivate Northern Soul—the British movement of dancing to African American rhythm and blues, often after taking copious amounts of speed. It became a way of life: escapist, maybe, and destructive, perhaps, but to know the music and how to move to it was a serious pursuit. It was a way of not just coping but of seeing the world. Levine brought into his mix obscure tracks with a shuffling, hypnotic beat. Because he was wealthy, Levine traveled to the States frequently; because he was gay, he went dancing at the Saint in New York City. Back in Blackpool, Levine introduced disco, a move that ruptured the Northern Soul scene.

At the Saint, the stamina-testing disco marathons were reminiscent of the amphetamine-fueled Northern Soul all-nighters, but with added gym-sculpted pecs and the weekend bender ending with men naked at New St. Marks Baths. Levine collaborated with the singer Miquel Brown, cowriting 'So Many Men, So Little Time'—and then 'Close to Perfection' especially for the Saint's early morning sleaze set. Moving to London, Levine used the energy of the Saint as a blueprint for his DJ sets at Heaven. Though the latter never reached the transcendence of the legendary New York club, it became a platform from which Levine pioneered the hi-NRG production sound. Hi-NRG, in turn, influenced teenybopper hits of the eighties—hyperactive singles by acts like Bananarama and Kylie Minogue produced by Stock, Aitken and Waterman. (*The Guardian* dubbed the team Schlock, Aimless and Waterdown.) The gay roots of pop culture is an embattled terrain of making the people happy and being readily dismissed as insipid.

———

Back in London a few weeks later, I screamed along until I lost my voice to a drag queen's rendition of Erasure's 'A Little Respect' at the Two Brewers in South London. In a room full of gay men, it was as though our collective trauma was being exorcised by the female impersonator and the synthesizers. A drag queen—a good drag queen—is not there to mock women, but to transcend the limitations of masculinity. A gay bar crowd—a good gay bar crowd—works the dance floor in a spirit of solidarity. Maybe, I thought, I'm a disco ball. I used to go out for attention. Now I only want to catch the light of the scene and throw glints back across the room.

Earlier that night, a woman demanded to borrow Famous's straw hat as a prop she could wear for a quick gay bar selfie. When Famous sharply turned her request down, she pleaded. Famous was triggered. (He happens to have an unhappy hat story.) Her continued persistence was a minor, maybe harmless incident. But both of us found ourselves wanting to say: An ally is there to join, not conquer. We aren't here to lend you props for a makeshift micro-appropriation. You can party with us, but give us a little respect.

Some things that are borrowed *feel* real. Like the Sylvester anthem—how *feeling* real can be a *good enough* mode of facing reality. It would be a betrayal of gayness for me to stomp around like authenticity police. We've always *troubled* authenticity. Not to mention, Famous's straw hat was made in Morocco, hardly his native costume to protect. He bought that signifier on Etsy. Still, he'll flinch if you try to take it off his head. Gays built a culture on the art of imitation. We formed an identity on the longing embedded in *feeling real*—on embracing that feeling, and refusing to accept realness as it's been constructed for us. That longing may be, for me anyway, at the crux of being gay. Going to the gay bar has always been about the expectation, the titivating at the mirror beforehand. Gay is false hopes and pre-drinking. Gay is backstage. I'm all for nongays coming along to this party. But those who want to *feel* gay should know something of the legacy of that *feeling*. It goes pretty deep.

Over the past couple of years, I've noticed standard pubs around South London have begun hoisting rainbow flags. At the sight of the first one, which I passed regularly on the bus, I turned different scenarios over in my head: Maybe it had been flown for Pride month and never taken down. Then other pubs started doing the same—huge ones, in the front window, repeated as bunting across the room, as stickers on the front door. It's hard to imagine that only fifteen years back, the Westminster City Council ordered all gay bars in Soho to remove their rainbow flags. They look so wholesome now, like they have a positive attitude, and a bit corporate, too. I presumed with these straight pubs it was a sign of inclusivity, but wasn't that laying it on a bit thick? Famous developed a theory: Maybe the flags weren't just inviting us in, but keeping certain other types at bay. Maybe the flag, which once proclaimed what a bar is, now proclaims what it isn't—a place for hooliganism, violence, machismo. We don't want trouble here, the flag now signals. *Cheaper than a bouncer,* Famous says.

We went back to the Royal Vauxhall Tavern, to attend a cabaret and disco to benefit a group called Lesbians and Gays Support the Migrants. Its name riffs on the mid-eighties activist group Lesbians and Gays Support the Miners, frequently upheld as an exemplary and amusing ('pits and perverts') instance of coalition politics—and the one which induced the Labour Party to take gay civil rights seriously. Playing off *miners* and *migrants* is doubly impactful in that it's a transversal across two blocks—entrenched blue-collar labor and arrivals from foreign countries—which certain media and politicians strategically position as adversaries.

When we arrived, an Irish lad with a nose ring was reciting 'Admin,' his spoken word piece about the tension between his Marxist ideologies and compulsion to purchase char-coal supplements and sunlight alarm clocks. Next, a mature woman in a suffragette costume came to the microphone and delivered a limerick about dildos in a plummy accent.

From the crowd, two lean, bendy men—one with black hair braided a few different ways, the other rocking a Sikh patka—moved like sexy insects onto the stage, where they hopped together with pendulous limbs. At intermission, I stood with Ben Walters, who wrote the RVT's successful listing application. *That's a new gold curtain,* he pointed out, pleased by this evidence of the place's rude health. We speculated about whether The Bar, that cruise club in the arches across the alley, had been already shuttered. It had. (The butch men's club XXL folded, too, which some saw as the management's comeuppance for refusing entry to a customer wearing high-heeled boots.)

As the show started up again, one of the hosts—gangly, with a laid-back confidence, barefoot through each of their costume changes—announced: *I see some people have just joined us.* A subdued cheer rose from a group of self-conscious men. *You're cricket fans?* the host asked. Apparently, there was a cricket championship at the Oval, a nearby stadium. *You're very welcome here,* said the host through a wide smile. *We're very inclusive here. Stick around and you'll find out what that entails.* Each word seemed underlined, and through a fixed grin, they'd become steely: *Just be sure to respect that this is a safe space.*

I went to the bar while a radiant woman danced in a golden sari. The cricket fans near me were enraptured. I was baffled that they'd each had the cash to hand for the suggested donation at the door, were happy to continue when informed it was a queer pub, persisted through all the hoops an inclusive space erects these days. On my way back to Famous, I saw an altercation was brewing between a couple of the cricket fans and a young South Asian man, who shot forth, *You don't GET to call US fascist. This is a queer space.* The older of the two cricket fans hung his head drunkenly. *I'm not trying to cause any trouble,* he muttered. Two security guards pounced, instructing the men to leave. *How's that for tolerance,* said the younger of the pair, and I could see how to him the scenario was a fait accompli. This is what it had come to: they used to be the winners—now we'd clipped their imperial wings. He shoved the distressed lad, who was half his size, then an even littler black woman, but she pushed back with velocity. We all seemed so small and *of color* compared with him. *I don't mean any trouble,* maintained the older cricket fan, who had much of his pint still to finish; hanging on to it seemed his priority. The younger wasn't having it: *he* did not need to apologize to *us.* He shouted into the faces of the people around him, who were all attempting to get him out the door like moving a rolled-up carpet. He came at the queer boy again, who was shaking, and I instinctively grabbed the boy's shoulder, then worried the resistance might tear his shirt. I could feel the long mane of Ben Walters behind me, but his gallantry was no longer needed. Security had ushered the cricket fans away. *Cricket?* we shrugged at one another.

It was then I realized a performer of striking appearance had taken the stage during the affray. Maybe their androgyny and albinism had prompted the whole thing. They were draped in a fantastic clash of patterns. Their eyes were closed as they recited poems about how desperately they wanted to be fucked by a nine-inch penis while high on ecstasy. They giggled at several of their own lines in delight. The audience was with them, all the more so in our newfound solidarity. Famous then trotted off to buy himself the fund-raiser t-shirt, which read NOT GAY AS IN HAPPY, QUEER AS IN FUCK YOUR BORDERS. The slogan comes off like all of queer theory in an aphorism—rejecting a constricting identity for an expansive subjectivity. It suggests queer as a starting point for coalition rather than staking a minoritarian status. But at the same time, it doesn't totally disavow gay, only *gay as in happy*—the carefree version the world wants to latch on to. The slogan reclaims gay as a *form of queer* (one that can still be about, as Famous put it, *outrage, activism, organizing*). What we do with these shifting definitions, where we go with them, is a complicated question, and bound to be contentious. It was such a positive night, speaking to the progress we've made and the next possibilities. And yet I've never witnessed that kind of clash in a gay bar before, that blatant tribalism. Does declaring a safe space from the stage anticipate trouble, and draw battle lines? Does a safe space require borders, even as it raises money to abolish them?

———

In 2019, *The Telegraph* published the results of a poll in which, compared with four years prior, young Britons were 'half as likely to identify as gay or lesbian and eight times more likely to identify as bisexual.' If the populace is more fluid and less gay, it is both less othering and more so. In this liberation from the binary, gay and lesbian become marginalized again, now as anachronistic categories. It used to be: *We are everywhere.* Now it's: *We are everything.* To create inclusive spaces for these morphing identities is an ambitious undertaking, like planning a house for a vagabond.

It also means thinking from the point of view of the most vulnerable, after years of nightlife rewarding the alphas in the room.

An organization called the Friends of the Joiners Arms formed after the closure of that ribald venue on Hackney Road—where I was trapped in a cubicle twice by randy men, danced to 'Bad Romance,' got myself a course of antiretroviral medication. The Friends of the Joiners Arms made gay bar history when it persuaded the local council to enact legislation demanding that any developer taking over the property must grant a twenty-five-year lease to a queer operator on the ground floor. The initial conditions were deemed inadequate—'a Trojan horse draped in a rainbow flag,' a representative of the campaign wrote in *The Guardian*, averring that the proposed space was infelicitous to a late night drinking establishment, certainly not one as life-giving as the aughts-era Joiners. Further stipulations were agreed: the former late hours would be maintained, one hundred and thirty thousand pounds given to the occupant toward the fit-out, the first year rent-free, nearly a quarter more floor space added, enhanced soundproofing.

Since then, the challenge has been for the Friends of the Joiners Arms itself to win the bid for that space. In the interim, the Friends took the form of itinerant queer parties which were in many ways different from its namesake. The group hosts sober nights and drag king showcases. From its early stages, the campaign did not only ask 'What are we losing?' but 'What didn't we have in the first place?' The script of Ian Giles's art film *Trojan Horse Rainbow Flag*, a study of the Joiners legacy and subsequent campaign, is based on a series of named and anonymous interviews. One of the latter put it this way: 'The pub was frequented and held together by a community that consisted of / gay misfits / whores / drug dealers / rent boys / taxi drivers / local East End men / criminals / homeless and the curious / They've all dispersed now as the area has been gentrified / Does that area need another gay venue? / yeah but not the Joiners.'

So like other young queer promoters, the Friends redrew the boundaries, and focused on the most marginalized populations—like trans people of color to whom a typical gay bar is often a hostile environment. The Friends has also issued a charter—provisional, as queers are dynamic beings who grow and change—but initially establishing zero tolerance of racism, sexism, homophobia, transphobia, xenophobia, ableism, fat phobia, body shaming, slut shaming; prejudice based on class, faith, religion, language ability, gender presentation, learning disability or mental health. It also forbids harassment of any kind, including nonconsensual touching, following, leering, ogling, persisting in a conversation or making nonverbal gestures when the other person has expressed they don't want to engage.

I'm afraid I'd be out at the *leering*. When drunk, I am a champion at projecting an unintentional hostility when I'm going for broodily seductive. I'm not proud to confess that more than once a cute fag has told Famous on the dance floor: *Your boyfriend looks like he wants to kill me.* We'd all laugh, and I didn't have to explain myself. But this came from a position of privilege. Other types of people now need spaces where they don't have to explain themselves, too. At the Friends' parties, guests can identify a support team by their LED halos—the Joiners Angels. They're on hand all night to deal with an incident, or to offer a helping hand, hug or chat. Again, I can't help but think that if I sought out an angel, I'd come across like I was ogling their halo.

The kids today, it turns out, want rules. They need a provisional constitution for what their new spaces will be. In 2018, *The Observer* ran a piece under the headline 'Clubbing's New Generation Want Good, Clean Fun, Not Hedonism.' One promoter explained that clubbers now chose to dance in a place that fits their ideology. Bad behavior is promptly reported. The consensus seemed to be that clubbing is now about promoters finding ways to create egalitarian, fair-minded, noncreepy environments, unlike the world outside—whereas clubs have often been microcosms of some of society's worst qualities.

We did not go out to be safe. I didn't, anyway. Not to the Joiners Harms. I went out to take risks. I went out to be close to other bodies. Perhaps that amounts to safety in numbers. It was more about being turned on in proximity. The idea of a safe space isn't coherent to me, but then again I now recognize that I'm privileged in ways I didn't previously comprehend. The kids have told me.

———

We went back to my first. The pilgrimage was as vague as the memory. In West Hollywood, I took Famous for a veggie with pickles at Astro Burger, where I once sat alone reading the *LA Weekly*. We went for a beer and tequila at the Gold Coast, and I told Famous about the man who didn't cop a feel when I ventured in alone, and how many years later a straight guy complained on Yelp that he had been groped there, now that gay bars were meant to be places where straights should feel at ease. I told Famous about how I'd read that a man was murdered upon leaving the place a few years back while his partner was at home awaiting his return. We went into Circus of Books, where I'd bought my first porn magazine. The shelves were half empty: it was a closing-down sale. When we left, Famous pointed out that the radio was playing 'Another One Bites the Dust.'

We did not go to Probe. (The site is now an opulent antiques showroom whose owners joke they once in a while catch a whiff of poppers.) On foot, Famous and I circled the Factory Building, which stretches between two city blocks east to west, in a kind of ritual that reminded me of the time we unintentionally circumscribed the whole of Vatican City in Rome because we couldn't find the entrance and just kept going. Now I saw the Factory in much more detail than I did in my youth: it was faded black with bog-green sides, rickety compared with its slick, glassy neighbors. It looked like a place of labor, humble and hardy like a pack mule.

It had been designated one of America's Most Endangered Historic Places by the National Trust for Historic Preservation in 2015. Conservationists got the Factory Building listed on the state level, and persevered until it was also eligible for the National Register of Historic Places; the building's owner did not accept the listing. The edifice was slated for demolition in order to erect a showy new hotel and retail complex. It seemed an affront: this is where Joan Rivers hosted an early AIDS benefit in the face of violent threats, where gay men were in charge of their own party, where later the weekly Girl Bar night gave rise to the lipstick lesbian scene. In 2016, the *Los Angeles Times* ran an opinion piece entitled 'Save This Eyesore.' Its author wrote,

'Places like Stonewall and the Factory turn conventional wisdom about historic preservation on its head: Sometimes, ugly architecture is important because of its ugliness. Many old gay bars have no windows...the patrons wouldn't have been safe drinking and flirting and dancing and conversing openly behind glass. Today, gay bars with wide windows and open patios and prominent rainbow flags surround the Factory—which is a great reason to preserve it.' The journalist was surely referring to the Abbey across the street—that festive patio bar crowded with bachelorette parties and real estate agents in movie-star sunglasses. In 2017, it was the focus of a reality TV series about buffed-up bar staff called *What Happens at the Abbey*. So this is what we fought for, apparently.

The *Times* then published a response by Don Kilhefner, the seasoned activist who led the uprising at the mob-owned bar the Farm. Kilhefner was aghast at the notion of the building as a monument: 'For most conscious gay and lesbian people of that period, Studio One stood for racist discrimination and white male privilege.' Some argued that problematic past made the building all the more worth preserving; perhaps it could be turned into a community center for queer youth. But in 2018, the West Hollywood City Council approved the developers' plans by a vote of four to one. At the meeting, council members indulged their own Studio One stories but cleared the way for partial demolition. As the mayor stated to the press, 'The whole nostalgia around Studio One is something I'm very familiar with. It's the first gay bar I went to. It's where I met my circle of friends and circle of lovers.' He did not, however, cast the sole dissenting vote. Rather, he insisted that the new facade pay tribute to the disco era. The younger generation, the rationale went, does not form a sequestered community amid industrial wrecks, but they do like that aesthetic.

Then the Los Angeles Conservancy announced, working alongside the project developers, a new iteration that incorporates a larger portion—supposedly nearly eighty percent—of the original building. The unfettered industrial shell will become industrial chic cladding that accents a glassy edifice. There's been promise of Studio One ephemera on display: the golden age of gay bars enshrined in vitrines the way the golden age of Hollywood is framed on the walls of the city's grand old hotels. This would make a very different impact than its unsettling presence as a haunted site. The building will no longer speak for itself. A presentation will provide the summary. Then again, the building was taciturn. I danced there with no clue of its history.

Famous and I spotted a deliveryman enter the building and slipped in behind him underneath an exterior chandelier. It was still just another nightclub inside. It didn't smell of anything, not really—a little of bleach, and the heat of the day in the big empty room.

———

In London, on occasion, Famous and I still wind up in gay bars—the unfashionable kind. In Soho, several are now run by the same corporation. This is easily detected: the same pump clips repeat from one bar to the next. The places seem to offer little more than end-of-day conciliation to office drones or minstrel shows for out-of-towners. *You're probably thinking where am I?* the drag queens shriek from a beglittered stage at the Admiral Duncan on Old Compton Street to a crowd they assume just happened to wander in. Gay bars used to operate on the presumption of prior knowledge. The catching-up was a part of it. In the case of the Admiral Duncan, the history includes the nail-bomb attack of April 1999, which killed two gay men and their pregnant friend, and injured dozens more. Crossing the threshold, always passing a bouncer, still evokes in me both a sense of solidarity and an irrational pang of fear. I'm fond of the place. A blond lad named Harry — or Scarlett Harlett several nights of the week — DJs and chomps gum as a queen belts musical-theater ballads. If the British Nigerian queen Son of a Tutu leads a sing-along of 'Take Me Home, Country Roads,' I feel included by the queer concept of home as elusive. I can sense Famous grin beside me. Then an overexcited birthday gal attempts to get the homos around her to sing into her hairbrush, and I'm annoyed by it all.

The last time we decided to stop in, after a Chinese dinner of jiao zi and dan dan noodles, the Admiral Duncan had a despondent air. The queen onstage was so wasted she'd actually begun to refuse shots. The men's bathroom had flooded, so that urine pooled with the spilled drinks on the dance floor by way of the soles of the customers' sensible work shoes. The speakers were so loud we sat away from the stage, near the front door. A pair of very old men stood across from us. Of course, I saw our future selves in them. They couldn't hear much, but obviously enjoyed each other's company. *This is a new number,* the younger of the two shouted as the queen massacred an Amy Winehouse tune, and his companion nodded. I noticed for the first time a dusty chandelier suspended from the beamed ceiling. The fixture comprised three candle-effect flickering bulbs in an abstract design. An abstraction of what? Famous described it as a commotion. It roughly resembled a tangle of unspooled tape. I asked a chipper bartender collecting glasses about it. He explained it was in remembrance of the 1999 bombing. *Yes,* I said, but I wondered if he knew whether the form was meant to approximate something specific. *Oh, I don't know that.* He whizzed his arms about. *You know what the gays are like. Always trying to outdo everyone else.*

Famous and I left soon after that. An uncrowded gay bar is morose. It's as if the cold beer is colder, and the air-conditioning blasting in anticipation of a later crowd brings the chill of wishful thinking. We moved through the night and decided to stop off at a twink bar neither of us had been to for years. *I don't think I've ever been, actually,* Famous corrected me. At the door, the bouncer told me I'd have to remove my cap. *We've had trouble,* he tried to explain. Famous speculated opportunists of some kind must be using cap brims to hide their faces from CCTV. I didn't want to take mine off. *Forget it,* I said. *I'm over tonight.*

We'd catch a train home from Charing Cross Station, which stretches across the once notorious Adelphi district, and leads onto a bridge over the Thames. We'd pass the lights of the London Eye and the other riverside attractions. Ours is only a few stops away, but Famous usually falls asleep. We'd pass hundreds of illuminated windows, in tall apartment buildings and Victorian terrace houses. I always find myself imagining the residents at home, cooking or watching TV or what have you—people who didn't go out.

ACKNOWLEDGMENTS

The book's editors, Jean Garnett at Little, Brown and Ka Bradley at Granta, approached this beast unflinchingly, then took it dancing. Laura Macdougall at United Agents made it happen. I'm very glad they were my trusty companions.

My gratitude also to Olivia Davies at United Agents; copyeditor Trent Duffy; everyone at Little, Brown, including Betsy Uhrig, Karen Landry, Marie Mundaca, Lucy Kim, Lena Little, and Ira Boudah; everyone at Granta, including Pru Rowlandson and Simon Heafield.

Thank you: Ben Walters, Andy Campbell, Shaun Cole, Josh Cheon, Olivia Laing, Sean Hart, Anh Do, Farika Holden, John Thomson, Ian Giles, Euan MacDonald, Colter Jacobsen, Don Kilhefner, Richard Dyer, Rictor Norton, Joe Parslow, Jack Fritscher, Rocco Kayiatos, Jasleen Kaur, Bobby McCole, Adrian Rifkin, Martin Meeker, Gayle Rubin, Jim Gleeson, Jay McCauley Bowstead, Bob Skiba, Jack Clarke and Ruth Pilston at Arcadia Missa, Hannah Quinlan and Rosie Hastings, Hal Fischer, Bus Station John, David Ghee, Gavin Watson, Marc Vallée, Jenny Hoyston, Wayne Koestenbaum, Eileen Myles, Michelle Tea, the Friends of the Joiners Arms, Jack Rollo, Elaine Tierney, Laurie and everyone at the Chateau, Paul Burston, Kirk

Read, Fitzcarraldo Editions, Liz Ohanesian, Karen Ocamb, Jeff Moen, PJ Mark, Russell Garnett and Chloe Gott at KBJ Management, Simon Amstell, Stuart Comer, Matt Connors, Travis Elborough, Isaac Fellman at the GLBT Historical Society, Sinead Evans, Bryony Quinn, Jeremy Millar and all my friends from Writing at the Royal College of Art, Ellis Moore at Bolinda and Elisa M. Rivlin.

There are several journalists, historians and critics who cleared the paths I decided to saunter down; their foundational work gave direction to my rambling. I'm compelled to mention Matt Houlbrook; Johan Andersson; Ben Campkin and the Urban Lab at UCL; Mark Simpson; Murray Healy on gay skins; Nan Alamilla Boyd on San Francisco queer history; Martin Meeker; Gayle Rubin for her brilliance generally and specifically 'The Temple of the Butthole,' where I first encountered many of the colorful details about the Catacombs; Simon Watney, whose papers in the nineties proposed a reaffirmation of gay when the challenges faced by the population were more urgent than quibbling over the identity's shortcomings. When I'd find myself down a rabbit hole of infighting and invective, such constructive thinkers shone a light.

Thank you to the staff of Rare Books & Music at the British Library, who brought me stacks of gay daily. Shout out to LAGNA at Bishopsgate Institute, Hackney Archives and the National Archives. Much appreciation to Loni Shibuyama, Jeanne Vaccaro and everyone at the ONE Archives in Los Angeles.

The title page photo is of Sundowners in Margate, England. The chapter photographs are of Vauxhall, London; the Factory Building before dismantling, West Hollywood;

ACKNOWLEDGMENTS

Lower Robert Street, London; Twin Peaks Tavern, San Francisco; Wild Side West, San Francisco; the London Apprentice pub sign, London; The Flying Handbag, Blackpool.

At the time of going to print, the Nelsons Head crew runs the Cock Tavern on Kennington Road, and the G&D team heads up the Queen Adelaide on Hackney Road. Long live the Triangle.

Much respect to the Phone Booth and El Rio in San Francisco, which must be my spirit bars.

Visit Blackpool!

Famous was named after 'Famous Blue Raincoat' by Leonard Cohen. That song and those by the Velvet Underground are entwined with how we've moved through the world, especially chapters 2 through 5.

Big hugs to those who were there making the memories (and blurring them), including Anh, Teebs, Stooves, Boobs, Ralpharoo, Jesse, Niki, Matt, Carl, Dawn, Richard, Steph, Carrie, Jeff, Ginny, Kyle, Warwick, Paul, Chandra, Markie, the MH crew, all the Sams. To the twinks, buddies, strangers, queens, bar staff, DJs and performers—cheers.

Love to Jenny for being a disco ball, Mom for 'Having a Coke with You,' Dad for the integrity.

Jamie Atherton was there each step of the way, then back over and again. He helped shape my notions into some semblance of reason, and gave this book a reason.

NOTES

EPIGRAPH

vii 'A long while amid': Walt Whitman, 'A Glimpse,' 'Calamus 29' (1860), in *Leaves of Grass: A Textual Variorum of the Printed Poems, 1860–1867* (1980; repr., New York: New York University Press, 2008), 397.

THE DARK WALKS

3 'Historically, gay bars': Hannah Quinlan and Rosie Hastings in conversation with Hatty Nestor, 'Our Work Poses Questions That Bridge the Gap Between the Past, Present and Future of Queer Culture in the UK,' *Studio International*, 22 August 2017.

5 'It may seem difficult': Gordon Westwood, *Society and the Homosexual* (London: Victor Gollancz, 1952), 127.

5 'in a pathetic kind': Ibid., 126.

5 'The pink shilling': Matt Houlbrook, *Queer London: Perils and Pleasures in the Sexual Metropolis, 1918–1957* (Chicago: University of Chicago Press, 2005), 81.

6 'We were ghosts': Andrew Holleran, *Dancer from the Dance* (1978; repr., New York: Harper Perennial, 2001), 130.

6 'I am the shadow...ghost am Iain': Wilfred Owen, 'I Am the Ghost of Shadwell Stair,' in *The Poems of Wilfred Owen* (Ware, Eng.: Wordsworth Classics, 1994), 34.

6 'I dance to save myself': Paul Verlaine, 'Mille e tre' ('A thousand and three'), in *Women/Men*, trans. Alistair Elliot (1979; repr., Greenwich, Eng.: Anvil Press Poetry, 2004), 91.

8 'to construct a queer consumer': Houlbrook, *Queer London*, 85.

285

NOTES

9 'The party is coming': Hugo Greenhalgh, 'Gay Bars Fall Victim to Soaring Property Prices,' *Financial Times*, 28 September 2015.

9 'I can't help wondering': June Thomas, 'The Gay Bar: Is It Dying?,' *Slate*, 27 June 2011.

10 '3 Deviates Invite': Thomas A. Johnson, '3 Deviates Invite Exclusion by Bars,' *New York Times*, 22 April 1966.

10 'all Heteros…in a gay area': Review of Gold Coast Bar, *yelp.com*, 1 January 2015 (accessed 19 May 2020).

10 'Do gay people still': 'Do Gay People Still Need Gay Bars?,' *BBC News*, 1 April 2014.

11 'How "Gay" Should': Jim Farber, 'How "Gay" Should a Gay Bar Be?,' *New York Times*, 24 June 2017.

11 'What are they doing': Donald Webster Cory, *The Homosexual in America: A Subjective Approach* (1951; repr., New York: Arno Press, 1975), 131.

12 'And then, when my part': Dave Cullen, 'Mass Murder at the Gay Bar: When a Refuge Becomes the Target,' *Vanity Fair*, 13 June 2016.

13 'When gays are spatially scattered': Manuel Castells, *The City and the Grassroots* (London: Edward Arnold, 1983), 138.

13 'Being Gay': Ofri Ilany, 'Being Gay Is Passé,' *Haaretz*, 7 June 2018.

14 'When there is a vaccine': Patrick Califia, 'The Necessity of Excess,' *Poz*, 1 October 1998.

18 'You meet men there': James Miller, *The Passion of Michel Foucault* (Cambridge, Mass.: Harvard University Press, 1993), 264.

19 'the transgression of transgression': Roland Barthes, *Roland Barthes by Roland Barthes*, trans. Richard Howard (1977; repr., New York: Hill and Wang, 2010), 66.

21 'secretly sodomizing': Robert Smithson, 'A Tour of the Monuments of Passaic, New Jersey,' in *Robert Smithson: The Collected Writings*, ed. Jack Flam (Berkeley: University of California Press, 1996), 71.

21 'Rather than being "pushed" out': Johan Andersson, 'Vauxhall's Post-industrial Pleasure Gardens: "Death Wish" and Hedonism in 21st-Century London,' *Urban Studies* 48, no. 1 (2010): 96.

22 'the dark walks': William Makepeace Thackeray, *Vanity Fair* (London: Bradbury and Evans, 1848), 47.

23 'visibility is a trap': Michel Foucault, *Discipline and Punish: The Birth of the Prison*, trans. Alan Sheridan (1977; repr., New York: Vintage, 1995), 200.

23 'notions of the queer's character': Houlbrook, *Queer London*, 63.

NOTES

23–24 'I think they get…to everything else': P.C. Butcher statement to Department Committee on Homosexual Offences and Prostitution, 7 December 1954, PRO, HO 345/12: CHP TRANS 8, Q633, 3, National Archives, London.

24 a ten-minute maximum: 'Lefties to "Clock" Cops in the Loo!,' *Sun*, 15 June 1985; available at Lesbian and Gay Newsmedia Archive, Bishopsgate Institute, London.

26 'fragile from fear': Ben Walters, application to English Heritage (now Historic England) to list the Royal Vauxhall Tavern, January 2015, p. 31, www.rvt.community/read-our-application-to-make-the-tavern-a-listed-building/ (accessed 19 May 2020).

26 'Instead…feminized domesticity': Ben Walters, 'The Police Wore Rubber Gloves,' nottelevision.net, 17 January 2017 (accessed 19 May 2020).

27 'onerous restrictions': Biographical note of James Lindsay, CEO/Managing Director, vauxhalltavern.com (accessed 19 May 2020).

27 'momentary excitements': Gayle Rubin, 'Geologies of Queer Studies,' in *Deviations: A Gayle Rubin Reader* (Durham, N.C.: Duke University Press, 2011), 355.

28 'London's Greatest Bohemian Rendezvous': Flyer, 1934, MEPO 3/758, National Archives.

28 'absolutely a sink': Note to Commissioner of Police, 1934, MEPO 3/758, ibid.

29–30 'coloured people'…'were freely used': Various police constable statements to Bow Street Police Station 'E' Division, August 1934, MEPO 3/758, ibid.

30 This certifies that I': Evidence at Bow Street Police Station 'E' Division, 26 August 1934, MEPO 3/758, ibid.

30 'I don't mind': Statement to Bow Street Police Station 'E' Division, August 1934, MEPO 3/758, ibid., quoted in Houlbrook, *Queer London*, 12.

31 'I ask one thing': Earl of Arran, statement to House of Lords regarding the Sexual Offences Bill (No. 2), 21 July 1967, api.parliament.uk (accessed 19 May 2020).

33 'And yet the question remains': Simon Watney, 'AIDS and the Politics of the Queer Diaspora,' in *Negotiating Lesbian and Gay Subjects*, ed. Monica Dorenkamp and Richard Henke (New York: Routledge, 1995), 61.

35 'Humiliation is always personal': Wayne Koestenbaum, *Humiliation* (London: Notting Hill Editions, 2011), 186.

36 'They were together...regularly gay': Gertrude Stein, *Geography and Plays* (Boston: Four Seas, 1922), quoted in *Oxford English Dictionary*.

36 'Went round': Kenneth Williams, 'Thursday, 16 January' (1947), in *The Kenneth Williams Diaries*, ed. Russell Davies (London: HarperCollins, 1994), 8.

36 'I have yet to meet': Sara H. Carleton, 'The Truth about Homosexuals,' *Sir!*, quoted by Jim Egan, *Challenging the Conspiracy of Silence* (Toronto: The Canadian Lesbian and Gay Archives/Homewood Books, 1998), 50.

37 '"I enjoy my double"': *Observer*, 17 January 1971, quoted in *Oxford English Dictionary*.

38 'Queer scenes': Michael Warner, *The Trouble with Normal: Sex, Politics, and the Ethics of Queer Life* (Cambridge, Mass.: Harvard University Press, 1999), 35–36.

39 'eventful to no one': Erving Goffman, *Stigma* (London: Penguin, 1963), 104.

40 'Our hearts pounded': Cleo Rocos, *The Power of Positive Drinking* (London: Random House, 2013), 47.

41 'There's more literature': Thomas, 'The Gay Bar: Is It Dying?'

41 'Today I write back': José Esteban Muñoz, *Cruising Utopia: The Then and There of Queer Futurity* (New York: New York University Press, 2009), 113.

Also:

Achilles, Nancy. 'The Development of the Homosexual Bar as an Institution.' In *Sexual Deviance*, edited by John H. Gagnon and William Simon. New York: Harper and Row, 1967.

Ackroyd, Peter. *Queer City: Gay London from the Romans to the Present Day*. London: Chatto and Windus, 2017.

Alabanza, Travis. 'Going to the Gay Bar.' *Archive on Four* (BBC Radio Four), 14 September 2019.

Berry, David. 'Chasing the Pink Pound.' *Guardian*, 14 May 1984.

Bersani, Leo. *Receptive Bodies*. Chicago: University of Chicago Press, 2018.

Borg, Alan, and David E. Coke. *Vauxhall Gardens: A History*. New Haven: Yale University Press, 2011.

Halperin, David M. *How to Be Gay*. Cambridge, Mass.: Belknap/Harvard University Press, 2012.

Miller, Russell. 'Please Excuse Him While He Puts On His Bra.' *Nova*, August 1968.

NOTES

Norton, Rictor. *Mother Clap's Molly House*. London: GMP, 1992.

Pry, Paul. *For Your Convenience: A Learned Dialogue Instructive to all Londoners and London Visitors*. London: Routledge, 1937.

'Segregation in the LGBTQ Community.' *Love Child Talks*, 13 March 2019.

Squires, Charlie. *What's a Girl Like You...* (London Weekend Television), 1969.

Tatchell, Peter. 'Don't Fall For the Myth That It's 50 Years Since We Decriminalised Homsexuality,' *Guardian*, 23 May 2017.

THE FACTORY

47 'When I was young': Derek Jarman, *At Your Own Risk* (1992; repr., New York: Vintage, 2019), 26. (Published by Cornerstone; reprinted by permission of the Random House Group Limited © 1991).

49 'the fastest proliferating type': Wayne Sage, 'Inside the Colossal Closet,' in *Gay Men*, ed. Martin P. Levine (New York: Harper and Row, 1979), 155.

49 'Probe invites all': Poster, 1983, Coll. 2018.001: Poster Collection, ONE Archives at the USC Libraries, Los Angeles.

49 'probe the darkness': Flyer, 1984, Coll, 2012.001, Subject Files: Probe, ibid.

50 'A Chilling Walk... I shivered': Flyer, 1992, ibid.

51 'In between the play': E. Michael Gorman, 'The Pursuit of the Wish: An Anthropological Perspective on Gay Male Subculture in Los Angeles,' in *Gay Culture in America: Essays from the Field*, ed. Gilbert Herdt (Boston: Beacon Press, 1992), 98.

51 'One interesting change': Ibid., 104.

55 'emphasize exchange-value': Mickey Lauria and Lawrence Knopp, 'Towards an Analysis of the Role of Gay Communities in the Urban Renaissance,' *Urban Geography*, 1985, quoted in Moira Rachel Kenney, *Mapping Gay L.A.: The Intersection of Place and Politics* (Philadelphia: Temple University Press, 2001), 42.

61 'Bejeweled, Balenciaga'd, trailing': John Hallowell, 'Somebodies and Nobodies,' *New York*, 16 September 1968.

61 'L.A. has the most beautiful men': Edmund White, *States of Desire Revisited: Travels in Gay America* (Madison: University of Wisconsin Press, 2014), 14.

61 'a futuristic inferno': Jack Slater, 'Discotheques Dance to Another Tune,' *Los Angeles Times*, 11 August 1976, Coll. 2012.001, Subject Files: Studio One, ONE Archives.

62 'Faces were smiling': *Data Boy*, June 1977, ibid.

62 'Total drama, that's what': Charles Solomon, 'Disco L.A.: Behind the Seen,' *Los Angeles Times*, 15 August 1979, ibid.

62 'Gay bars are not...gay establishments': Sage, 'Inside the Colossal Closet,' 148.

62 'Disco to a gay person': Dennis Hunt, 'Disco Clubs: Down but Not Out,' *Los Angeles Times*, 8 April 1980, ONE Archives.

62 'Even the dances...dance by ourselves': Jack Slater, 'Discotheques Dance to Another Tune,' *Los Angeles Times*, 11 August 1976, ibid.

62–63 thirty-five instances: Dave Johnson, 'Studio One Hit with Charges of Racism, Sexist Discrimination,' *Los Angeles Free Press*, 13–19 June 1975, ibid.

66 'This was established': Slater, 'Discotheques Dance to Another Tune.'

66 'The secret to a discotheque's longevity...you don't get in': Ibid.

66 'Because they only go out': Ibid.

66 'freaks...they are associated': Sage, 'Inside the Colossal Closet.'

67 'are not sisters and brothers': Flyer, 1975, ONE Archives.

77 'It's not against...We're Americans, too!': Lillian Faderman and Stuart Timmons, *Gay L.A.: A History of Sexual Outlaws, Power Politics, and Lipstick Lesbians* (New York: Basic Books, 2006), 158.

78 'gladioli, mums': Dick Michaels, '"Patch" Raids Police Station,' *Los Angeles Advocate*, September 1968, quoted in Marc Stein, *The Stonewall Riots: A Documentary History* (New York: New York University Press, 2019), 106.

84 'Skinny glam-indie': *i-D*, October 1995.

85 'hormone queen': Joanne J. Meyerowitz, *How Sex Changed: A History of Transsexuality in the United States* (Cambridge, Mass.: Harvard University Press, 2002), 191.

Also:

Aletti, Vince. *The Disco Files: 1973–78*. New York: Distributed Art Publishers, 2018.

Altman, Lawrence K. 'AIDS Is Now the Leading Killer of Americans from 25 to 44.' *New York Times*, 31 January 1995.

Architectural Resources Group. 'Robertson Lane Hotel and Commercial Redevelopment Project Historical Resources Technical Report.' 19 December 2016, weho.org (accessed 19 May 2020).

Armstrong, Elizabeth A., and Suzanna M. Crage. 'Movements and Memory:

The Making of the Stonewall Myth.' *American Sociological Review* 71, no. 5 (2006).

Durden, E. Moncell. *Beginning Hip-Hop Dance.* Champaign, Ill.: Human Kinetics, 2019.

Frye, Douglas, et al. '2010 Annual HIV Surveillance Report.' County of Los Angeles Public Health HIV Epidemiology Program, 2011.

Guzman-Sanchez, Thomas. *Underground Dance Masters: Final History of a Forgotten Era.* Santa Barbara: Praeger, 2012.

Lawrence, Tim. 'The Forging of a White Gay Aesthetic at the Saint, 1980–1984.' *Dancecult: Journal of Electronic Dance Music Culture* 3, no. 1 (2011).

Negrón-Muntaner, Frances. *Boricua Pop: Puerto Ricans and the Latinization of American Culture.* New York: New York University Press, 2004.

Shapiro, Peter. *Turn the Beat Around: The Secret History of Disco.* New York: Faber and Faber, 2005.

Simpson, Mark. *Male Impersonators: Men Performing Masculinity.* London: Continuum/Bloomsbury, 1994.

Swil, Warren, with Stewart Barkal. 'The Black Party at Probe Was a Special Event Where the Audience *Was* the Show.' *Frontiers Newsmagazine,* 1 April 1986.

Wat, Eric C. *The Making of a Gay Asian Community: An Oral History of Pre-AIDS Los Angeles.* Lanham, Md.: Rowan and Littlefield, 2002.

White, Edmund. 'Fantasia on the Seventies.' In *The Burning Library: Essays.* 1994. Reprint, New York: Knopf Doubleday, 2010.

THE ADELPHI

89 'If coming out isn't': Mark Simpson, 'Gay Dream Believer: Inside the Gay Underwear Cult,' in *Anti-Gay,* ed. Mark Simpson (London: Continuum/Bloomsbury, 1996), 6. (Copyright © Mark Simpson; reprinted by permission of Bloomsbury Publishing, Plc.).

89 'I'm a connoisseur...Have a nice day': Gus Van Sant, *My Own Private Idaho,* dir. Gus Van Sant (New Line Cinema, 1991).

90 'Out with the gay look': *Attitude,* December 1995.

90 'real music': Ibid.

90 'the inevitable result': Mark Simpson, 'Preface,' in Simpson, ed., *Anti-Gay,* xvii.

91 'the new pieties': Adam Phillips, *On Flirtation* (London: Faber and Faber, 1994), 124.

91 'What exactly is the queer appeal': Paul Burston, *Attitude*, September 1994.

95 'a new gay night...types queue here': 'Starz in Their Eyes,' *i-D*, October 1995.

96 'Substation, Backstreet and the Fort': Johan Andersson, 'Hygiene Aesthetics on London's Gay Scene: The Stigma of AIDS,' in *Dirt: New Geographies of Cleanliness and Contamination*, ed. Ben Campkin and Rosie Cox (London: I.B. Tauris, 2007), 109.

96 'spoiled identity': Susan Sontag, *AIDS and Its Metaphors* (London: Penguin, 1990), 15.

97 'a failed attempt at stylishness': Johan Andersson, 'Homonormative Aesthetics: AIDS and "De-Generational Unremembering" in 1990s London,' *Urban Studies* 56, no. 14 (2019), 3008.

97 'the emphasis would be': Dominic Lutyens, 'The Gay Team,' *Observer*, 26 October 2003.

97 'factory-farms stereotyped': Talia, 'Simon Hobart' (obituary), *Londonist*, 28 October 2005.

97 'tapping into a younger': Lutyens, 'The Gay Team.'

98 'The easiest way': Peter Paphides, *Attitude*, November 1994.

105 'I've called myself a bisexual': Mark Simpson, 'The Persueders,' *Attitude*, October 1994.

106 'I think I'll have two of you': Jonathan Harvey, *Beautiful Thing*, dir. Hettie Macdonald (Channel Four Films/World Productions, 1996).

107 'One wanders into the bar': Donald Webster Cory, *The Homosexual in America: A Subjective Approach* (New York: Arno Press, 1975), 120.

107 'I hate it': Harvey, *Beautiful Thing*.

107 'Yanks Go Home!': *Select*, April 1993.

108 'dear dad...child and wife': David M. Bergeron, *King James and Letters of Homoerotic Desire* (Iowa City: University of Iowa Press, 1999), 175.

109 'I naturally so love': Ibid., 203.

109 'I was fond of': Charles Dickens, *The Personal History of David Copperfield* (London: Bradbury and Evans, 1850), 116.

110 'resort of persons': Inspector Woods, statement to Bow Street Station 'E' Division, 17 July 1933, MEPO 2/4309, the National Archives, London.

110 'the operations of municipal power': Matt Houlbrook, *Queer London: Perils and Pleasures in the Sexual Metropolis, 1918–1957* (Chicago: University of Chicago Press, 2005), 63.

111 'What I hate': *Gay Life*, dir. Nigel Wattis (London Weekend Television, 1980).

111 'gay until he was thirty': Ibid.

111 'the only club': J.M. Barrie, *The Greenwood Hat* (privately printed, 1930), 284.

111 'a ghost on the back': Ibid., 287.

112 'read backward in time': John D'Emilio, 'Capitalism and Gay Identity,' in *The Lesbian and Gay Studies Reader*, ed. Henry Abelove, Michèle Aina Barale and David M. Halperin (New York: Routledge, 1993), 468.

112 'For gayness to be': Wayne Koestenbaum, 'Wilde's Hard Labor and the Birth of Gay Reading,' in *Engendering Men: The Question of Male Feminist Criticism*, ed. Joseph A. Boone and Michael Cadden (New York: Routledge, 1990), 188.

Also:

Bersani, Leo. *Homos*. Cambridge, Mass.: Harvard University Press, 1995.

Colman, David. 'A Night Out With: James Collard; The Corner of Straight and Gay.' *New York Times*, 19 July 1998.

Dyer, Richard. *The Culture of Queers*. London: Routledge, 2001.

——. "In Defence of Disco." *Gay Left*, no. 8, 1979.

Lemmey, Huw, and Ben Miller. 'King James VI and I.' *Bad Gays* (podcast episode #4), 9 April 2019.

Medhurst, Andy, and Sally R. Munt, eds. *Lesbian and Gay Studies: A Critical Introduction*. London: Cassell, 1997.

Muñoz, José Esteban. *Disidentifications*. Minneapolis: University of Minnesota Press, 1999.

Norton, Rictor. *The Myth of the Modern Homosexual: Queer History and the Search for Cultural Unity*. London: Cassell, 1997.

Parkes, Taylor. 'A British Disaster: Blur's Parklife, Britpop, Princess Di and the 1990s.' *The Quietus*, 28 April 2014.

'Sexual Politics; New Way of Being.' *New York Times*, 21 June 1998.

Simpson, Mark. 'Sing If You Cringe to Be Gay.' *Independent*, 25 January 1998.

Turner, Luke. 'Modern Life Isn't Rubbish: The Trouble with Britpop Nostalgia.' *The Quietus*, 10 April 2014.

Watney, Simon. *Imagine Hope: AIDS and Gay Identity*. London: Routledge, 2000.

——. "The Spectacle of AIDS." In *The Lesbian and Gay Studies Reader*. Edited by Henry Abelove, Michèle Aina Barale and David M. Halperin. New York: Routledge, 1993.

NOTES

THE WINDOWS

117 'But back to when': Michelle Tea, *Valencia* (2000; repr., Seattle: Seal Press, 2008), 105.

119 'As for the famous gay life': Edmund White, *States of Desire Revisited: Travels in Gay America* (Madison: University of Wisconsin Press, 2014), 31.

120 'a carnival where': Frances FitzGerald, *Cities on a Hill* (New York: Simon and Schuster, 1986), 12.

120 'I was white, male': Ibid., 29–30.

121 'as if every individual': Les Wright, 'Clone,' in *Encyclopedia of Gay Histories and Cultures*, ed. George Haggerty (2000; repr., London: Routledge, 2013), 200.

121 'a slightly hostile air': FitzGerald, *Cities on a Hill*, 54.

121 'The new gay fashion': Randy Shilts, *The Mayor of Castro Street: The Life and Times of Harvey Milk* (1982; repr., London: Atlantic Books, 2009), 101.

121 'drugstore cowboys eyed': Ibid., 207.

121 'doped-up, sexed-out': Martin P. Levine, 'The Life and Death of Clones,' in *Gay Culture in America: Essays from the Field*, ed. Gilbert Herdt (Boston: Beacon Press, 1992), 69.

122 '"mefirstism" implicit': Ibid., 71.

122 'a new kind of mindless': Edward Guthmann, 'Stars,' *San Francisco Sentinel*, 2 June 1978, quoted in Richard Myer, 'Warhol's Clones,' in *Negotiating Lesbian and Gay Subjects*, ed. Monica Dorenkamp and Richard Henke (New York: Routledge, 1995), 110.

122 'a mask of masculinity': *Gay San Francisco*, dir. Jonathan Raymond (1970).

122 'nice mustache...shampoos for days': Armistead Maupin, *Tales of the City* (1978; repr., London: Random House, 2012), 160–61.

124 'Business space on Castro': J. Stark, 'Who's Minding the Store?,' *San Francisco Examiner*, 11 February 1979, quoted in Nan Alamilla Boyd, 'San Francisco's Castro District: From Gay Liberation to Tourist Destination,' *Journal of Tourism and Cultural Change* 9, no. 3 (2011).

124 'painting and refurbishing': FitzGerald, *Cities on a Hill*, 59.

127 'desexualizing': David M. Halperin, *How to Be Gay* (Cambridge, Mass.: Belknap/Harvard University Press, 2012), 76.

127 'the spread of the gay bar': John D'Emilio, *Sexual Politics, Sexual Communities: The Making of a Homosexual Minority in the United States 1940–1970* (Chicago: University of Chicago Press, 1983), 32.

128 'All was not so gay': Nan Alamilla Boyd, *Wide-Open Town: A History of Queer San Francisco to 1965* (Berkeley: University of California Press, 2005), 121, citing a 1949 article in the *San Francisco Chronicle*.

129 'swishing movements': Ibid., 139.

129 'you're a cute...to wit: Homosexuals': J. White, opinion, California Supreme Court, *Vallerga v. Department of Alcoholic Beverage Control*, 23 December 1959, scocal.stanford.edu (accessed 19 May 2020).

130 'The only moral': Boyd, *Wide-Open Town*, 214, citing a 1961 column by Herb Caen.

131 'It was for the best': MaryEllen Cunha interviewed by Moses Corrette et al., 'Article 10 Landmark/Historic Preservation Commission Case Report Initiation of Designation: Twin Peaks Tavern,' 19 September 2012, commissions.sfplanning.org (accessed 19 May 2020).

132 'I actually liked': Simeon Wade, *Foucault in California* (Berkeley, Calif.: Heyday, 2019), 71.

133 'the first urban zone': Allan Bérubé, 'Resorts for Sex Perverts: A History of Gay Bathhouses,' in *My Desire for History: Essays in Gay, Community, and Labor History* (Chapel Hill: University of North Carolina Press, 2011), 71.

134 'Just walking into': Gayle Rubin, 'The Catacombs: Temple of the Butthole,' in *Deviations: A Gayle Rubin Reader* (Durham, N.C.: Duke University Press, 2011), 229.

134 'a firm sense...my cupped hand': Patrick Califia, 'The Necessity of Excess,' *Poz*, 1 October 1998.

135 'sexual heretics...the hostile': Rubin, 'The Catacombs,' 224.

135 'A secret world': Paul Welch, 'Homosexuality in America,' *Life*, 26 June 1964.

137 'At the Black and Blue': White, *States of Desire Revisited*, 52.

140 'was about gender': Joshua Gamson, *The Fabulous Sylvester: The Legend, the Music, the Seventies in San Francisco* (New York: Picador, 2005), 130.

141 'community of memory': Robert N. Bellah, Richard Madsen, William M. Sullivan, Ann Swidler and Steven M. Tipton, *Habits of the Heart: Individualism and Commitment in American Life* (Berkeley: University of California Press, 1985), 153.

141 'celebrates the narcissism': Ibid., 72.

141 'When we hear phrases': Ibid., 74–75.

142 'Living people had their hearts': Gamson, *The Fabulous Sylvester*, 248.

NOTES

142 'the institutions of culture-building': Michael Warner, 'Introduction,' in *Fear of a Queer Planet*, ed. Michael Warner (Minneapolis: University of Minnesota Press, 1993), xvi–xvii.

143 'The bars were seedbeds': D'Emilio, *Sexual Politics, Sexual Communities*, 32.

144 'the second annual baseball game...to our amusement': Bill Kruse, 'POLICE BEATEN! Play Ball!,' *Bay Area Reporter*, 11 July 1974.

145 'their melting sirens': Shilts, *The Mayor of Castro Street*, 388.

149 'conversation-stopper': Adam Phillips, *Attention Seeking* (New York: Penguin, 2019), 40.

149 'I don't think': Elspeth Probyn, *Blush: Faces of Shame* (Minneapolis: University of Minnesota Press, 2005), x.

151 'Those arrested at the Center': Mattilda, aka Matt Bernstein Sycamore: 'Gay Shame: From Queer Autonomous Space to Direct Action Extravaganza,' in *That's Revolting: Queer Strategies for Resisting Assimilation*, ed. Mattilda Bernstein Sycamore (2004; repr., New York: Soft Skull Press, 2008), 252.

152 'Shame measures the distance': Phillips, *Attention Seeking*, 56.

Also:

Butler, Judith. *Gender Trouble*. New York: Routledge, 1990.

Fritscher, Jack. 'Fistfucking in a Handball Palace.' *Drummer*, 23 July 1978.

Gorman, Michael R. *The Empress Is a Man: Stories from the Life of José Sarria*. London: Routledge, 1998.

Halperin, David M., and Valerie Traub, eds. *Gay Shame*. Chicago: University of Chicago Press, 2009.

Meeker, Martin. *Contacts Desired: Gay and Lesbian Communications and Community, 1940s–1970s*. Chicago: University of Chicago Press, 2006.

Murray, Stephen O. 'Components of Gay Community in San Francisco.' In *Gay Culture in America: Essays from the Field*. Edited by Gilbert Herdt. Boston: Beacon Press, 1992.

Jones, Cleve. *When We Rise*. London: Constable, 2016.

Levine, Martin P. *Gay Macho: The Life and Death of the Homosexual Clone*. New York: New York University Press, 1998.

Love, Heather. *Feeling Backward: Loss and the Politics of Queer History*. Cambridge, Mass.: Harvard University Press, 2007.

Macey, David. *The Lives of Michel Foucault*. London: Hutchinson, 1993.

Miller, James. *The Passion of Michel Foucault*. Cambridge, Mass.: Harvard University Press, 1993.

Muñoz, José Esteban. *Disidentifications*. Minneapolis: University of Minnesota Press, 1999.

Newton, Esther. *Mother Camp: Female Impersonators in America*. Englewood Cliffs, N.J.: Prentice-Hall, 1972.

Rubin, Gayle. 'Elegy for the Valley of the Kings.' In *Sexualities*. Vol. 3, *Difference and the Diversity of Sexualities*. Edited by Kenneth Plummer. London: Taylor and Francis, 2002.

Sedgwick, Eve Kosofsky, and Adam Frank, eds. *Shame and Its Sisters: A Silvan Tomkins Reader*. Durham, N.C.: Duke University Press, 1995.

Solnit, Rebecca. 'Rattlesnake in Mailbox: Cults, Creeps, California in the 1970s.' In *The Encyclopedia of Trouble and Spaciousness*. San Antonio: Trinity University Press, 2014.

Stanley, Eric. 'The Affective Commons: Gay Shame, Queer Hate, and Other Collective Feelings,' *GLQ: A Journal of Lesbian and Gay Studies* 24, no. 4 (October 2018).

THE NEIGHBORS

157 'I was not thinking': Wayne Koestenbaum, 'My 1980s,' in *My 1980s and Other Essays* (New York: Farrar, Straus and Giroux, 2013), 11.

157–158 'super cool...you might like it': Betty Pearl and Pansy, *Betty & Pansy's Severe Queer Review of San Francisco*, 7th ed. (Berkeley, Calif.: Cleis Press, 2003), 129.

159 'INTERNATIONAL FAGGOT': *Butt*, August 2002.

161 'I sloshed away': Michelle Tea, *Valencia* (2000; repr., Seattle: Seal Press, 2008), 11.

161 'a kind of reverse serenade': Ibid., 77.

162 'we felt so much better': Eileen Myles, *Chelsea Girls* (1994; repr., Los Angeles: Black Sparrow Press, 1997), 47.

162 'queen of the dykes': Benjamin Moser, *Sontag: Her Life and Work* (London: Penguin, 2019), 84.

163 'big happy...a community': Jane Kramer, *Allen Ginsberg in America* (New York: Random House, 1968), 48.

163 'a pack of unleashed zazous': Herbert Gold, 'Hip, Cool, Beat—and Frantic,' *Nation*, 16 November 1957, quoted in John D'Emilio, *Sexual Politics, Sexual Communities: The Making of a Homosexual Minority in the United States 1940–1970* (Chicago: University of Chicago Press, 1983), 179.

164 'Almost coincident': Robert Duncan, 'The Homosexual in Society,'

in *A Selected Prose,* ed. Robert J. Bertholf (New York: New Directions, 1995), 41.

164 'where the whole atmosphere... rehearsal of unfeeling': Ibid., 47.

164 'taking on the modulations': Ibid., 46.

164 'a wave surging': Ibid., 47.

167 'a sort of gay finishing school': Edmund White, *States of Desire Revisited: Travels in Gay America* (Madison: University of Wisconsin Press, 2014), 65–66.

167 'gray bar': Camper English, 'The Gray Agenda,' *SF Gate,* 11 June 2006.

167 'Just before I left': White, *States of Desire Revisited,* 32.

170 'Is not the most erotic': Roland Barthes, *The Pleasure of the Text,* trans. Richard Miller (1973; repr., New York: Hill and Wang, 1975), 9.

171 'I'm 28': Betty Pearl and Pansy, *Betty & Pansy's Severe Queer Review,* 32.

171 'greatest gay bar... poets went there': D'Emilio, *Sexual Politics, Sexual Communities,* 186.

172 'blue fungus... getting caught': Randy Shilts, *The Mayor of Castro Street: The Life and Times of Harvey Milk* (1982; repr., London: Atlantic Books, 2009), 60.

173 'freedom of speech... one of the best': Guy Strait, 'What Is a Gay Bar,' *Citizens News,* December 1964, lib.berkeley.edu.

173 'They had long hair': Aaron Shurin, 'Full Spectrum,' in *Infinite City: A San Francisco Atlas,* ed. Rebecca Solnit (Berkeley: University of California Press, 2010), 49.

179 'the golden age of gay': Bill Picture, 'Flashback,' *Out,* May 2006.

181 'There's not just a gap': Ryan Kost, 'At the Edge of the Tenderloin, a Gay Disco Rages,' *SF Gate,* 13 May 2015.

181 'so authentic': Mark Mardon, 'Got Tubesteak?,' *Bay Area Reporter,* 17 March 2005.

185 'The White Horse': Jenny Hoyston, 'The White Horse Is Bucking,' performed by Erase Errata (Inconvenient Press and Recordings, 2003).

188 'a big ol' boy... a bore': Bill Motley, 'Cruisin' the Streets,' performed by Boys Town Gang (Moby Dick Records, 1981).

188 'Too many bosses': David Diebold, *Tribal Rites: San Francisco Dance Music Phenomenon* (Northridge, Calif.: Time Warp, 1988), 106.

188 'I thought I was at home': Ibid., 111.

189 'hangout for... faint cologne': Betty Pearl and Pansy, *Betty & Pansy's Severe Queer Review,* 19.

NOTES

Also:

Castells, Manuel. *The City and the Grassroots: A Cross-Cultural Theory of Urban Social Movements.* London: Edward Arnold, 1983.

Fischer, Hal. *Gay Semiotics: A Photographic Study of Visual Coding among Homosexual Men.* 1977. Reprint, Los Angeles: Cherry and Martin, 2015.

hooks, bell. 'Choosing the Margin as a Space of Radical Openness.' In *Yearning: Race, Gender, and Cultural Politics.* 1990. Reprint, New York: Routledge, 2015.

Jay, Karla, and Allen Young, eds. *Lavender Culture.* 1978. Reprint, New York: New York University Press, 1994.

Stimpson, Catharine R. 'The Beat Generation and the Trials of Homosexual Liberation.' *Salmagundi*, no. 58/59 (1982).

Timpson, John. *Requiem for a Red Box.* London: Pyramid Books, 1989.

THE APPRENTICE

195 'Because there was such a thing': Eileen Myles, 'Live Through That?!,' in *Live Through This! On Creativity and Self Destruction*, ed. Sabrina Chapadjiev (New York: Seven Stories Press, 2008), 220.

198 'has emerged as a grittier': Aric Chen, 'Where the Club Boys Are,' *New York Times*, 20 May 2007.

209 An article ran in *The Independent*: Lena Corner, 'A Brush with Death: Why Britain's Coolest Art and Fashion Names Have Rallied Around a Victim of Random Knife Crime,' *Independent*, 30 August 2009.

210 groups of 'Asian guys': Rebecca Taylor, 'Gay Londoners See Attacks Rise,' *Time Out*, 21 April 2010, timeout.com (accessed 19 May 2020).

210 'The area's already crawling': Michelangelo Antonioni, Edward Bond and Tonino Guerra, *Blow-Up*, dir. Michelangelo Antonioni (Premier Productions/Carlo Ponti Production/MGM, 1966).

211 'East London has seen...their culture': Johann Hari, *Attitude*, January 2011.

212 'like a homosexual': 'Killed—for Smiling,' *Gay News*, 17 April 1980, Lesbian and Gay Newsmedia Archive, Bishopsgate Institute, London.

212–13 'Even if this unfortunate man': 'Man Who Killed with Karate Kick Is Freed,' *Guardian*, 4 March 1980, ibid.

215 'clone-a-billies': Shaun Cole, *Don We Now Our Gay Apparel* (London: Bloomsbury Academic, 2000), 170.

215 'hard times': Ibid., 174.

215 'Somehow the atmosphere': Robert Elms, 'Hard Times,' *The Face*, September 1982.

215 'to flaunt your': Sue Tilley, *Leigh Bowery: The Life and Times of an Icon* (London: Hodder and Stoughton, 1997), 33.

215 'no one was': Ibid., 39.

217 'assembly line': Peter Hall, 'Industrial London: A General View,' in *Greater London*, ed. J. T. Coppock and H. Prince (London: Faber, 1964), cited by Joanna Smith and Ray Rogers, *Behind the Veneer: The South Shoreditch Furniture Trade and Its Buildings* (London: English Heritage, 2006), 4.

218 'Has discos, fairly pricey': *East London & City Beer Guide* (London: The Campaign for Real Ale, 1983).

218 'Used by gays': *East London & City Beer Guide* (London: The Campaign for Real Ale, 1986).

218 'In fact, so dark were': Derek Jarman, *Modern Nature* (New York: Vintage, 1991), 96.

218 'Ideal Friend': J. R. Ackerley, *My Father and Myself* (1968; repr.: New York: New York Review Books, 1999), 174.

220 'Is not this conduct…simpler walk of life': Harold Sturge opinion, Old Street Magistrates Court, November 1954, HO 345/7, National Archives, London.

221 'with shafts…at the London Apprentice': Rupert Haselden, 'Gay Abandon,' *Guardian*, 7–8 September 1991.

224 'Those nights out': Neil Bartlett, *Ready to Catch Him Should He Fall* (1990; repr., London: Serpent's Tail, 2017), xii.

224 'I know there's not always': Ibid., 236.

224–25 'a challenge…one was looking for': Alan Hollinghurst, *The Swimming-Pool Library* (1988; repr., New York: Vintage, 2015), 246.

225 'I acted out…he knew what I liked': Ibid., 247.

225 'For 20 years': Haselden, 'Gay Abandon.'

226 'People look at': Ibid.

226 'not a man': 'Skin & Bona: Interviews with Gay Skinheads,' *Square Peg*, 1986.

226 'For me, the gays': Murray Healy, *Gay Skins* (London: Cassell, 1996), 208.

226–27 'Who's copying who here?': Ibid., 190.

227 'remain an unidentifiable body': Ibid., 8.

NOTES

229 'I saw him riding around': Jon Kelly, 'Nicky Crane: The Secret Double Life of a Gay Neo-Nazi,' *BBC News Magazine*, 6 December 2013.

230 'Camp, on the other hand ... "perverse" angle?': Eve Kosofsky Sedgwick, *Epistemology of the Closet* (1990; repr., Berkeley: University of California Press, 2008), 156.

231 'Behind the "straight" public sense': Susan Sontag, 'Notes on Camp,' in *Against Interpretation and Other Essays* (New York: Penguin, 2009), 281.

231 'The Camp insistence': Ibid., 290–91.

231 'In all their uses': Susan Stewart, *On Longing* (Durham, N.C.: Duke University Press, 2007), 168.

231 'Where the dandy': Sontag, 'Notes on Camp,' 289.

232 'No, no, no': David S. Reynolds, *Walt Whitman's America: A Cultural Biography* (1995; repr., New York: Vintage, 1996), 396.

232 'louche and pungent bouquet': Eve Kosofksy Sedgwick, *Between Men: English Literature and Male Homosocial Desire* (New York: Columbia University Press, 1985), 202.

233 'hang up my picture': Walt Whitman, 'Recorders Ages Hence,' 'Calamus 10' (1860), in *Leaves of Grass: A Textual Variorum of the Printed Poems, 1860– 1867* (1980; repr., New York: New York University Press, 2008), 380.

235 'a poseur of truly colossal': Reynolds, *Walt Whitman's America*, 161.

239 'Is Slumming': James Granville Adderley, 'Is Slumming Played Out?,' *English Illustrated Magazine*, August 1893, cited by Seth Koven, *Slumming: Sexual and Social Politics in Victorian London* (Princeton, N.J.: Princeton University Press, 2004), 6.

239 'to please others': Marcel Proust, *In Search of Lost Time*, vol. 2, *In the Shadow of Young Girls in Flower*, trans. James Grieve (London: Penguin, 2002), 253.

240 'the disquieting delights': Ibid., 256.

Also:

Andersson, Johan. 'East End Localism and Urban Decay: Shoreditch's Re-Emerging Gay Scene.' *The London Journal* 34, no. 1 (2009).

Bridge, Haydon. 'The Mysterious East,' *QX*, qxmagazine.com (accessed 19 May 2020).

Core, Philip. *Camp: The Lie That Tells the Truth*. Medford, N.J.: Plexus, 1984.

Eade, John. 'Nationalism, Community, and the Islamization of Space in London.' In *Making Muslim Space in North America and Europe*. Edited by Barbara Daly Metcalf. Berkeley: University of California Press, 1996.

NOTES

GALOP Third Annual Report: 1986–1987. London: The London Gay Policing Group, 1987.

Hari, Johann. 'Can We Finally Talk about Muslim Homophobia in Britain?,' *Huffington Post*, 24 February 2011, huffpost.com (accessed 19 May 2020).

Hennessy, Patrick, and Melissa Kite. 'Poll Reveals 40pc of Muslims Want Sharia Law in UK.' *Telegraph*, 19 February 2006.

Rowbotham, Sheila. *Edward Carpenter: A Life of Liberty and Love*. London: Verso, 2008.

Schaefer, Max. *Children of the Sun*. London: Granta, 2010.

Smith, Joanna, and Ray Rogers, *Behind the Veneer: The South Shoreditch Furniture Trade and Its Buildings*. London: English Heritage, 2006.

Wilson, Andrew. 'The Love That Dare Dress How It Likes.' *Guardian*, 20 April 1992.

THE BORDERS

245 'I was so nervous': Simon Amstell, *Simon Amstell: Set Free*, dir. Julia Knowles (Netflix, 2019).

246 'In the queer world': Michael Warner in conversation with Harry Kreisler, 'Publics and Counterpublics,' *Conversations with History*, University of California Television, 21 March 2018.

246 'You can end up': Ben Walters, 'Closing Time for Gay Pubs—A New Victim of London's Soaring Property Prices,' *Guardian*, 4 February 2015.

246 'they're thrown into a pen': Ryan Thaxton, 'Gay Bars Were Never a Safe Space,' *Huffington Post*, 28 June 2016, huffpost.com (accessed 19 May 2020).

260 'drag queens are catnip': Marke B., '655 Tubesteak Connections—and Still Growing!,' *48 Hills*, 9 November 2016.

261 'Amusement under late capitalism . . . grooves of association': Theodor W. Adorno and Max Horkheimer, 'The Culture Industry: Enlightenment as Mass Deception,' in *Dialectic of Enlightenment*, trans. John Cumming (London: Verso, 1979), 137.

270 'half as likely': Gabriella Swerling, 'Young People Are Far More Likely to Consider Themselves as Bisexual than Gay, New Data Reveals,' *Telegraph*, 3 July 2019.

271 'a Trojan horse': Amy Roberts, 'We Fear the Joiners Arms Proposal

Is a Trojan Horse Draped in a Rainbow Flag,' *Guardian*, 9 August 2017.

272 'The pub was frequented': Ian Giles, *Trojan Horse Rainbow Flag* (London: Hato Press, 2019).

273 clubbers now chose to dance: Tess Reidy, 'Clubbing's New Generation Want Good, Clean Fun, Not Hedonism,' *Observer*, 4 March 2018.

275 'Places like Stonewall': Ann Friedman, 'Save This Eyesore,' *Los Angeles Times*, 27 July 2016.

275 'For most conscious': Don Kilhefner, letter to the editor, *Los Angeles Times*, 30 July 2016.

275 'The whole nostalgia': Christopher Kane, 'West Hollywood Divided over Fate of the Factory,' *Los Angeles Blade*, 3 July 2018.

Also:

Brewster, Bill. 'Interview: Ian Levine, Northern Soul Legend,' *DJ History*, 1999, via redbullmusicacademy.com, 2016.

Massey, Doreen. *Space, Place and Gender*. 1994. Reprint, Cambridge, Eng.: Polity Press, 2007.

Quinlan, Hannah, and Rosie Hastings. *UK Gay Bar Directory*. London: Arcadia Missa, 2017.

Where a description of a person or group is not self-identification, it's based on cultural and geographical context. Contemporary terms are not used for historical figures except as deliberate wordplay. Lingo is not always ideal or neutral, but reflects the experience of the moment.

Some further reading on lesbian, trans, inclusive queer sites—*Mapping Desires: Geographies of Sexualities* (Valentine/Bell, Routledge, 1995); *Queers in Space: Communities, Public Places, Sites of Resistance* (Ingram/Bouthillette/Retter, Bay Press, 1997); *Queer Constellations: Subcultural Space in the Wake of the City* (Chisholm, U of Minnesota Press, 2004); *Planning and LGBTQ Communities: The Need for Inclusive Queer Spaces* (Doan, Routledge, 2015); *Queer Premises: LGBTQ+ venues and identities in London since the 1980s* (Campkin, Zed / Bloomsbury Academic, 2021).

ILLUSTRATION CREDITS

THE DARK WALKS

p. 29: Unknown photographer, crime photograph of Caravan Club interior, Endell Street, London, 1934. PRO, ref. 2/224. National Archives, London.

THE FACTORY

p. 50: Unconfirmed artist, flyer for event at Probe, s.d. Courtesy of ONE Archives at the USC Libraries, Los Angeles.

p. 64: Pat Rocco, photograph of dancing at Studio One, s.d. Courtesy of ONE Archives at the USC Libraries, Los Angeles, and the estate of Pat Rocco.

p. 75: Unknown photographer, documentary photograph of the Black Cat demonstration, 1967. Courtesy of ONE Archives at the USC Libraries, Los Angeles.

THE ADELPHI

p. 109: Benedetto Pastorini, engraving of the Adelphi and Thames riverside, circa 1772, reproduced in *The Works in Architecture of Robert and James Adam, Esquires*, vol. 3, 1822.

ILLUSTRATION CREDITS

THE WINDOWS

p. 137: R. Michael Kelley, photograph of Chuck Arnett's Tool Box mural, 1975. Courtesy of the photographer.

THE NEIGHBORS

p. 170: Hal Fischer, *Street Fashion: Basic Gay*, from the series *Gay Semiotics*, 1977. Copyright © Hal Fischer. Courtesy of the artist.
p. 179: DJ Bus Station John, collage flyer for Tubesteak Connection, circa mid-2000s. Courtesy of the promoter.

THE APPRENTICE

p. 228: Gavin Watson, *STRENGTH THRU OI!*, 1981. Courtesy of the photographer.

All other photos by Jeremy Atherton Lin. Every effort has been made to confirm copyrights on the artwork included in this book. The author and publisher would be pleased to rectify any omissions in subsequent editions.